Giving

Philanthropic Studies

Robert L. Payton and Dwight F. Burlingame, general editors

Karen J. Blair. *The Torchbearers: Women and Their Amateur Arts Associations in America*

Dwight F. Burlingame, editor. *The Responsibilities of Wealth*

Dwight F. Burlingame and Dennis Young, editors. *Corporate Philanthropy at the Crossroads: The Need for Research Informed by Practice*

Marcos Cueto, editor. *Missionaries of Science: The Rockefeller Foundation and Latin America*

Gregory Eiselein. *Eccentric Benevolence: Literature and Humanitarian Work in the Civil War Era*

Thomas H. Jeavons. *When the Bottom Line Is Faithfulness: Management of Christian Service Organizations*

Mike W. Martin. *Virtuous Giving: Philanthropy, Voluntary Service, and Caring*

Mary J. Oates. *The Catholic Philanthropic Tradition in America*

J. B. Schneewind, editor. *Giving: Western Ideas of Philanthropy*

Giving

Western Ideas of Philanthropy

edited by J. B. Schneewind

Indiana University Press

Bloomington and Indianapolis

The paper used in this publication meets the minimum requirements of American National Standard for Information Sciences—Permanence of Paper for Printed Library Materials, ANSI Z39.48-1984.

Manufactured in the United States of America

Library of Congress Cataloging-in-Publication Data

Giving : Western ideas of philanthropy / edited by J. B. Schneewind.
       p.   cm. — (Philanthropic studies)
  Includes bibliographical references and index.
  ISBN 0-253-33072-6 (cl : alk. paper)
  1. Charities—History.   I. Schneewind, J. B. (Jerome B.), date.
  II. Series.
  HV16.G58   1996
  361.7′09—dc20   95-51749

1 2 3 4 5   01 00 99 98 97 96

Contents

Acknowledgments

THIS VOLUME IS the outgrowth of a suggestion from Robert Payton. It was planned while I was a Fellow at the Center for Advanced Study in the Behavioral Sciences. The assistance and the unsurpassable atmosphere for research that the Center provided, and discussions with other Fellows there, greatly aided the initial stages of the project.

I drew on many people for advice about contributors: Martha Howell, Judith Walkowitz, Daniel Rubinfeld, Sidney Mintz, William Werpehowski, John Saillant, Jeffrey Stout, Marcello Suarez-Orozco, and Alfred Moss. Without their expertise I would not have known who were the best people to bring together from so many different fields. I am most grateful to them.

Robert Payton's initial interest in the project and his guidance along the way have been indispensable. Dwight Burlingame provided much-needed assistance at crucial moments. David Kaufman was quietly expert in arranging the conference at which all the contributors met to discuss the papers before submitting final versions. My thanks go to them for their continuous support. Judy Kopec graciously and skillfully helped out at the last minute. I am particularly indebted to Natalie Brender for her knowledgeable and thoughtful hard work in preparing the manuscript for publication. My deepest thanks are due, of course, to the contributors, for agreeing to write, confer, and rewrite, and so to make the book possible.

J. B. Schneewind

Introduction

Robert L. Payton

In his foreword to *Ways of Worldmaking*, Nelson Goodman said, "This book does not run a straight course from beginning to end. It hunts; and in the hunting, it sometimes worries the same raccoon in different trees, or different raccoons in the same tree, or even what turns out to be no raccoon in any tree" (Goodman 1978, p. ix).

What was true of one author could well be true of ten, a fortiori, as they say. This book is also a hunt with many different notions of what is being hunted and where it is to be found. When we began to plan this volume, we did not think we were hunting for a single "idea" of philanthropy. We thought we would start a search for some of the many faces that charity wears. We would ask how it looks to donors, to receivers, and to societies. "Faces" could mean, after all, simply facts or perspectives or approaches; but faces, here, could also recall the complex images Picasso and Braque created more than a half-century ago. Those who prefer to be skeptics or even cynics would see the faces as masks—charity as an illusion; charity not as virtue at work but manipulation or self-deception. The facades of buildings lining the main streets of old western towns come to mind: charity as a way of claiming more about ourselves than the truth will support. Faces are also sources of expression, expressions which are presumably readable; perhaps we should seek to discern the character of the culture in its charity.

"Charity" itself, of course, is a mare's nest of ambiguity. The authors here speak of charity as a virtue, as a religious value, as voluntary and obligatory, as religious and secular; as justice, social behavior, irrationality, and mutual aid; as organizational behavior and as tradition; and, of course, as always problematic. What Paul Veyne says about euergetism might apply: "No word in the languages of antiquity corresponds exactly to euergetism. . . . Never mind. Even if the word is lacking, the thing is none the less a wide and well-defined field of study" (Veyne 1990, p. 10). In our case we have the word but we differ about its meanings; we can't agree about how many raccoons in how many trees, but we agree we aren't snipe hunting.

I will use this book in my seminar on "The Philanthropic Tradition." I will learn much from it—directly from the authors and their sources and indirectly from the unexpected connections that spin off from both. I am always daunted by the rigor of Jerry Schneewind's thought, and startled by the deceptive simplicity of Mary Douglas's insights. Allen Buchanan, Jerry Schneewind, and I have been in occasional conversations about the ideas developed in their papers for this volume for almost a decade; it has been twenty years or more since I first marveled at the wisdom of Mary Douglas, and more than a decade since I first had the pleasure of meeting her.[1] I have also long known Alan Ryan through his work but met him for the first time at the authors' conference that was the basis for this book. Robert Frank's *Passions within Reason* has been on my reading lists since it was first published in 1988; he, like Buchanan, Douglas, and Schneewind, has taken part in other Center on Philanthropy conferences.

Scott Davis, Suzanne Roberts, Ellen Ross, and Adrienne Lash Jones are new colleagues because of this book. I share with Alex Rondos, the token "practitioner" in this group, continuing interests in the former Yugoslavia, the refugee crisis, and Catholic Relief Services.

The point of this recitation of connections is to applaud the way Jerry Schneewind has brought fields and generations together in a common hunt or exploration. New fields need new people as well as old hands, and Schneewind has succeeded in bringing them together here.

Jerry Schneewind, Richard Rorty, and Quentin Skinner edit a well-known Cambridge University Press series entitled "Ideas in Context." To what extent may ideas be dealt with abstracted from their historical setting, to what extent must they be understood as "contingent," to what extent should historians and philosophers be doing each other's work? As the series description puts it:

> The books in this series will discuss the emergence of intellectual traditions and of related new disciplines. The procedures, aims and vocabularies that were generated will be set in the context of the alternatives available within the contemporary frameworks of ideas and institutions. Through detailed studies of the evolution of such traditions, and their modification by different audiences, it is hoped that a new picture will form of the development of ideas in their concrete contexts. By this means, artificial distinctions between the history of philosophy, of the various sciences, of society and politics, and of literature, may be seen to dissolve.[2]

In the introduction to the first volume in the series, a formidable essay in its own right, the editors discuss this approach in the complex interrelationship between what they call intellectual history and the history of philosophy:

> We do not offer any concrete suggestions about how present disciplinary matrices might be reformed in order to make the inevitable interdependence between these two fields [intellectual history and the history of philosophy] more visible, but we hope the essays in this volume (and further volumes in the series of which this volume is a member) may make people in both fields more aware of the possibility of such reforms. (R. Rorty et al., eds. 1984, p. 14)

In the first volume and in others that have followed it, there are many authors in search of varied fauna, not just hunting raccoons in trees. I became interested in the "Ideas in Context" project at an early stage of its development and have followed it, off and on, ever since. It still holds out promise for me as a model for work to be done in philanthropic studies. Philanthropic studies is, at this point, far more diffuse and tentative than the history of philosophy; it has no "disciplinary" home, as yet.

Thank God.

As is fully evident in this volume, anthropology, philosophy, economics, history, sociology, religion, the history of ideas, and a dozen other fields and subfields are engaged in this common enterprise. No one that I know has the depth of erudition or experience to be on a par with all ten of the authors. The frustration as well as the great delight of interdisciplinary work is that it forces one to dog-paddle toward the unknown deep end of the pool rather than to follow the clearly marked lanes up and down, back and forth, simply ignoring what is deep and what is shallow.[3]

Philanthropy is a liberal art; it is also a human art. It is a practice as well as a concept, acts as well as ideas. People who study philanthropy sometimes try to hold in mind complex external economic forces and complex internal psychological motivations as they leaf through ancient correspondence or diaries or prayer books or county records of marriage and mortality rates. Philanthropy is to be practiced as well as studied. Because of its deep human values and mundane practices, it forces scholars to reflect on subjective personal experience and understanding.

What is most intriguing to me about this book is the chance to "apply" the theory to the practice. How can Alex Rondos "make use" of Schneewind's reflections on perfect and imperfect duties? How can we examine the recorded experience of medieval charity described by Suzanne Roberts or the Victorian attitudes toward children described by Ellen Ross under the cultural glass that Mary Douglas offers us? Is the history of African American philanthropy that Adrienne Lash Jones discusses illuminated by Allan Buchanan's uncompromising words about justice? What can practitioners like Alex Rondos learn from the study of virtue that Scott Davis and others pursue?

Mary Douglas and Robert Frank both make use of the research by Tversky and Kahneman on the way expected future gains are often sacrificed to prevent more immediate losses. Douglas also refers to work by Larry Siedentop on "two liberal traditions." Siedentop's essay is in a book edited by Alan Ryan honoring Isaiah Berlin (Ryan, ed. 1979, pp. 153–74). We might next seek to persuade Alan Ryan to write an essay on philanthropy seen through the lens of Isaiah Berlin much as Ryan does here with Kant and the Idealists.

One set of questions might address the differences between disciplinary perspectives; a second set might address the differences between doing philanthropy and thinking about it, the impact of action on thought, or of passion on both. The barriers between disciplines, the barriers between thought and action are implicit in this book, presumably brought to the surface by the reader's own experience and worldview.

This book is one of more than two dozen the Center on Philanthropy has helped bring into being. The ten authors are among hundreds and perhaps thousands of scholars and practitioners the Center has thus far touched in its work. Yet some see ominous signs in the academic world of philanthropic studies:

> I think that these centers for the study of philanthropy are thoroughly perni-
> cious and destructive things for foundations to support. You would think that
> nothing would make more sense than providing good training for new re-
> cruits in the noble profession of philanthropy. But when I visit some of these
> centers and look at the curricula, it seems to me that they are exaggerated ver-
> sions of the academic approach to life. They're encapsulated, self-satisfied, and
> inclined to rise into high theoretical formulations and to flee from any specific
> matters.[4]

The source of those comments hasn't visited the Center on Philanthropy at Indiana University, at least not recently, and so I will assume he's talking only about other centers. In either case it is a diatribe worth examining briefly here.

"You would think that nothing would make more sense than providing good training for new recruits to the noble profession of philanthropy": I value the distinction often drawn between training and education; I come down firmly on the importance of both. Education should underlie training, however; education illuminates the cultural context, if you will, while training helps to function within it. The practical training we offer in fund-raising and are be-ginning to offer in grant making is intended to help people do that kind of work. The educational programs we offer—the curriculum of our master of arts degree in philanthropic studies, for example—attempts to explore the ethics and values of philanthropy, its religious traditions and practices, the history of philanthropy, the literature of philanthropy, the economics and politics and so-ciology and anthropology of philanthropy. We encourage everyone to talk with everyone else along the way, and sometimes that works; often it doesn't.

We are interested in philanthropy "warts and all"; the study of philan-thropy without a serious attempt to be disinterested and critical is not serious. Nielsen, of course, knows that; he prides himself on his revealing the foibles and weaknesses of "the noble profession." As is evident in this book, the authors are determined to examine what is going on—"the conversation we are in" is *about* something.

There is no current definition of "profession" that would include philan-thropy. It is, for some, an occupation, just as studying it is, for others, an occupation. There are also amateurs who practice philanthropy as well as study it. There are no clear standards for "professionals" or for amateurs—any more than there are for consultants. (Nielsen is a consultant.)

What should people engaged in the work of philanthropy know? What would improve their competence? What would enhance their empathetic understanding of the people they serve? What would make them "reflective practitioners"?

The authors of this book draw on many of the same sources I do in trying to think my way through such questions. Ideas about virtue, for example, seem relevant to acts that intervene in the lives of others for their benefit. Which acts of charity might be thought to be obligatory in some "perfect" way? How do motives and incentives change in different settings and different cultures? How has the Western world dealt with the troubling notion of "desert"?

One incentive to do the hard work of scholarship has been to tie it to the requirements of scholarly careers: publish or perish.[5] Good scholarly work was supposed to lead to the once-valued notion of job security. The best-known contributors to this volume are as many as several decades beyond the award of tenure; there is reason to believe that the other scholars will follow in their footsteps and continue to publish serious work because they are serious about it.

Despite the current fashion in political discourse, I won't be persuaded by anecdotal evidence about the weaknesses of academe to denigrate scholarship of this kind and quality. I am instead prompted to reaffirm the values of the academic culture I know best and seek ways to strengthen them. The best way is to encourage books like this, to help authors like these, to support centers like the one at Indiana, to read the books of publishers like this one, to use them in my own work, and to urge them upon my students. My students include foundation executives and trustees, fund-raisers and other "nonprofit" executives, graduate and undergraduate students, and unsuspecting passersby. They would all benefit, in my opinion, from thinking seriously about the difference between saints Augustine and Thomas on the idea of charity, between perfect and imperfect duties, between charity and justice, between medieval and modern notions of desert, between the philanthropy of African Americans, other minorities, and the tainted if not polluted mainstream. The reader of Ellen Ross's essay on school lunches for the poor in London a century ago will have a far better sense of the present debate about the subject in the United States. Well-known historians like Gertrude Himmelfarb and amateur historians like Marvin Olasky have written best-selling books imploring us to relearn the moral lessons of nineteenth-century England. I applaud their goal even when I differ from their conclusions.

Those who claim that something as multifaceted as the faces of charity can be seen one-dimensionally are either obtuse or unobservant.

I would invite other readers of this book to join me in trying to think about what's left out. That is a serious suggestion because we want to encourage more good books about charity and philanthropy in the spirit of this one. Here are some of the ideas I've been reading and thinking about and hope to write about that will be influenced by what I've read here:

The notion of "life chances:" The term is from Max Weber but I am indebted more directly to Ralf Dahrendorf, who defines life chances as "the social conditions in which individuals realize their potential."[6] Dahrendorf says that politicians want to claim they are seeking to improve life chances; I will argue that philanthropy is also engaged in the effort to enhance the life chances of people. Dahrendorf says that life chances are shaped by *ligatures* and *options*, what Donald Horowitz elsewhere refers to as "birth and choice."[7]

The culture in which people define themselves and are defined by others can put greatest emphasis on birth characteristics and other aspects of ethnicity; such was life in most of the premodern world. The modern culture is arguably one in which individuals have far greater choice in determining and shaping their own identity.

Philanthropy, it seems to me, falls at the choice end of the spectrum. It is not a matter of indifference to the philanthropic tradition that premodern racism and ethnic fundamentalism are on the rise.

Giving gives us useful tools and information to examine the question of life chances.

Civil society: It is in the language of the notion of civil society that scholars in Europe and the United States have come together. Civil society bridges worldviews that were defined either as nonprofit or nongovernmental. That is a very important distinction, of course, and has practical consequences in the enabling legislation that is being written in Central and Eastern European countries. American scholars now have to read Hegel, and European scholars have to read Madison. People who teach philanthropy will use Habermas as well as, say, Rawls (even though both are now getting long in the tooth).

It is also the case that the decline of governments everywhere has made the most insistent demand on all the "centers on philanthropy" the provision of training in fund-raising. How does one teach Course 101 of The Fund Raising School in Thailand? in Mexico City? in Ljubljana? We need Mary Douglas's help as well as that of Alex Rondos.

Ernest Gellner's recent book, *Conditions of Liberty*, helps me to think about the role of philanthropy in civil society, even though Gellner doesn't mention philanthropy at all. As Dahrendorf and Horowitz help me to think about philanthropy and ethnic conflict, Gellner makes me realize how many people there are in the world who are not in this conversation at all.

"Civil society" generally calls positive images to mind, as "life chances" does. The term has not yet taken on the pejorative associations that still plague "charity" and "philanthropy." More important, talking about this subject in terms of civil society makes more compelling the links between philanthropy and democracy.

Religion and philanthropy: Mary Douglas once told me that "you don't need religion to explain that" when I spoke of the "origins" of philanthropy in religious values. Despite her caveat, most of the time Occam's razor remains in the bathroom cabinet at my place. A few years ago some colleagues of mine at Indiana suggested that it would be easier to bring other scholars into the discussion if we were to talk about "philanthropy and culture" rather than "philanthropy and religion."

One of the reasons is that religion plays a problematic role in philanthropy. It also plays a problematic role in ethnicity and nationalism. Because I'm interested in the role of philanthropy in resolving or preventing ethnic conflict, and because religion plays such a major part in American philanthropy, there seems to me much work to do to better understand what is going on. The conflict in Northern Ireland is a case in point: both the combatants and the peacemakers carry a cross. And in Northern Ireland as well as in Yugoslavia, it can be argued that religious action for and against peace masks deeper economic issues than ethnic issues. Certainly in the former Yugoslavia there is evidence of leaders "playing the ethnic card" to advance political aims in the midst of economic disorder and decline. Alex Rondos has been organizationally as well as intellectually and perhaps religiously confronted with these issues. But religious morality also permeates the Victorian culture Ellen Ross writes about; it is central to Suzanne Roberts's essay on the shift from the "evangelical" to the "discriminating" charity of the Middle Ages; the African American philanthropy Adrienne Lash Jones describes is singularly influenced by religious congregations. Religious values and religious practice are deeply intertwined with religious charity and philanthropy.

Some of these ideas and impressions will be in the back of my mind over the coming months when I return to places like Northern Ireland and the former Yugoslavia, and perhaps Israel, in a search for better understanding of the faces of charity in the context of civil war. The faces of charity see children starving, smell gunpowder, and often taste despair.

The people I am closest to, where Walzer's thick and thin mesh most comfortably, read books like *Giving* with a conviction that they will help us advance the causes we are concerned about. They also help us to ferret out the weaknesses and illusions of those causes and to face more squarely our own biases and self-deceptions.

Notes

1. And her husband, James, whose *Why Charity? The Case for a Third Sector*, Sage, 1983, was an important contribution to the early conceptual discussions of the topic.

2. *Ideas in Context* series description, Cambridge University Press, 1984ff.

3. Rorty et al. (1984) quote Gadamer on "the conversation we are in" (p. 1) and refer to "what have been called 'rational bridgeheads'—not high-level criteria but rather low-level platitudes—which have made conversation possible across chasms" (p. 2). Those interested in the point might also read with great profit Michael Walzer's little book, *Thick and Thin* (Walzer 1994).

4. Waldemar Nielsen in an interview reported in the newsletter of The Philanthropy Roundtable.

5. I am reminded of the *New Yorker* cartoon that shows a headstone in a cemetery; under the name the epitaph: "Published, but perished anyway."

6. Dahrendorf 1979, p. 11: "Life chances are the moulds of human life in society; their shape determines how and how far people can unfold."

7. Horowitz 1985; cf. p. 55 on "the continuum from birth to choice."

Giving

1 | Philanthropy as a Virtue in Late Antiquity and the Middle Ages

Scott Davis

"PHILANTHROPY," "CHARITY," and related concepts were well known to late antiquity and the Middle Ages. Rulers, wealthy individuals and, early on, the Christian church founded hospitals, distributed food, and established forms of relief for the needy of various sorts throughout the period. The problem comes in interpreting these activities, their motives, and their goals. Is the *philanthropia* of a pre-Christian philosopher of a piece with the *agape*, or Christian love, of a fourth-century bishop? When the Roman emperor provides bread and circuses, what does he intend and why does he do it? Does the twelfth-century nobleman intend the same? As with so many of our social, moral, and political concepts, placing "philanthropy" and its premodern cognates in their historical and intellectual context highlights our contemporary understanding of philanthropic work and its place in our moral world.

Consider two respected scholars in the field. Demetrios Constantelos, revising a major study of East Roman social welfare that he had published twenty-five years earlier, writes that in the intervening period he has come to believe "the Christian agape developed as a direct inheritance of ancient Greek philanthropia." And he adds that he now sees "more continuity in the social ethos of ancient Hellenism with Christian Hellenism than I was willing to acknowledge" (Constantelos 1991, p. ix). On the other hand, the celebrated French historian Paul Veyne argues persuasively that the appearance of continuity between classical philanthropy and Christian charity "is an illusion," that the grand expressions of pagan benevolence, as opposed to the "pious and charitable works" of Christians, "differ in ideology, in beneficiaries and in agents, in the motivations of agents, and in their behaviour" (Veyne 1990, p. 19).[1] Neither Veyne nor Constantelos denies that from late antiquity on there were hospitals and orphanages, poor relief and patronage.[2] But knowing what happened is only part of the story. What we would like to know is why they were established and what they meant, how they fitted into the fabric of ancient and medieval moral thought and political life.

Unfortunately, this is easier said than done, for it is not entirely clear what we want to know, or how to discover it. In imperial Rome the doing of grand public works is reserved to the emperor, at least in the capital; is this intended to stamp out popular rivals or encompass the city in the godlike embrace of the first citizen? Are the foundations of hospitals and the like power plays, penance for evils done, acts to ingratiate the doer with the gods or expressions of compassion at the plight of the indigent? Is the patronage of Maecenas, so indispensable to Virgil and Horace, an instance of philanthropic support for the arts, the ostentatious display of a powerful aristocrat, or both? Veyne, reflecting on the family allowances instituted by Trajan, notes that "its humble beneficiaries thanked the Emperor for his liberality, while the political world praised him for ensuring the survival of the Italian race . . . whether it was beneficence or birthrate policy, he had spent his money on a new and gracious task" (Veyne 1990, p. 367). The point, of course, is that we have no clear way of determining whether these pensions were established for "philanthropic" purposes or for reasons of state, to secure a stable agricultural base. How could we tell? But this needn't mean that we can learn nothing about the motives and goals of giving in antiquity and the Middle Ages. My goal in what follows is to sketch what was meant by philanthropy in various social contexts, from late antiquity to the end of the thirteenth century, focusing not so much on the facts of who gave what to whom, but on the ideals and motives that inspired such giving.

From Aristotle to Seneca: Virtue, Prudence, and Concern for Others

For several reasons it will prove useful to begin with Aristotle, for he not only sets out to write the first self-conscious "ethics," he insists on its continuity with the political world and is committed to a level of detail in analysis that makes him a useful foil for understanding the implications of his rivals. Although "philanthropy" as a noun occurs very rarely in his works, the adjectival form is common and its use instructive. For example, at the beginning of his discussion of friendship, Aristotle notes that friendship seems to be a natural instinct, "for which reason we praise those who love their fellow men (tous philanthropous epainoumen)" (Aristotle 1975, 1155a).[3] Here "philanthropic" means "benevolent" or "humane," without the sense of public giving or aid to the needy carried by its modern cognate. It is the attitude with which we should approach our dealings with other people, the foundation of that friendship which, if properly reciprocated, would make recourse to law rare and unnecessary. We praise philanthropy not because it promotes a certain kind of act, but because it is the way we feel toward others if we are properly brought up.

The Aristotelian virtues directly associated with giving have little to do with love of humanity. Liberality, the virtue associated with small sums, is the disposition to "give for the nobility of giving," and the noble "will give to the right people, and the right amount, and at the right time, and fulfill all the other conditions of right giving" (Aristotle 1975, 1120a). Right giving, like all of Aristotle's virtues, stems directly from the character of the individual and from his desire to achieve happiness through living the most choiceworthy life and doing the most praiseworthy deeds. The right people are his family, friends, and fellow citizens, who share his penchant for virtue and will, in their turn, give rightly. To give excessively, either to the wrong people or when it is ill timed, is prodigal, while failure to give when giving is appropriate is meanness. Aristotle's student and successor, Theophrastus, paints the mean character as likely:

> to borrow of a stranger that is staying in his house; to say as he carves the meat that the carver deserves a double portion, and help himself without more ado. . . . When a friend or a friend's daughter is to be married, he is like to go into foreign parts some time before the wedding to avoid the giving of a present. (Theophrastus 1953, XXX)

The mean person, like the prodigal, we condemn not so much for the consequences of his actions as the quality of his character, and this should alert us to something important about classical ethics. Whatever their differences, the classical authors on ethics begin by asking what a good and choiceworthy life looks like. After determining what our lives should look like, the task is to make ourselves the sort of people for whom that life is natural, people of character, for whom virtuous action flows unimpeded. This is why the liberal individual gives freely and with pleasure, while to give at all pains the mean man. His desires are shaped by the virtues, and thus he wants to give, while the mean man wants to keep what he has and gives only under constraint.

When large sums and public display come into play we graduate from liberality to magnificence, but the basic account of virtue does not change. Thus, writes Aristotle, "the magnificent man is an artist in expenditure: he can discern what is suitable, and spend great sums with good taste." If the situation calls for it "he will spend gladly and lavishly, since nice calculation is shabby; and he will think how he can carry out his project most nobly and splendidly, rather than how much it will cost and how it can be done most cheaply" (Aristotle 1975, 1121a–b). The forms such magnificence takes are varied, and include public banquets and dramatic choruses, as well as "the service of the gods—votive offerings, public buildings, sacrifices—and the offices of religion generally" (Aristotle 1975, 1122b). In all, however, he observes the mean with regard to his resources and his position in the community, otherwise he becomes prodigal, profligate, and a fool.

The association of magnificence with religious practice deserves comment. The magnificent man underwrites a building or offers a sacrifice in thanks for benefits received or in hope of benefits to come. It is a display of prudence, a form of reciprocity through which he maintains his status with the powers that be. Through such acts the city as a whole benefits, but should there be any benefit to the poor it is at best secondhand. Their families and kin, not strangers, are expected to take care of them. The severely underprivileged might gather round the temple in hope of food or alms, but they have no formal recourse and must rely on the goodwill of those who have paid for the sacrifice or come to share in the magnificence of their friend.

This is not to imply that no thought was given to the indigent. Poor relief and exemption from certain civic duties are incorporated into the Athenian constitution, but the motive is neither sympathy, in the modern sense, nor identification with the poor (cf. Aristotle 1984, 69). It seems, rather, to reflect the interaction of legal justice and common decency, what older translations call equity. "Equity," Aristotle writes, "though just, is not legal justice, but a rectification of legal justice." It is the virtue that adjusts the letter of the law to particular cases, not necessarily because there is a defect in the law, but because "the material of conduct is essentially irregular. When therefore the law lays down a general rule, and thereafter a case arises which is an exception," the person of common decency attempts to "rectify the defect by deciding as the lawgiver would himself decide if he were present" (Aristotle 1975, 1137b). Equity, common decency, is what we expect from our neighbors. If they are properly reared they will exercise this decency in conjunction with the philanthropy, or benevolence, that we also praise as exemplifying what is well bred in our fellow citizens. Those among us endowed with exceptional wealth, assuming always that *they* are well bred, will be naturally disposed to express themselves, in the right way and at the right time, in acts of magnificence, and they are to be recognized as such.

This excursion into the vocabulary of Aristotelian virtue highlights several points. It alerts us to the dangers of identifying our use of a word with its earlier uses and opens up the complexity of the classical vocabulary of ethics. Even more important, it points up the dangers in assuming that our contemporary vocabulary is sufficiently supple to capture the arguments and presuppositions of our precursors. The modern contrast of "egoism" with "altruism," for instance, is an anachronism when imported into classical ethics.[4] Despite her judicious attempts to avoid such anachronisms, Julia Annas seems to me to reverse the source of paradox in her recent discussion of the debate between Aristotelians and Stoics on concern for others. "Aristotle," she writes, "sees morality as developing from self-love, and also argues that the end result is self-love—a highly special and refined form of self-love, of course. The latter point is universally rejected after Aristotle, as being unnecessarily paradoxical" (Annas 1993, p. 288). Later departures aside, Annas mislocates the paradox, by taking impartiality as an obvious moral desideratum, assigning thereby Aristotle and others to the ethical margins (cf. Annas 1993, p. 270ff.).

The debate Annas presents centers on whether "self-love," *philauton*, is properly a term of reproach or a presupposition of rational action. "It is those who take too large a share of things," Aristotle writes, "whom most people usually mean when they speak of lovers of self" (Aristotle 1975, 1168b). His use of popular proverbs and the like indicate that the person guilty of *pleonexia,* taking too much, is the same character satirized by Theophrastus. This is obviously a bad sort, and if this is all there is to self-love, then it is a bad quality. But, *this* is the paradox, for if taken at face value what could be more natural than to love ourselves? We naturally want what is good, and even if we also want it for others, we assuredly don't deny it to ourselves. By book nine of the *Nicomachean Ethics,* Aristotle thinks he has clarified where the good lies, and so the paradox of "self-love" as a term of opprobrium stands out with clarity. Thus he can write that "it is our reasoned acts that are felt to be in the fullest sense *our own* acts, *voluntary* acts" (Aristotle 1975, 1169a), assuming that his readers will understand that the most perfectly reasoned and voluntary acts are precisely those in accord with virtue, as he argued in book two, and since virtue is intrinsically lovable, and those acts which are most ours are acts of virtue, we should love ourselves. The common criticism of self-love is nothing but a sloppy way of condemning "sordid greed" and the sort of character we describe as "niggardly, close-fisted, and stingy" (Aristotle 1975, 1221b–1222a).

For Aristotle, concern for others is a consequence of being well brought up, having a sense of common decency grounded in an education that enables us to discern the demands of virtue and act accordingly. While nothing guarantees that we always manifest the virtues, or even common decency, few communities of any size can tolerate too much deviation from their norms, for that would render any attempt to pursue and secure the goods of life unstable. This, at least, seems the import of Aristotle's remark that "friendship appears to be the bond of the state," and his noting that "to promote concord, which seems akin to friendship," is what wise lawgivers desire, "while faction, which is enmity, is what they are most anxious to banish" (Aristotle 1975, 1155a). The wise lawgiver knows that benevolent acts stem from those virtues, such as liberality and magnanimity, that incline us to do good for the sake of good, particularly to our friends. Friendship, it would seem, is the ideal relation, both for individuals and for the community as a whole. After that, the law and common decency attempt to rectify less-than-ideal relations and states of affairs. Beyond that, giving is not systematically related to the moral life.

If there is anything novel in Aristotle's treatment of our relations with others, it is not his accounting for other-concern in terms of self-concern and our relations to friends, but his replacing obligations derived from divinely sanctioned relations of reciprocity with reasons based on virtues. Constantelos writes that:

> In the Homeric age philanthropy was associated with assistance to beggars as well as to the poor and to strangers. . . . The ancient Greeks were also very philanthropic and affectionate toward the aged. Not only was reverence for

aged parents advocated, but also respect and consideration for all persons of advanced age. . . . The spirit of brotherhood and friendship which is the basis of philanthropy is well expressed by Sophocles in his Antigone. (Constantelos 1991, pp. 4–6)

But he cites as evidence for this general spirit Xenophon's remark that "if one desires the protection of the gods, one must practice piety toward them; if a man would be loved by his friends he must help them; if he would be honoured by a city he must serve it" (Constantelos 1991, p. 6). Rather than the spirit of Christian charity, much less contemporary altruism, this reflects the understanding of gift giving studied by Marcel Mauss in his classic, *The Gift.* According to Mauss, gift giving in traditional and ancient societies is a matter of reciprocal obligation. At the most basic level a gift carries with it a supernatural energy that remains unstable and potentially dangerous until it has been satisfied by a return of equal value. There is a spiritual economy that obliges the recipient to give and the giver to receive, and the sanctions that secure this circulation of goods are not merely social but spiritual in the sense that "to refuse to give, to fail to invite, just as to refuse to accept, is tantamount to declaring war" (Mauss 1990, p. 13). Mauss argues that almsgiving, for example, has its roots in this "morality of the gift," for to receive the blessings of wealth and power without an effort to keep them circulating offends against the order of things. Generosity becomes an obligation when the gods either demand or tolerate that a portion of what "had been hitherto destroyed in useless sacrifice should serve the poor and children" (Mauss 1990, p. 18). Where Aristotle innovates is in arguing that virtue and happiness, as opposed to the gods and the spirits, require this recognition of the underprivileged. Nonetheless, the principal motivation behind our actions remains our quest for happiness, informed by those virtues that make us praiseworthy, both in our own eyes and in the eyes of our compatriots.

Placing the matter in this context sheds a different light on the debate Annas lays out between Aristotelians and Stoics in the Hellenistic period. She argues that the Stoics "are the first ethical theorists clearly to commit themselves to the thesis that morality requires impartiality to all others from the moral point of view" (Annas 1993, p. 265), and goes on to present this as a consequence of the demand for rigorous rationality in reaching practical conclusions. The argument seems to be that difference in moral treatment must depend exclusively on difference in intrinsic worth, and since we are all humans we are all identical in our intrinsic worth. Preferences of one sort or another must, therefore, depend on acquired qualities or relationships, which may modify particular obligations at particular times, but do not affect our basic relations as moral agents. This is different from the requirement of common decency, which insists on impartiality in our legal system and related institutions. Those institutions answer to the good of the public as a whole, and to use them for personal or family gain would be unjust. The debate Annas points to centers on our fundamental reasons for action, pitting our search for happiness against the ostensible claims of even "the furthest Mysian" (cf. Annas 1993, ch. 12). For the Stoic, not only does the stranger *in our midst* have a claim on our common decency, but so does the distant stranger as well. When pressed as to the source of this claim, the Stoic response seems to be "in virtue of our shared fellowship in the family of humankind." Aristotle, not to mention the ancient and traditional cultures discussed by Mauss, must find this simply specious. I might, as an act of compassion or magnanimity, go to the aid of that "furthest Mysian," but *claim* he has none. That, as Annas puts it, "later Aristotelians simply caved in to the Stoics on this point and accepted the impartiality requirement without even integrating it to the rest of the theory very satisfactorily" (Annas 1993, p. 290) reflects poorly on those later thinkers, while leaving the Stoics themselves with no very good reason for their claim.

That at least some Stoics didn't fully understand the point comes out in Seneca's discussion of gift giving, penned toward the middle of the first century of the common era. Early in his discussion of benefits Seneca insists on the study of "the rules for a practice that constitutes the chief bond of human conduct . . . a law of conduct in order that we may not be inclined to the thoughtless indulgence that masquerades as generosity" (Seneca 1979, I.4). Here he remarks the need for the giver to "make no record" and the recipient "to feel indebted for more than the amount," going on to cite the Stoic Chrysippus on "this most honourable rivalry in outdoing benefits by benefits." Whatever the status of impartiality, gift giving remains securely tied to the traditional system of reciprocity traced in Mauss to the ancient Indo-Europeans (Mauss 1990, pp. 47–63). Seneca cites Chrysippus yet again for the example of the ball game in distinguishing the good player from the novice. The skilled player "must of necessity use one method of hurling the ball to a partner who is a long way off, and another to one who is near at hand. The same condition applies to a benefit" (Seneca 1979, II.17). Giving is like a game in which all work together to keep the play going smoothly, the goal being to sustain the sort of life appointed us by nature. Giving creates friendship and hence sustains the social fabric, thus "I must be far more careful in selecting my creditor for a benefit than a creditor for a loan." I should seek to give and receive benefits only from those whose character is worthy, for:

> even after I have paid my debt of gratitude, the bond between us still holds; for, just when I have finished paying it, I am obliged to begin again, and friendship endures; and, as I would not admit an unworthy man to my friendship, so neither would I admit one who is unworthy to the most sacred privilege of benefits, from which friendship springs. (Seneca 1979, II.18)

As with Aristotle, the motive for giving has little to do with the material circumstances of the recipient, and when it does the relevant issue is whether or not he is in a position to return the benefit. To give to an unworthy person, or in a way that does not sustain the friendships that make up our social relations, is simply wasteful. From Aristotle to Seneca, albeit with differences of emphasis, public giving, whether by individuals or the state, is intended to secure those goods most desirable to the givers, not necessarily the recipients. When the Christians come to reinterpret pagan virtue in the fourth century, it is precisely the self-conscious sense of *discontinuity* that stands out, and it is to that we now turn.

Splendid Vices: Pagan Virtue in Ambrose and Augustine

The fourth century began with the last Roman persecution of Christians, that of Diocletian, and ended with the emperor Theodosius proclaiming edicts against the pagans and in favor of the church. Though battles of Christian against Christian loomed, the traditional gods of Rome were now on the defensive, and, at least in some quarters, their traditional virtues as well. When, in February of 362, Julian the Apostate proclaimed religious freedom it was in the vain hope of restoring the temples and protecting their worshipers from Christian depredations. In a long fragment Julian writes that a Roman priest "must above all exercise philanthropy, for from it result many other blessings, and moreover that choicest and greatest blessing of all, the good will of the gods." But he goes on almost immediately to remark that:

> philanthropy has many divisions and is of many kinds. For instance it is shown when men are punished in moderation with a view to the betterment of those punished, as schoolmasters punish children; and again in ministering to men's needs, even as the gods minister to our own. (Julianus 1954, II, 289a–c)[5]

Despite the intervening six centuries, philanthropy remains much what it was for Aristotle. While it is now identified, at least in part, with helping the needy, that help is an expression of a much broader attitude that may as easily include moderating legally mandated punishments or disciplining children. When Julian speaks of giving to the poor he embraces the "paradox" of giving to the unworthy, though he notes that we must not ignore "the poor who go about in our midst, especially when they happen to be of good character—men for instance who have inherited no paternal estate, and are poor because in the greatness of their souls they have no desire for money" (Julianus 1954, II, 290a). The truly magnanimous individual cares for all, but the well born and the philosophically inclined have a *special* claim on his attention. When Julian talks of why we should condemn those who ignore the poor, or blame the gods for their plight, he does not reprove their lack of humanity, but cites the more mundane vice of "insatiate greed." As with Aristotle and Seneca, it is individual virtue, deployed to attain happiness and the most choiceworthy life, that motivates giving. Julian's immediate concern with the neglect of the poor by the upholders of Roman tradition centers on the rise of Christianity:

> for when it came about that the poor were neglected and overlooked by the priests, then I think the impious Galilaeans observed this fact and devoted themselves to philanthropy. And they have gained ascendancy in the worst of their deeds through the credit they win for such practices. For just as those who entice children with a cake, and by throwing it to them two or three times induce them to follow them, and then, when they are far away from their friends cast them on board a ship and sell them as slaves . . . they have led very many into atheism. (Julianus 1954, 305c–d)

Philanthropy is, quintessentially, the attitude of the gods toward mortals, and thus, as Norman Baynes put it, "when subjects speak on the streets or in the public baths—wherever it may be—of that which they desire from their emperor, the one word is *philanthropia*" (Baynes 1955, p. 55). As a good emperor, Julian attempts to let this philanthropy flow from the top down, and by obliging his lesser magistrates to follow his example he hopes to secure the noble traditions of Greece and Rome against the impiety of the Christians. Even when provoked by the sophistries of the Christians, philanthropy should shine through and strive to cure them, "even against their will, as one cures the insane, except that we concede indulgence to all for this sort of disease. For we ought, I think, to teach, but not punish, the demented" (Julianus 1954, 37: III, 424a).[6] By his piety and philanthropy, expressed in reason and moderation, Julian hoped to retrieve even those fallen into atheism, regardless of their social and material station.

He failed. By the middle of the fourth century the momentum gathered by the Christian movement easily withstood the short-reigned apostate, and Christian intellectuals began to turn the works of the classical tradition against themselves. Such, at least, was the intent of Ambrose, Bishop of Milan, who recast Cicero for Christian use. Thus, he says, while meditating on Psalm 39, "it has come to my mind to write on the duties. . . . And as Cicero wrote for the instruction of his son, so I, too, write to teach you, my children" (Ambrose 1979, I, 7). A bit of Ambrose's popular etymology is illuminating here. He asks, having introduced the subject, whether *officium* is a proper word for Christians to reflect on, concluding that such a discussion is not only supported by scripture, but "is not inconsistent with reason, since we consider that the word *officium* [duty] is derived from *efficere* [to effect], and is formed with the change of one letter for the sake of euphony; or at any rate that you should do those things which injure [*officiant*] no one, but benefit all" (Ambrose 1979, I, 8). The play on duty, effect, and injury introduces a subtle but important twist to Cicero's original. For where Cicero's duties devolve upon us in virtue of our natural endowments and social status, Ambrose suggests that they derive from our relations to other people in general, in virtue solely of their status as human beings, created by God. The ordinary state of human beings, he goes on, is typically miserable and only rectified in the life to come, as in the example of Lazarus in Luke 16, "who endured evil things here, there found comfort." In fact, the great distinction between Christians and pagans is where they locate their true goods. Pagans value conveniences, resources, and wealth, while the Christians "state nothing useful but what will help us to the blessings of eternal life," and do *not* "recognize any advantages in opportunities and in the wealth of earthly goods, but consider them as disadvantages if not put aside, and to be looked on as a burden, when we have them, rather than as a loss when expended" (Ambrose 1979, I, 9). By themselves, these remarks are consistent with the popular Stoicism of Cicero's text, and thus with one strain of the tradition of reciprocity, but Ambrose does not stop here. He adopts Cicero's distinction between "the sort of duty that is called common and that called perfect" (Cicero 1961, I, 3; I have given a more literal translation) and identifies the common duties with those codified in the Decalogue, going on to cite that passage of Matthew where Jesus counsels the rich young man that "if thou wilt be perfect, go and sell all thy goods and give to the poor, and thou shalt have treasure in heaven; and come and follow Me" (Ambrose 1979, I, 11). Here we have Cicero's notion of a perfect duty being given both concrete content and divine ordination in terms of forsaking material gain and giving it to the poor, not as an expression of your own magnanimity, but because the poor are in need and the seeker after eternal life will wish to escape the entrapments of this world.

Ambrose carries his critique of pagan morality further in book three, where he attacks profit seeking at the expense of the public. To the merchant who says, "I have sown freely. I have tilled actively. I have gathered good increase . . . in time of famine I sell it, and come to the help of the hungry," Ambrose replies "thou collectest wealth from the misery of all, and callest this industry and diligence, when it is but cunning shrewdness and an adroit trick of the trade. Thou callest it a remedy, when it is but a wicked contrivance." Here the classical distrust of the retailer meets the Christian reversal of classical values. Citing both the Gospel of Luke and the Proverbs of solitude he concludes that "the gains of avarice have nothing to do with the rights of succession" (Ambrose 1979, III, 6). Those in need have a right to the fruits of nature. To insist on your own work as an entitlement to profit from the prevailing situation is duplicitous.

Nevertheless, Ambrose remains within the pale of classical culture. Thus, concluding his discussion of Christian duty, Ambrose naturally employs the traditional language of friendship, noting that a friend is "a partner in love, to whom thou unitest and attachest thy soul. . . . It is produced, not by money, but

by esteem; not by the offer of rewards, but by a mutual rivalry in doing kindness" (Ambrose 1979, III, 22). What makes Christian friendship different is the
rejection of material goods in favor of the kingdom of God. It is still natural to
desire the enjoyment of fellowship and mutual obligation, particularly now that
it is freed from the taint of money. The mutual reciprocity of man and man, man
and God, remains. Ambrose's identification of Christ's injunction to give to the
poor with Cicero's notion of a perfect duty is a key step toward a novel concept
of the virtue of giving. As in the case of Seneca, this is a view of human relations
that did not see itself in conflict with the reciprocity of benefits. In order to develop our notion of charity as giving motivated by the plight of the stranger,
regardless of our relation to that stranger, a markedly different account of the
virtues will be necessary. A key figure in this transformation is Ambrose's
younger contemporary, and sometime student, Augustine of Hippo.

Augustine's thought is notoriously protean, driven more often than not by
the exigencies of ecclesiastical and doctrinal dispute. A detailed and secure un-
raveling of the strands of his moral thought would be far too ambitious for the
present occasion. Nonetheless, the key text and its centrality to Augustine's
thought is not in doubt. In 425, just five years before his death, Augustine composed for the nineteenth book of his *City of God* the following simple, but devastating argument:

> For though the soul may seem to rule the body admirably, and the reason the
> vices, if the soul and reason do not themselves obey God, as God has com-
> manded them to serve Him, they have no proper authority over the body and
> the vices. . . . It is for this reason that the virtues which it seems to itself to
> possess, and by which it restrains the body and the vices that it may obtain
> and keep what it desires, are rather vices than virtues so long as there is no
> reference to God in the matter. For although some suppose that virtues which
> have a reference only to themselves, and are desired only on their own account,
> are yet true and genuine virtues, the fact is that even then they are inflated
> with pride, and therefore to be reckoned vices rather than virtues. (Augustine
> 1948a, XIX, 225)

From seemingly unexceptional premises Augustine concludes not merely that
the classical tradition of moral thought is confused or defective in various
places, but that it is vicious, root and branch, and to the extent that its followers
succeed in internalizing and acting upon its recommendations they make themselves, albeit splendidly, damnable in the eyes of God. For it is a matter of justice, "whose office it is to render to every man his due" (Augustine 1948a, XIX,
4), that we acknowledge the sovereignty of God. Failure to do so is unjust. God's
law for us is clear in Matthew 22:37–40, where Jesus states unequivocally that
the first mandate of the law is to love God with all your heart, all your soul, and
all your mind, while the second is to love your neighbor as you love yourself.

But the classical virtues, inflated as they are with pride, fail to acknowledge this law. They are self-serving, willful, and godless, hence they and all their fruits are unjust.

Peter Brown rightly sees this brusk condemnation as "the last round in a long drama" (Brown 1967, p. 302), and a full account of Augustine's moral theology and its relation to the classical tradition would qualify it in myriad ways.[7] Nonetheless, the argument itself stands as the cornerstone of the theology of the subsequent 12 centuries in the west and remains central to the moral vision of many in the Christian tradition (cf. Davis 1991). Jesus, on this account, delivered the new law, superseding the old law of the Hebrew Bible and establishing thereby the true church, entry into which is through faith, which comes as a free gift from God. What will become the orthodox understanding of this grace, the doctrine being laid down by Augustine, insists that it alone makes possible the love of God and neighbor that the Lord demands.

Recent interpreters have focused on the conflict between *agape* and *eros*, charity and erotic love, but for many reasons this seems misguided. It is more fruitful to think, with Augustine, in terms of the transformation of the individual needed to recognize the propriety of God's new law, for the problem is not that each and every pre-Christian was a creature of pride, bent on his own virtue and the enjoyment of that virtue's rewards. It is, rather, that the noblest and most praiseworthy of pagans is doomed to fail in his quest for happiness by an inability to feel, and thus to perceive the truth about his relation to others. The preeminent example of the need for the transformation worked by grace is Augustine himself. On the brink of his conversion he is all but persuaded of the intellectual and the moral superiority of Christianity; this is no longer the problem. "Grant me chastity and continence, but not yet," he had prayed, but "the day had now come when I stood naked to myself, and my conscience complained against me: 'Where is your tongue?' . . . I threw myself down somehow under a certain figtree, and let my tears flow freely. . . . 'Why not now? Why not an end to my impure life in this very hour?' " Why not indeed? But the choice cannot be made unaided, by Augustine himself:

> As I was saying this and weeping in the bitter agony of my heart, suddenly I heard a voice from the nearby house chanting as if it might be a boy or a girl (I do not know which), saying and repeating over and over again "Pick up and read, pick up and read." At once my countenance changed, and I began to think intently whether there might be some sort of children's game in which such a chant is used. But I could not remember having heard of one. I checked the flood of tears and stood up. I interpreted it solely as a divine command to me to open the book and read the first chapter I might find. For I had heard how Antony happened to be present at the gospel reading, and took it as an admonition addressed to himself when the words were read: "Go, sell all you have, give to the poor, and you shall have treasure in heaven; and come, follow

me." . . . with a face now at peace I told everything to Alypius. (Augustine 1992, *Conf*: VIII, 12)

He is turned around, converted in the literal sense of the word, and he is now able to see what he should do. The androgynous voice floating into the garden comes from the Holy Spirit and renders Augustine capable, at last, of hearing and acting upon what his intellect already tells him. His internal conflicts are healed, and it now becomes natural and easy to perceive what needs to be done and make the decisions necessary to that end.

Once his conversion is effected Augustine becomes capable of recognizing that true virtue does not stem from the desire for individual attainment and happiness, but from the desire to serve his neighbor that flows from the love made possible by grace. As he wrote not long after his conversion:

> temperance is love keeping itself entire and incorrupt for God; fortitude is love bearing everything readily for the sake of God; justice is love serving God only, and therefore ruling well all else, as subject to man; prudence is love making a right distinction between what helps it towards God and what might hinder it. (Augustine 1948b, XV)

Grace imparts love of God, and thus the preeminent desire to do God's bidding. God commands not merely good works, but love of the neighbor, and this, on Augustine's account, constitutes a qualitative and unbridgeable gap between the motives and actions of pagan and Christian. The relevant distinction is not institutional allegiance, but the difference in heart and soul between the person who has received grace, now capable of genuine moral discernment, and the one who still labors under the constraints of sin. The Stoics were, it now appears, on the right track, but without an awareness of God's law they could not coherently articulate the ties that bind us to the most distant Mysian, mediated as they are through the creative and providential activity of God. The particularities of our place in time and space will modify what we can do for strangers, and hence qualify the blame that accrues to our failures, but in principle everyone is our neighbor, and we are bound and beholden to do what we can for them in this life, up to and including the sacrifice of ourselves and our immediate loves. This is perfect virtue. Anything less is mundane and tainted by our own self-interest.

The Appearances and the Realities:
Occasions for Giving in the Medieval Context

Michel Mollat, the preeminent student of medieval poverty and its relief, writes that the uniquely Christian argument for poor relief "derived straight from the Gospels: Christ is found in the poor; we possess earthly goods only to administer them; all excess belongs to the poor; alms wipe away sin, but God cannot be corrupted by charity; it is the duty of all Christians to give alms" (Mollat 1986, p. 39). But the reality is much more complex. Medieval thought on giving is fluid and responsive to changes in the social and intellectual context. In illustration, I shall comment briefly on the monastic tradition, an influential English lord and his milieu, the movement initiated by St. Francis of Assisi, most famous of high medieval saints, and Thomas Aquinas's attempt to come to grips with all this in the *Summa Theologica*, his self-described manual for beginners.

About the time Augustine pens the nineteenth book of his *City of God*, John Cassian, in a religious house in Marseilles, writes that the earliest monks:

> men of perfect life, were, if I may say so, a stem from which grew many flowers and fruit—the hermits. Everyone knows the founders of this way, Abba Paul and Antony . . . this second way of perfection sprang out of the first. Its followers are called anchorites, that is *withdrawers*. They have not remained satisfied with defeating the attacks which the devils secretly plan in human society, but have been ready to meet them in open war. (Cassian 1958, 18, 6)

The image of monk as warrior is central, for although the great figures of monastic tradition are typically well versed in Augustine's thought, true perfection expresses itself not in the doing of good works, but in encountering the temptations of the devil and proving your fealty to your lord. The most influential training manual for this battle against God's opponents, as far as western Europe goes, is the *Rule* of St. Benedict, composed sometime in the sixth century and given great impetus in the seventh by the spiritual authority of Gregory the Great.[8] The follower of Benedict internalizes his love of God by climbing the ladder of humility, giving up his own will in obedience to his abbot, "bearing injuries and adversity with patience. But more: Struck on one cheek they offer the other," until they reach the point "when the monk's inward humility appears outwardly in his comportment," at which point the monk "will quickly arrive at the top, the charity that is perfect and casts out all fear. And then the virtues which he first practiced with anxiety, shall begin to be easy for him, almost natural, being grown habitual" (Benedict 1958, 7). For the monastic, charity is the perfection of virtue, the service out of love for God and the neighbor that comes with the gift of faith. The monk works to internalize this in his struggles against the temptations thrown up by the forces of evil.

Among the 70-some precepts enumerated in rule four are "to relieve the poor, to clothe the naked, to visit the sick, to bury the dead, to help those that are in trouble, and to comfort the afflicted," but they are explicitly "instruments of spiritual progress," and "the best place to practice these things is the monastery with its seclusion—provided that we remain steadily in the community and do not leave it" (Benedict 1958, 4). Although the office of almoner emerged well before the twelfth century, his special duty is not mentioned by name in the rule. Almsgiving, as a practical activity, may be a duty, but it is not the attainment of perfect charity sought by those who enter the lists of spiritual combat.

This is not to say that the monasteries had no impact on charitable giving, or that they did not teach the duty to relieve the poor. Quite the opposite, for "the brutal reality of poverty and greed contradicted the ideal of the Sermon on the Mount" (Mollat 1986, p. 42). Within the church the monastic houses in particular considered assistance to the poor "an evangelical obligation," that enjoined the almoner not merely to aid the poor and ill who came to him, but in some cases "to make a weekly tour of the township to seek out any who were sick and in need of food or medicaments" (Lawrence 1989, p. 122). The church could sustain this welfare because religious opinion "considered that offering the material things of this world to God's servants was an act of piety deserving salvation," which meant that "any act of mortal sin was an occasion for a devout man to make a gift of atonement. . . . Benedictine abbeys and cathedral churches were the chief beneficiaries" (Duby 1962, p. 174). The church was expected to devote its material resources to the care of the community, and those suitably endowed were expected to give, and they intended those gifts to secure their own spiritual, as well as physical, well-being. In an important sense the spiritual power derived from combat with demons, and stored up in the monasteries, could be circulated to protect the spiritual welfare of the rich, whose alms to the monasteries made it possible both for the monks to continue their battles and give succor to the poor. Richard Southern, discussing this system of circulation, cites a rousing passage from the twelfth-century chronicler Orderic Vitalis:

> Look carefully at the things which are provided for you by trained monks living in monasteries under a Rule: strenuous is the warfare which these castellans of Christ wage against the Devil; innumerable are the benefits of their struggle. . . . I earnestly advise you to build such a castle in your country, manned by monks against Satan. Here the cowled champions will resist Behemoth in constant warfare for your soul. (Southern 1970, p. 225; ellipses mine)

The evangelical duty embedded in the *Rule* plays an important unifying factor in the larger spiritual and material economy of the time. The great fathers of the Latin church—Ambrose, Augustine, and Gregory—may have set the stage for the transformation of classical into Christian virtue, but the overarching framework remains the reciprocal exchange of goods articulated by Mauss and evidenced in Veyne.

Duby captures this ethos of spiritual and material reciprocity particularly well in his account of William Marshal's last hours, in April of 1219. This regent of England, who rose from humble beginnings to wield immense power, leaves to his second son a seigneury in Normandy "so that unlike so many disinherited second sons he will not envy and torment and execrate his older brother" (Duby 1985, p. 8). The third son's place in the church has been secured, at considerable expense, the fourth given a small manor, and the fifth an income in trust. The daughters, all but one, are properly and advantageously disposed and it is now left to divest himself of his liquid assets, "whose weight risks dragging his soul down to hell. That is what the churchmen keep telling him. For they are here now, increasingly numerous, drawn by this windfall" (Duby 1985, p. 17). Distribute it he does, first to his own people, then to the lords and prelates who, he assumes, will remember his largesse in working for the continued stability of his family, and finally in death, he presides over a final meal, "as master of the house, the seigneur who is never better loved than when he distributes bread and wine. He has told his heir that he desires that one hundred poor men be present and fed . . . there are on this day many more than are needed" (Duby 1985, p. 23). To be mindful of others, and of your duties to God and to those less fortunate is part and parcel of a noble's self-interest, and failure in this regard will cause you to suffer duly. In the comparatively small world of Anglo-Norman nobility William may well have heard tell of Alais of Soissons, who "after dining exceedingly well on the first day of Lent . . . lost the use of her tongue and became infirm throughout her body, and, what was worst of all, after that she had no understanding of the things of God and lived the life of a pig" (Benton 1970, pp. 209–10). In a world where all our acts have consequences both natural and supernatural it is a mark of wisdom to do as much as we can to secure the circulation of goods in our favor. In this way there is a constant exchange going from monk to noble to the indigent poor, watched over by God.

But even as William Marshal lay dying things had begun to change. In January or February of 1206 an exasperated father brought his rebellious son before the local bishop, insisting that if he would not renounce his ways he should at least renounce all claim on his patrimony. Appearing before the bishop the well-to-do young man, not quite 25, "did not wait for any words nor did he speak any, but immediately putting off his clothes and casting them aside, he gave them back to his father. Moreover, not even retaining his trousers, he stripped himself completely naked before all" (Habig 1973, p. 241). So began the spiritual career of Francis of Assisi. A generation earlier the attempt of Peter Waldo and his followers to embrace poverty and lay preaching got them hounded out of Lyon, but from this dramatic beginning Francis went on to become the most famous saint of the high Middle Ages. The order of "little brothers" that he founded became wealthy and powerful to the point of internal fracture, and like never before the source of contention was money.[9] But while visionary, Francis's new understanding was not without its precursors.

In the earlier Middle Ages alms circulated from the landed few to the monasteries and cathedral churches, who added to the work of divine service the responsibility for assisting the publicly needy. The solitary hermits who chose poverty and life in the forest were rarely in a position to help the needy. Lay giving, as in the example of William Marshal, was "ostentatious by design, and pride and condescension were integral components of the act of giving" (Mollat 1986, p. 71). But with the growth of a money economy and the revival of city life came new reflections on the status of the poor, returning self-consciously to the central texts of Augustine and the other fathers to unite Christian charity with justice for the poor. The rich now have a "duty" to give, not simply as a hedge against hell, but as a matter of proper Christian intention.[10] These reflections bore fruit in various public responses to the calamities of the twelfth century. Mollat notes the upsurge in founding or refurbishing hospitals, the establishment of a royal almonry in France, and the appearance of charitable associations in the cities (Mollat 1986, pp. 87–101)—all this as part of a rethinking of Christian charity and its place in the social and economic systems.

Where the Benedictines of earlier days stored up spiritual power through battle with demons, the followers of Francis made their spiritual ascent by forsaking all forms of wealth, but especially money, and dedicating themselves to preaching and to serving the poor. Whatever its relation to the official lives of Francis, the life attributed to his earliest followers is striking for its emphasis on the role of money in his conversion.[11] Thus it opens, "the father of the blessed and evangelical man Francis was named Peter, the son of the merchant Bernadone; and he was absorbed with making money" (Habig 1973, p. 890). The saint they describe as:

> a spendthrift, and all that he earned went into eating and carousing with his friends. . . . he spent much more on his clothes than was warranted by his social position. He would use only the finest materials. . . . Although a merchant, he squandered his wealth, never counting the cost. One day when he was in the shop selling cloth, a beggar came in and asked for alms for the love of God; but Francis was so intent on the business of making money that he gave nothing to the poor man. (Habig 1973, pp. 891–92)

It is involvement with money for money's sake that characterizes Francis before his conversion, and his subsequent rejection of money is linked to a new understanding of the demands of the gospel. We do not sell all we have and give it to the poor in order to take on the demons in the desert, but in order to minister directly to the needy, whose demand on us is pressing for no other reason than that they are Christ's poor.

The work of Francis and his older contemporary, Dominic, "represent something new in the history of poverty" (Mollat 1986, p. 119). New is the identification with the poor, not merely as recipients of soul-salving alms, or Cassian's voluntary "withdrawers," but as the objects of God's highest affection and hence a reprimand to all who are not committed to their love and care. But

Francis combines love for the poor with two other notions that are key to understanding the novelty of his position. First, he feels compelled himself to live the life of the poor. In all the early biographies Francis insists on the poorest of garments, eschews shoes, and embraces extremes of hunger and discomfort. From early on his followers are forbidden to take money or own real property and must rely on the goodness of others for their daily needs. In the final version of his *Rule*, in 1223, Francis insists that even if the brothers allow spiritual friends to provide their barest necessities, "this does not dispense them from the prohibition of receiving money in any form," going on to permit them to accept what they need as wages, when they work, "except money in any form. And they should accept it humbly as is expected of those who serve God and strive after the highest poverty" (Habig 1973, p. 61, rules 4 and 5). Second, Francis insists that whatever good the friar performs comes not from him, but from God. In itself this is hardly a novel idea, but Francis takes it to a new intensity, not only in his own life, but in the *Admonitions* collected after his death and kept as a Franciscan book of guidance. Thus in the 12th admonition the test of the truly religious is that "his lower nature does not give way to pride when God accomplishes some good through him, and if he seems all the more worthless and inferior to others in his own eyes" (Habig 1973, p. 83). The sentiment is reiterated in the 17th, which extols "the religious who takes no more pride in the good that God says and does through him, than in that which he says and does through someone else" (Habig 1973, p. 84). This is still clearer in the 25th admonition, lauding "that friar who loves his brother as much when he is sick and can be of no use to him as when he is well and can be of use to him" (Habig 1973, p. 86). Neither Aristotle nor William Marshal would himself be so callous as to abandon a sick friend, for Francis's point is that Christian brotherhood extends to "all peoples, tribes, families and languages, all nations and all men everywhere, present and to come" (Habig 1973, p. 51). Here, as nowhere before, the virtues reinterpreted as forms of Christian love are conjoined with the call to work actively and in your own person on behalf of the most needy.

The novelty, not to mention the difficulty of living out this ideal is nowhere more evident than in the subsequent history of Franciscan poverty. Within a generation of Francis's death in 1226, the order had become the object of severe criticism from outside, and inside the Franciscans bickered over discipline, government, and, most especially, over the requirements of poverty. Within a century internal factions turned militant, and argument turned to outright rebellion. On May 7 of 1318 Pope John XXII had four recalcitrants burned in Marseilles for their refusal to submit (Moorman 1968, p. 311). In subsequent years various groups were persecuted as heretics and even within the order divisions proliferated to accommodate competing ideals. But this fascinating story goes well beyond the limits of this essay. To conclude I turn to the remarkable *Summa Theologica* of St. Thomas Aquinas.

It is common to treat the work of St. Thomas as a watershed in the thought of the Middle Ages, and in a sense this is correct. The *Summa*, though unfinished, is a masterpiece of synthesis, argument, and organization. In later centuries it became the centerpiece of much mainstream Catholic thought. Nonetheless, identifying medieval thought with the work of St. Thomas risks obscuring the innovative, in many ways radical, qualities of Thomas's work. For Aquinas wishes both to continue the tradition of Ambrose, Augustine, and Gregory *and* take advantage of the now inescapable legacy of Aristotle, recovered for the Latin West only within the century. The body of Aristotle's work was little known in the early Middle Ages, and it burst on the culture of the emerging universities like a dam breaking. Teaching Aristotle's natural philosophy was banned at Paris in 1210, and the ban was renewed in 1215 and again in 1231, but by 1255 its study was required by the statutes of the university (Kretzmann et al. 1982, pp. 70–73). The institutional impact of Aristotle, not to mention the intellectual excitement of the work, made it more than expedient that his place within the teachings of the faith be clarified and integrated, particularly in the teaching of young clerics. Thomas undertook this in his various commentaries, disputed questions, and the *Summa contra Gentiles*, but nowhere more deeply than in the *Summa Theologica*.[12]

The *Summa Theologica* takes for its architectonic the derivation of all things from God's creative act and the manner in which creation reflects the perfection of that act. Most of nature, of course, reflects this simply by behaving as it was designed, though humanity, as a result of disobedience, fell away from God, and its perfection is only realized in the return to God made possible through grace. This structure falls naturally into three parts: The nature of the created order in general; the nature of human action, both in its perfection and in its defect; and the steps by which a fallen humanity may be brought back to God. In the process of return all aspects of man's created nature are perfected, including the senses, leading naturally to his discerning things as they are and treating them as they should be treated, and indeed "this is effected by charity which operates consent in us men. Wherefore even the perfection of the senses consists radically in the perfection of charity" (Aquinas 1989, 2a2ae, 184, 1 ad 1). In good Aristotelian fashion, there is a continuity in the perceptions, emotions, and habits that incline us to act, so when charity reshapes the senses, it allows them to grasp what was previously obscured. At the same time the emotions are brought into line and the virtues transformed so that the truly good may be seen and done. In this fashion Aquinas melds Augustine's transformation of the virtues with Aristotle's account of how those virtues work.

Another aspect of Thomas's Aristotelianism is his tendency toward the specific. Thus if charity is the general state toward which the Christian moves, it may have specific forms, so that "we may consider a threefold perfection. One is absolute, and answers to a totality not only on the part of the lover, but also on the part of the object loved, so that God be loved as much as He is lovable." This sort of perfection is only possible for God, who is infinitely lovable and also the only being capable of infinite love. A second form of perfection in charity would be to love God as much as the lover, given his created nature, is capable, but "perfection such as this is not possible so long as we are on the way, but we shall have it in heaven." It is not possible on earth because we are constantly being distracted from the love of God by our own concerns and the concerns of those around us. But despite the fact that these two forms of perfection are not available in this life, we can achieve the love of God that disposes us to remove from our affections "all that is contrary to charity, such as mortal sin," as well as "whatever hinders the mind's affections from tending wholly to God." This is the perfection appropriate to human life in this world, though Aquinas goes on to point out that charity is possible, and when achieved it is worthy, even when it is not perfect, "for instance in those who are beginners and in those who are proficient" (2a2ae, 184, 2).

If perfection is found in charity, it is still necessary to discover what charity is, and how it relates to human interaction. For Thomas, the answer is that "charity is the friendship of man for God" (2a2ae, 23, 1). In good Aristotelian fashion, friendship seeks happiness through achieving the good for the friend. In the case of God, this is obedience to his law as communicated through Jesus. To be a genuine friendship, however, the interaction, and thus the communication must be continuous, and, in the sense that perfection is possible in this life, this friendship extends not only to our immediate friends, but to everyone in respect of God:

> as when a man has a friendship for a certain person, for his sake he loves all belonging to him, be they children, servants, or connected with him in any way. Indeed, so much do we love our friends, that for their sake we love all who belong to them, even if they hurt or hate us; so that, in this way, the friendship of charity extends even to our enemies, whom we love out of charity in relation to God, to Whom the friendship of charity is chiefly directed. (2a2ae, 23, 1 ad 2)

Charity is first and foremost friendship with God, which becomes love of our friends for God's sake, and then love of those "belonging to him," which means all people, at all times. Thus we find ourselves naturally disposed to care for all humanity as a consequence of our charity.

Aquinas contrasts such charity with liberality. Liberality, as we saw earlier, deals specifically with money and its proper disposition. It is a part of justice only insofar as it is concerned with the appropriate distribution of goods to others, and far from being the perfection of virtue, liberality rests on a friend-ship that is not "based on virtue, as though he were better than others, but that which is based on utility, because he is more useful in external goods, which as a rule men desire above all others. For the same reason he becomes famous" (2a2ae, 117, 6 ad 3). Liberality, by itself, may be related to charity, but only as a subordinate virtue that must itself be judged by the precepts of charity.

Almsgiving provides a more complex example of the melding of Augus-tinian with Aristotelian. Thus Thomas acknowledges seven forms of corporal almsgiving, "to visit, to quench, to feed, to ransom, clothe, harbor or bury," which go hand in hand with the spiritual alms, "to counsel, reprove, console, to pardon, forbear, and to pray" (2a2ae, 32, 2 ob. 1). To the extent that almsgiving is a part of charity, as opposed to an expression of pagan pride, it comprises both the spiritual and corporal duties that are due members of the community from their fellows. Here Thomas rejects reciprocity in the sense of Mauss. He insists, for example, that "to invite our friends and kinsmen . . . so that they may invite us in return" is unacceptable, "an act not of charity but of cupidity" (2a2ae 31, 3 ad 1). Nonetheless, almsgiving in practice must be subsumed under the general Aristotelian account of virtue as rational action in accord with na-ture and congruent with the mean. Thus, in addressing the question of whether one ought to give alms out of what one needs, Thomas concludes that "it is al-together wrong to give alms out of what is necessary to us" in the sense of being required for the maintenance of station and family. "For instance," he notes, "if a man found himself in the presence of a case of urgency, and had merely sufficient to support himself and his children, or others under his charge, he would be throwing away his life and that of others," albeit he qualifies this by granting that such sacrifice would be acceptable in

> such a case as might happen, supposing that by depriving himself of neces-saries a man might help a great personage, and a support of the Church or State, since it would be a praiseworthy act to endanger one's life and the lives of those who are under our charge for the delivery of such a person, since the common good is to be preferred to one's own. (2a2ae, 32, 6)

We must, as a matter of the reason, exercise discretion in giving and acknowl-edge the ties of nature that lead us to prefer our near neighbors and family over distant neighbors. We must respond selflessly to the distress of even the stranger who suffers in our midst, but not to the extent of endangering ourselves and our charges, *except* in the case where the person to be helped is of particular importance to the community whose common good now resides in the spiritual realm.

Neither the unbridled self-sacrifice of Francis nor the studied reciprocity of the Stoic commonwealth, this alloy of Augustine and Aristotle on the virtues stands as a backdrop for charity in all of its forms. St. Thomas may serve as a summary of the medieval consensus on giving not because he brings a single theory to its culmination, but because he succeeds in holding several strands of the tradition in a reasonably stable synthesis. Aquinas articulates the common wisdom that the sacrifice of Francis cannot be obligatory on all, while acknowledging it as an ideal to be applauded. For those incapable of such sacrifice, giving must be ordered by the doctrine of the mean found in Aristotle, interpreted in terms of the good represented by the church. When Dante, in the *Paradiso*, has Thomas extol the relation of Francis and Lady Poverty, whose "harmony and their glad looks, their love and wonder and their gentle contemplation, served others as a source of holy thoughts" (Dante XI, 76–78), he acknowledges one among many forms of life, all of which must be cultivated as long as Christians remain pilgrims in this world.

Conclusion

I began with a dispute over the continuity of philanthropy from late antiquity into the Middle Ages. By and large I have sided with Veyne and his claim for the *discontinuity* of the classical with the late antique and medieval meanings of philanthropy. But there was still an important story to be told about philanthropy, charity, and their related vocabulary. This is the story I have tried to sketch, and it involved the spectrum of medieval thought, institutions, and common presuppositions. If there is a medieval consensus, St. Thomas represents it as well as anyone else, but it is important to recognize the continuing plurality of forms and understandings that underlie the medieval concept of philanthropy. While Thomas measured giving against the norms of nature and virtue, Benedict counseled his charges to climb the solitary ladder of humility. Francis left an example that stood in judgment against even Aquinas's analysis. Whatever the dictates of practical reason, the plight of the poor *should* inspire the total sacrifice of Francis, and while failure to go as far as the saint may not be a moral failure, it points nonetheless to our spiritual limits. To do at least something, even for the furthest Mysian, is not just a duty, it should be a desire.

Notes

1. Veyne uses the term "euergetism" which is derived from two Greek roots meaning "good" and "to do." "Euergetism," Veyne writes, "means private liberality for public benefit. The word euergetism is a neologism—nay, even a new concept—for which we are indebted to André Boulanger and Henri-I. Marrou. It was created from the wording of the honorific decrees of the Hellenistic period by which cities honored those persons who, through their money or their public activity, 'did good to the city' " (Veyne 1990, p. 10). Veyne's book was first published in 1976, in French; an abridged English translation appeared in 1990. See also Veyne (1987).

2. The evidence for ancient Greece and Rome is surveyed in Hands (1968). Jones

(1964) remains fundamental for the early centuries of the common era, while Constantelos (1991) takes the eastern empire into the Middle Ages, with considerable bibliography. For fascinating details of case studies in the medieval West, see Suzanne Roberts's chapter in this volume.

3. It is traditional to cite Aristotle by referring to the nineteenth-century edition of Immanuel Bekker. Although Bekker's text has been superseded, his consecutive numbering of pages and lines continues to be printed in almost all editions and translations, allowing users to find a text regardless of the edition.

4. "Altruism" appears to be a neologism introduced by Compte "to denote a devotion to the interests of others as an action-guiding principle" (Paul et al., eds. 1993, p. vii). It should probably be seen as part and parcel of the French critique of British liberal individualism that also motivated Durkheim and issued in Marcel Mauss's classic work on gift giving in traditional cultures. See Mary Douglas's forward to Mauss (1990).

5. References to Julian take as their standard the pagination of the 1696 edition of Spanheim, but this is problematic for some works, so in addition I have added the volume number of Wright's text, from which all my citations come. Thus (II, 289a–c) indicates Wright volume two, Spanheim 289A to 289C.

6. That this last is intended as a mark of Julian's philanthropy could hardly be lost on those who might remember the brutality of the last persecutions, particularly in the east, where market goods were sprinkled with the blood of pagan sacrifices, propaganda circulated to rouse the hatred of the mob and, as Robin Lane Fox puts it, "prostitutes were tortured to confess to Christian debaucheries, while bishops were directed to a new, invigorating life as keepers of the Imperial camels or stable boys for the Imperial horses" (Fox 1986, p. 596).

7. The secondary literature on Augustine is of oceanic proportions. Chadwick (1986) is an adequate introduction, with a sensible bibliography, though rather unhelpful on the specifics of philosophical argument. Look at Wetzel (1992) for a sensitive and philosophically sophisticated account of Augustine on grace, virtue, and freedom, with serious attention to the relevant bibliography.

8. Knowles (1969) is a popular, though authoritative, survey of the sweep of monastic history. Lawrence (1989) concentrates in more detail on the medieval west and brings the bibliography up to date. Straw (1988) is an important presentation of the spirituality of Gregory the Great.

9. Little (1978) explicitly relates these movements to an urban spiritual crisis under the advent of a profit economy. Morris (1989) provides further bibliography on all of these topics. Note particularly the works of David Knowles, R. I. Moore, M. D. Lambert, and Kajetan Esser.

10. In addition to the discussion in Mollat (1986, pp. 102–13), see the seminal essays in Chenu (1968), particularly 1, 6, and 7.

11. Habig's "omnibus" is a gold mine of sources with an exhaustive bibliography through 1969. Fleming (1977) is a systematic survey with an emphasis on the social and literary. Moorman (1968) is the standard history of the early Franciscans in English, but should be supplemented by the bibliography found in Morris (1989), particularly the works of Rosalind Brooke and David Knowles.

12. The standard way of referring to Thomas's *Summa* is by part, question, article, and section. Thus in my first citation below "2a2ae, 184, 1 ad 1" should be read "second part of the second part, question 184, article 1, response to the first objection." Although the French original appeared in 1950, Chenu (1964) remains an indispensable guide to Thomas's work as a whole. Weisheipl (1974) supplies the narrative, but there is no outstanding guide to the details of his thought, though many have tried. Of the more recent, Kenny (1980) is very readable.

2 | Contexts of Charity in the Middle Ages

Religious, Social, and Civic

Suzanne Roberts

THROUGHOUT THE Middle Ages, charity was inextricably bound with the theory and practice of the Christian religion, with its liturgy, theology, and spirituality. Yet this paper would dispel the notion that medieval charity was an entirely ecclesiastical enterprise throughout its thousand-year span. There was a clear shift from the early medieval period when it was administered by ecclesiastical institutions largely for liturgical ends to the laicized charity of the high Middle Ages. This period, which is the focus of this paper, saw the growing involvement of the laity and civic institutions in charitable activity; motives remained predominantly religious although blended with civic and social concerns. The late Middle Ages witnessed the beginnings of the secularization of poor relief as royal and municipal authorities played an increasing role in rationalizing the administration of relief for civic ends. This change was grounded, as we shall see, in the legal thinking of the high Middle Ages.

Major shifts in the nature of society and religious aspirations in the high Middle Ages brought dramatic changes in the practice and the meaning of charity on personal and social levels. The significance of charitable activity in this period sprang from a remarkable confluence of economic, social, and religious forces. The growing monetary economy facilitated charitable giving, which in turn became a means for individuals and communities to cope with the moral dilemmas and social problems of economic expansion. As part of the spiritual revival and codification of religious doctrine, charity became one of the forces that bound Christian communities together. In the crises of the late medieval period this convergence of forces disintegrated; new structures and new attitudes arose to deal with the problems of poor relief.

The medieval experience thus constitutes one chapter in what Mary Douglas has termed elsewhere in this volume "the great historical debate on poverty." It provides a case study of the two classic positions on the proper relationship of individuals and societies to the poor: one values and embraces the poor while the other blames and excludes them. The medieval experience sheds light on the historical conditions which cause one view to prevail in a given society and those which favor the other.

Background: Early Medieval Charity

To appreciate the transformation of charity in the high and late Middle Ages, we must understand the character of charity in the early medieval period and the economic and social forces which altered it. Largely the responsibility of the bishops and monasteries, charity became primarily a liturgical function until the economic and religious revivals of the twelfth century.

In the fifth and sixth centuries, the urban economy of the ancient world retreated from the Latin West, and Roman civil administration declined and with it public secular responsibility for poor relief. Bishops assumed this obligation, which was reinforced by papal decretals and decrees of church councils, in particular that of Orleans in 511. Church property was considered the "patrimony of the poor"; as the "fathers of the poor" bishops were to devote one-fourth of their revenues to care of the poor, and in rural areas one-third of charitable gifts belonged to the poor. Bishops were expected to set an example of personal generosity and to exhort clergy and laity to charitable acts.[1]

As poverty moved from the shrinking cities into rural areas in the seventh century, charitable services migrated from urban episcopal seats to rural abbeys and monasteries where hospices took on responsibility for assistance to the poor as well as hospitality for travelers and pilgrims. *Matricula* (lists of poor people who were cared for at church expense) and hostels were still maintained in cathedral churches, but by the ninth century, under the growing influence of the Rule of Saint Benedict, monastic hostels played an increasingly important role (Mollat 1986, pp. 41–42).

Charity and hospitality were an integral part of monastic life in the Middle Ages. Chapter four of the sixth-century Rule of Saint Benedict enjoined monks to perform good works, to give their old clothing to the poor, to wash paupers' feet on Holy Thursday (the *mandatum*), and to make distributions to the poor as part of observances for the dead (Roberts 1977, p. 38). In addition, Chapter fifty-three of the Rule outlined the obligation and forms of monastic hospitality. Guests were treated as if they were Christ himself; they were greeted with a kiss of peace, had their feet washed, and were conducted to a hospice (Roberts 1977, pp. 34–35). By the ninth century Benedictine monks distinguished between rich and poor guests and had hospices for the former and *hospitalia pauperum* for the latter. The distribution of alms in the latter was closely associated with religious rituals and liturgical customs. In addition to the ritual *mandatum* and distributions to the poor during Lent and at Easter, a symbolic number—often twelve—of paupers were regularly nourished in the monastery. By the tenth and eleventh centuries in the West, charity had become a function of liturgy and ritual (Little 1978, pp. 67–68).

Liturgical acts were of primary importance in Benedictine spirituality; assistance to the poor was a secondary concern. Poverty in this period was considered a phenomenon of power; the poor were contrasted with the powerful rather than with the rich. Monks were viewed, and viewed themselves, as the "poor of Christ"; having forsaken personal power and property, they lived in the security of their corporate wealth and were entitled to the charitable donations of the faithful. In the eyes of wealthy donors the true poor were these voluntary paupers, the monks who would pray for their salvation; the spiritual rather than the social benefits of charity were foremost in their minds.

All of these early medieval institutions, episcopal as well as monastic, persisted into the high and late Middle Ages, only slightly modified by the monastic and religious revival of the eleventh and twelfth centuries. The new religious orders, especially the Cistercians in the twelfth century, elaborated these patterns of charity without changing them in fundamental ways. The cartularies of the Cistercian houses in a region of southwestern France such as the Rouergue, for example, give evidence of extraordinary distributions of food in times of famine as well as of hospices and regular almsgiving.

By the late twelfth century, however, bishops and monks had lost their monopoly on charitable services. Beginning in the eleventh century the Latin West was transformed by major economic and demographic changes. With the commercial revival and the development of a money economy came a dramatic increase in population, its mobility and its concentration in urban areas where trade and industry flourished again. The poor, both itinerant and urban, became more numerous and more evident. A religious and intellectual regeneration accompanied the economic and social revival, transforming the medieval approach to poverty and poor relief on both intellectual and practical levels. The intersection of powerful economic forces and religious ideas forged new personal and social meanings of charity. Charity came to be directed more and more toward the less fortunate members of earthly society. At the same time lay men and women as individuals and as groups became increasingly involved in the practice of charity.

New Theories of Charity in the High Middle Ages

Against this background we can examine the concept of charity in the high Middle Ages. To illustrate the place of charity in the religious and intellectual movements, I will focus on two themes that shaped the meaning and practice of charity.

Throughout the Middle Ages, charity was closely tied to the theological and practical evolution of Christianity. Christian writings from the Bible and the writings of the Fathers to the decrees of councils, monastic rules, scholastic reasoning, and canon law provided a rich array of reflection and prescriptions to guide charitable activity. Two interpretations of the Christian duty of charity emerge from this body of material—an inclusive "evangelical" model and a "discriminating" one. The evangelical notion grew out of the eleventh- and twelfth-century spiritual revival; in the model charity was religious, spiritual, personal. The discriminating concept developed in the intellectual and legal ferment of that period and was based on concerns for law, justice, community, and right relations in human society.

The Evangelical Model

The religious revival of the twelfth century brought noticeable shifts in the idea and practice of Christian charity. Several elements of the new spirituality influenced changing notions of charity. Most important was the emphasis on apostolic poverty; Christ had admonished his followers to sell all their goods and give to the poor. Wealth was an impediment to salvation, and to aid the least of one's brethren was to succor Christ himself, who identified with the poor. The evangelical notion of charity was thus radically inclusive; it grew out of a desire to return to the *vita apostolica*, to the life and teachings of Christ as manifested in the New Testament, in particular the four gospels. One of the best-known passages of the Gospel, Matthew 25:34–46, evokes the Last Judgment and explicitly links works of charity—giving food to the hungry and drink to the thirsty, clothing the naked, sheltering the stranger, visiting the sick and the imprisoned—with salvation. Christ tells the blessed they will inherit His kingdom for "inasmuch as ye have done it unto one of the least of these my brethren, ye have done it unto me." Those who have not "shall go away into everlasting punishment." This vivid and moving passage, with its very broad and inclusive vision of the proper recipients of charity, was the foundation of the medieval doctrine of seven works of mercy, which will be discussed below.

The second important feature of the new spirituality was the humanization of religious experience; the emphasis on the humanity of Christ and the growing cult of the Virgin Mary were part of a broad movement which placed greater value on human experience. Charity, as love of one's neighbor, was seen as an essential part of the love of God, love best expressed by action in the world as well as in the soul.

The notion of intercession by the living for the dead is another element of twelfth-century spirituality which came to permeate the concept of charity. In spite of its increasingly social orientation, charity remained embedded in a family- and salvation-oriented piety. Charity indeed began at home. Donations to hospitals, almshouses, and leperhouses became a new way to intercede for one's relatives; donation charters nearly always state that the gift is intended to provide for the salvation of the donor's soul and those of his or her parents. The pious act itself secured intercession for the dead, but donors also expected the recipients of their charity to pray for them and their families. By the thirteenth century the evolution of charity had opened up a whole new category of intercessors; the poor, the sick, lepers, needy folk of gentle birth, poor women of marriageable age, widows, and orphans all had acquired a special spiritual value as instruments of salvation.

The final aspect of twelfth-century religious life that shaped the development of charity was the general tightening up of doctrine and its vigorous promulgation. The codification of charitable obligations and their firm integration into the doctrine of salvation were a product of this movement. The idea of works of mercy goes back, as seen above, to the New Testament and the Gospel of Matthew 25:34–46. The early church Fathers such as Cyprian, Lactantius, and Augustine commented on this passage, insisting that active mercy was important for attaining salvation. To the six works enumerated in Matthew, Saint Augustine added a seventh: burial of the dead. By the sixth century all the works of mercy had been spelled out along with their role in the final judgment (Vicaire 1978, pp. 26–27). In the twelfth century medieval thinkers elaborated two lists of works of mercy, corporal and spiritual, and fixed their content and number. The seven corporal works of mercy, following Augustine, included feeding the hungry, giving drink to the thirsty, clothing the naked, sheltering the homeless, visiting the sick, ransoming captives, and burying the dead. These were accompanied by seven spiritual works of mercy: instructing the ignorant, counseling the doubtful, admonishing sinners, bearing wrongs patiently, forgiving offenses, comforting the afflicted, and praying for the living and the dead. The systematization of these acts of mercy owed something to the medieval predilection for mystical numbers; numerous other theological notions were reduced to sevens at this time: capital sins, virtues, gifts of the holy spirit, beatitudes, and sacraments. It also received impetus from the intense effort of preaching and popularization in southern France which aimed at instructing the faithful in what they should believe and do to avoid heresy and obtain salvation. As the two septenaries of works and mercy came to be tied to other groups of seven (sacraments, sins, and virtues), the charitable obligations of Christians were spelled out as part of a systematic moral teaching. The fear of damnation served to direct the energies and resources of the faithful toward charity and good works. More important, however, was the dissemination and reception of these elements of Christian doctrine by a laity newly awakened to its spiritual needs and responsibilities (Vicaire 1978, p. 28).

The Popularization of Doctrine

The religious energy of the twelfth and thirteenth centuries produced several means of teaching religious doctrine to medieval people of all classes. Visual representations of the works of mercy appeared on the facades of churches, in stained glass windows, and on baptismal fonts. The didactic message was strongest, most evangelical, most charged with meaning on the portals of churches. The most famous of these is the tympanum of the Romanesque church of Saint Foy of Conques in southwestern France. Situated on the well-traveled pilgrimage routes to Saint James of Compostela, this Benedictine abbey received, sheltered, and instructed pilgrims in great numbers. The tympanum depicts the Last Judgment with a procession of the elect under the right hand of Christ. Angels carry banners inscribed with abbreviated verses from Matthew 25:31–46; others bear in Latin the words "charity" and "humility." The elect are described as virgins, martyrs, peaceful people, and *pietatis amici*, those who practice works of piety and charity. This moving sculpture impressed upon ordinary Christians the importance of works of mercy in the scheme of salvation (Vicaire 1978, pp. 29–31).

Sermons were a second means of spreading the gospel teachings on charity. The critical passages from the Gospel of Matthew were among the best known in the twelfth and thirteenth centuries; they were read on the Wednesday after Easter and at other times in the liturgical year when the theme of the Last Judgment arose. In addition, they figured prominently in the homilies of twelfth-century evangelical groups and itinerant preachers such as Raoul l'Ardent, who urged Christians to perform the specified works of mercy in order to be fed, clothed, welcomed, and comforted in eternity by the Supreme Judge (Vicaire 1978, pp. 30–31).

The third principal way the notion of charity reached medieval Christians was through penitential catechism. Works written to guide priests and confessors in their pastoral work appeared in the mid-thirteenth century. Like the *Penitential Book* of Alain of Lille, written between 1199 and 1203, they stress the importance of good works as a counterweight to avarice. Alain's *Art of Preaching* counseled priests to show how the works of mercy prepared the just to confront the Last Judgment and argue for them on the final day (Vicaire 1978, pp. 33–34).

The emphasis on charity as an antidote to avarice was quite new in the twelfth century. Traditional medieval morality was hostile toward most elements of the new economy including money, exchange, and profit making. While these attitudes were slowly changing, avarice joined pride as the major sin in the late eleventh and twelfth centuries. Numerous vivid, visual representations of and a large body of satirical literature about avarice in this period testify to the anxiety about the moral effects of money, the "root of all evil." Contemporaries thought that the best weapons against its corrupting influence were voluntary poverty and charity. Even thirteenth-century thinkers, who came to see money in more rational terms—as a measure of the value of things and as a medium of exchange—saw the ability to make charitable donations as a way to legitimize profit taking (Little 1978, pp. 35–36, 111–12, 178–79).

Numerous sets of statutes from episcopal synods of the thirteenth century contain manuals of penance and guides for instructing the faithful. They advise priests to teach people about the Trinity, the Incarnation, the seven sacraments, and the seven works of mercy which opposed the seven deadly sins. The works of mercy are enumerated and linked to the Day of Judgment (Vicaire 1978, pp. 34-36).

In other ways too the church encouraged pious and charitable works; from the twelfth century onward indulgences promised the faithful abbreviated stays in Purgatory in exchange for charitable donations to institutions that cared for the poor. In 1176, for example, the Bishop of Rodez granted an indulgence of seven days and participation in all its good works to those who contributed to the construction and adornment of a chapel in the leprosary of Combecrose which was located on the pilgrimage road outside Rodez. In 1228, his successor granted an indulgence of five days for the reconstruction of the same chapel.[2]

The Model of Discriminating Charity

The medieval emphasis on charity as a means to salvation has led modern historians to characterize medieval charity as indiscriminate and to criticize it for ignoring the real needs and merits of the poor. The dole at the monastery gate, the funeral gifts of shirts or pennies were even harmful, according to some, for they encouraged idleness and begging.[3] There was, however, another strain in medieval thinking about charity—a this-worldly emphasis which concerned itself directly with the perennial problem of discrimination in almsgiving and poor relief. This intellectual endeavor emerged in the second half of the twelfth century at the same time as the religious evangelical movement was reaching its high point.

The intellectual ferment of the twelfth century manifested itself in a desire to order and systematize the knowledge that had been transmitted across the centuries. Schools developed in the important urban centers of Bologna, Paris, and Oxford, producing reflections on charity in the disciplines of philosophy, theology, and law. Here I will focus on the group of canon lawyers who considered the obligations of almsgivers, the rights of the poor, and the social implications of charity. Their legalistic attempt to resolve contradictions in ancient authorities reinforced a more discriminating notion of individual charity and laid the groundwork for later discrimination in the administration of public poor relief. The canonists elaborated "a whole legal philosophy which related the claims of the poor to a coherent theory of natural law and property" (Tierney 1958-59, p. 361; see also Tierney 1959). Within this framework, they discussed the legal status of the poor, the right attitudes of benefactor and recipient, and the administration of public relief through ecclesiastical institutions.

The canonists in the second half of the twelfth century held that the poor had certain rights to the property of the rich. These were based in natural law according to which all property is common property in time of necessity. The poor had the right to use, though not to own, the property of others; they had a claim on the surplus wealth of the community. All classes had rights to church property, especially the poor whom it was supposed to support (Tierney 1959, pp. 27–44).

Considering the obligations of individuals to give alms, the canonists took up the problem of discrimination in poor relief: should eligibility be based solely on need, or should the desire to reform or punish the poor give rise to an order of preference among eligible recipients or criteria of selection (Tierney 1958–59, p. 361)? Their point of departure was the work of Gratian, whose *Decretum* (1140) had assembled without resolving the contradictory statements of the Church Fathers on the matter. The opinions of the early Christian writers covered the gamut from "indiscriminate" to truly punitive charity. Gratian presented the case for the former thus: "In hospitality there is no regard for persons, but we ought to welcome indifferently all for whom our resources suffice" (Tierney 1959, p. 55). He cited in support Saint John Chrysostom's opinion that one should help unquestioningly someone who asked only for food, for the generosity and goodwill of the giver were more important to God than the merits of the recipient (Tierney 1958–59, p. 362).

In support of more discriminating charity Gratian cited the *De officiis* of Saint Ambrose, the fourth-century bishop of Milan, himself an excellent administrator of poor relief. To guide clergy in fulfilling their pastoral duties, Ambrose delineated the groups of people who should receive preferential treatment in the dispensing of ecclesiastical charity. Faithful Christians had first claim to the generosity of the church along with those who because of age or sickness could not work and those who were plagued by misfortune. Special consideration should be given to those in need who were ashamed to beg publicly. Gratian also cited Saint Augustine, who maintained that no alms should be given to practitioners of vile professions such as actors, prostitutes, and gladiators. A more extreme view of Augustine also appears in the *Decretum*: "It is more useful to take bread away from a hungry man than to break bread for him if, being sure of his food, he neglected righteousness."[4]

In the second half of the twelfth century decretists or commentators on the *Decretum* attempted to reconcile these divergent authorities. In doing so they cited further texts and raised new distinctions. The influential Bolognese canonist Rufinus writing in the 1150s was the first to discuss discrimination in almsgiving in detail. He cited Saint Ambrose's order of charity (*caritas ordinata*) which "required a man to love first God, then his parents, then his children, then those of his own household and finally strangers" (Tierney 1958–59, pp. 363–64). Subsequent canonists strongly emphasized this notion that "charity begins at home" and the obligation to provide for family members who were needy. Rufinus proposed that beggars known to be dishonest and capable of working should receive nothing. Those dying of starvation should be helped regardless of other criteria. All unknown recipients who asked for food should be helped, but those who claimed to be preachers should be examined. If resources were ample, all honest persons could be aided. If resources were limited, Saint Ambrose's advice on discrimination in charity should be followed (Tierney 1958–59, pp. 363–64).

Most canonists in the French and Bolognese schools shared these views and agreed that poverty did not imply a moral defect on the part of the poor though some of them were more deserving than others. There was disagreement, however, on one important matter. Some held that there was a class of undeserving poor who should not receive aid even if there were sufficient resources; others felt that inadequate resources were the only reason to deny assistance.[5]

This central problem for poor relief, viz., should it simply alleviate want or should it attempt to correct or discipline those with great need but undesirable lifestyles and morals, received its definitive medieval treatment in the *Summa* (c. 1190) of the great Bolognese canonist Huguccio. Studied and accepted throughout the Middle Ages as the standard exposition of the problem, Huguccio's discussion incorporated the opinions of his predecessors. He maintained that funds permitting, strangers should receive assistance without investigation unless they claimed to be priests. Nonstrangers should receive aid unless they would be morally harmed by charity; able-bodied people capable of working but choosing to be idle fell into this category. Members of the vile professions should be assisted when they were needy. When resources were insufficient to help everyone, Saint Ambrose's rules of preference should be the guide, with severe cases of need receiving priority (Tierney 1958–59, pp. 369–70).

The canonists' discussions thus resulted in a doctrine on poor relief according to which one group of poor people were undeserving and ineligible for charity; this group was limited to the willfully idle while other objectionable lifestyles were tolerated. But in the most common situation of limited resources, the righteous were to be helped before the wicked (Tierney 1958–59, p. 370).

Canon lawyers thus provided society with a theory of property justifying the claims of the poor to assistance as well as strategies for deciding how to allocate limited resources. These guidelines served for individuals as well as institutions. Canonists adapted early patristic writings on the public, largely episcopal, administration of charity to the realities of the high Middle Ages where the parish system had come to play a prominent role in the administration of church property. In doing so they reinforced the notions that the established public authorities in society had to provide for the poor, that each parish had to provide for its own poor, and that authorities could enforce the obligation to contribute to poor relief. Much of their work was devoted to showing that episcopal responsibilities for poor relief had devolved on parish priests and to ensuring that priests had adequate resources to carry out this responsibility. Canon law required that all parishioners contribute through their tithes to the maintenance of the church and the poor. Lawyers found it necessary, however, to protect these revenues from being diverted from their intended use. Alienation, appropriation by monasteries (albeit for poor relief), and the absenteeism of parish priests were some of the abuses that prevented the appropriate use of ecclesiastical revenues in the thirteenth century. By the end of the thirteenth century they had developed a law of parochial incomes and responsibilities that suited the needs of the age (Tierney 1959, pp. 67–88).

They had in that time, however, developed little legislation about hospitals. In the fourteenth century abuses in the administration of hospitals provoked discussion among canon lawyers which centered on defining the legal status of these institutions in relation to parish and diocesan authorities (Tierney 1959, pp. 86–87).

The discussions and conclusions of canonists reached a wider audience through some of the channels mentioned above. Papal bulls, the decrees of general church councils, and the statutes of episcopal synods instructed the clergy and through them the laity in the rights of the poor and the duty of Christian charity for individuals, for ecclesiastical institutions and for the communities represented by parishes. Canon law, thus transmitted, provided for a modest redistribution of wealth in these communities and at the same time a rationale for a more discriminating approach to charity in case of insufficient resources. It also provided a model for an active role of public authority in poor relief.

By public authority, however, canonists understood the ecclesiastical hierarchy. What they did not take into account was the important role that lay men and women and secular authorities would play in the foundation and maintenance of charitable institutions as we will see below. Thus when the bull *Quia contingit* of Pope Clement V in 1311 required bishops to examine the affairs of all hospitals in their dioceses to ensure that revenues were not diverted from charitable purposes,[6] episcopal attempts at oversight ran into stiff resistance from municipal authorities which had been supervising hospitals for decades.

The Role of Recipients

Both the religious and legal modes of thinking about charity converged on a unique view of the place and responsibilities of its recipients. For medieval people charity was not aimed solely at those who would be described as poor by nineteenth- and twentieth-century standards, that is, the economically deprived. Poverty in the high Middle Ages had a broader meaning, or set of meanings, that shifted in the period under consideration. It meant, for one thing, the voluntary poor, those who had forsaken for religious reasons the wealth and comforts of this world. The term "poverty" also designated the involuntarily poor; those who were powerless, miserable, or sick; widows, orphans, and children, prisoners, and distressed gentlefolk were included along with the hungry, thirsty, naked, and homeless.

The shame-faced poor, or distressed gentlefolk (*pauperes verecundi*) are a category that deserves special note. "Reduced status was one of the most important medieval meanings of poverty" (Shaw 1993, p. 228). Those who had fallen temporarily or more permanently from their station in life had a prominent place in Ambrose's order of charitable giving. Subsequent centuries saw the development of a doctrine which accorded them the right to assistance, often in secret, from their fellow Christians, an exemption from work, and a higher standing among the poor in virtue of their reticence about their condition (Ricci 1983, pp. 158-77). They appeared with increasing frequency as objects of charity in the late thirteenth century, evidence that a contracting economy was taking its toll on the fortunes of the comfortable classes. The prominence of this category of recipients underscores the profoundly conservative nature of medieval charity; to the extent that it had social aims, they were focused on preserving the social order rather than changing it. Although poor beggars were increasingly seen as the embodiment of Christ, it was accepted that begging was a source of dishonor and humiliation for the well born. A high priority among charitable acts was the prevention of this form of pain and suffering. Poor girls of marriageable age were another category of recipient linked to this concern for maintaining people in their proper station (Trexler 1973, pp. 64-109).

To fall into any of the above categories of poverty was not viewed as a sin or a crime, although willful idleness was; paupers were not degraded or debased. Indeed, poverty was a positive virtue when practiced by pious men and women. The poor themselves were a theological rather than a sociological or economic category (Hildesheimer and Gut 1992, p. 13). The poor were not viewed, at least in the high Middle Ages, as outside the medieval community. They were recognized as neighbors, family, embodiments of Christ Himself. They were ashamed, perhaps, depending on their status, but not alien. Nor was acceptance of alms considered corrupting or degrading. A proper act of charity was good all around; the giver exhibited the virtue of generosity and the receiver that of humility (Tierney 1959, p. 53).

The poor, then, had a definite place in the medieval community. Charitable acts involved a reciprocal relationship. In the spiritual community and in the process of salvation, the poor had a clear and important role. As the representatives of Christ, their prayers had special intercessory value. The poor had legal rights in the temporal and social community. In case of extreme need they had a claim, based in natural, immutable law, to the property of others (Tierney 1959, p. 39).

The Practice of Charity in the High Middle Ages

The new enthusiasm for succoring one's neighbor and the clarification of the church's position on the relation of good works to salvation had an effect on the growth and development of new institutions. The effect is evident, first of all, in the shifting focus of pious activity. The foundations and gifts to monasteries which dominated the first part of the twelfth century yielded to a great wave of foundations of, gifts to, and service in hospitals and leperhouses in the latter part. Since works of mercy were held to be of little value without the proper attitude, many individuals went beyond merely endowing such institutions to consecrating themselves to the service of the poor and the sick. Charitable service became a new way of fulfilling a religious vocation and pursuing salvation without monastic renunciation of the world.

The conjunction of economic forces and religious ideas combined to produce a revolution in the theory and practice of charity in the high Middle Ages. In it we can see the impact of both the evangelical and the discriminating models on medieval people. The burgeoning of charity in the high Middle Ages was closely linked to economic expansion; demographic growth, urban growth, the acceleration of the economy and of money and commerce increased both need and the ability to meet it. Prosperity—and anxiety about it—rather than misery prompted the outpouring of mercy and aid.[7] In the twelfth and thirteenth centuries, evangelical spirituality dominated charitable giving, which has been described as "radically inclusive" vis-à-vis the recipients of alms (Miller 1993, p. 92). Any poor or miserable person could be a symbol of Christ. Charity was directed increasingly toward all the unfortunate members of society, and it was practiced increasingly by lay men and women both as individuals and groups. As the economy contracted and the poor continued to multiply in the late thirteenth and fourteenth centuries, a more cautious and discriminating approach gained ground.

We can best comprehend the personal and social meanings of charity for medieval people by considering the actions of individuals, groups, and communities. My primary evidence for this discussion of charitable activity comes largely from urban communities in southern France. Their members were involved, slightly in advance of their northern counterparts, in creating and supporting charitable institutions on several levels: through their private benefactions, their collective organizations, and their community governments. Regional studies from other parts of Europe support the general trends described.

Individual Charity

Personal charity as an expression of personal piety took numerous forms. Individuals founded, endowed, and supported hospitals and leperhouses, they devoted themselves and their lives to these institutions to serve the poor, and they made bequests to charitable institutions, to specified needy groups, and to the poor in general. In all these acts, their paramount concerns were to find through assistance to their fellow men, to Christ in the poor around them, salvation for their souls. As the period progressed, individuals became increasingly concerned for the salvation of other family members, living and dead.

The spiritual revival of the high Middle Ages created a great wave of institutional foundations. These institutions were more concerned with charity than with liturgy, and a new compassion for the sick, the weak, and the suffering is apparent in the naming of new institutions, both churches and charitable foundations. Many were dedicated to Saint Mary, the protectress of the weak and powerless, to Saint Lazarus, the patron of the sick and poor, and to the Holy Cross and the Holy Sepulchre, emblems of the humanity and suffering of Christ (Miller 1993, pp. 93–94).

In the south of France, the late twelfth century saw the founding of hospitals and leperhouses in large numbers. The enthusiasm for charitable establishments paralleled the intense religious experience that accompanied the development and repression of the Albigensian heresy (Mundy 1955, p. 188). In Toulouse, for example, over half of the nineteen medieval hospitals in the city were founded between 1160 and 1220, with only six appearing after the Albigensian Crusade (Mundy 1966, p. 236).

The importance of salvation as a motive in creating charitable institutions is unmistakable. Individuals founded and made donations to them for the love of God, the redemption of their sins, and the salvation of their souls and those of their kin (Roberts 1977, p. 267). The Church encouraged the link between charity and redemption by granting indulgences for contributions to charitable institutions.

Charitable donations and foundations were not just the acts of dying penitents. Hospitals and leperhouses appeared to offer opportunities for pious fellowship similar to those of monasteries. In the twelfth century the poor and sick, a Christ-like presence in their suffering, were felt to lead a religious life. The healthy laity could participate in this holiness by contributing to the institutions that sheltered them and by caring themselves for the wretched and unfortunate. Many people supported hospitals and leperhouses regularly throughout their lives; in exchange they participated in the spiritual fraternity, that is, in the prayers and benefits of the inhabitants. Following the monastic model, the poor and sick had a role as intercessors for the souls of their benefactors. Many hospital communities evolved into religious communities with rules and a cloistered life that resembled those of monastic or canonical establishments (Roberts 1977, pp. 178–88).[8] Whether or not a cloistered and regular community ran the daily operations of hospitals and leperhouses, many of these were considered religious institutions because they had consecrated chapels and cemeteries as well as priests in attendance; they were thus able to offer spiritual benefits, including masses for the souls of their benefactors. This became an increasingly common practice in the later Middle Ages.[9]

The desire for a spiritual life impelled some individuals a step further; they dedicated their bodies and souls to God and the service of Christ's poor in a particular hospital or leprosary; they thus participated more directly in the spiritual benefits of the establishment.[10] Often they were received into these houses as brothers or sisters and as paupers and members of the community. Motives for joining hospital or leprosary communities, however, were rarely simple. In exercising charity toward others, one could also take care of oneself not only spiritually, as has been noted, but also physically. In addition to devotion to Christ and the desire to consecrate oneself to the service of the poor in hope of more certain salvation, individuals often sought refuge from the world in their old age or widowhood. Some widowed donors entered as soon as they made their donations; others patronized an institution for years before claiming their right to retire there (Roberts 1977, pp. 279, 328–30).

Medieval hospitals opened their doors to a wide range of people. With the exception of leperhouses and their obvious specialization, hospitals represented the medieval attitude of unconditional welcome and hospitality that John Chrysostom and Gratian had articulated. Any visitor might be Christ himself, and accordingly all were received in that spirit: pilgrims, travelers, the sick, the poor, the aged, women in childbirth, prostitutes, foundlings, and orphans—all the unfortunate, the déclassé, the wretched, and rejected (Roberts 1977, 187–90, 294). There was, however, a measure of social control lurking in this all-inclusive welcome: undesirable elements were kept, cared for, and isolated from the rest of the community, particularly in urban areas. In Montpellier, for example, prostitutes were taken in during the Easter season, presumably to purify them and to keep them off the streets during the holiest time of the Christian calendar (Revel 1978, p. 343). Most hospitals did not specialize in caring for a particular type of disease or misfortune until the late thirteenth and fourteenth centuries, and then specialization occurred primarily in urban hospitals. Exceptions were those dedicated to Saint James and the care of pilgrims.

The care given to the poor in medieval hospitals was as much spiritual as physical or medical. Many hospitals had chapels with priests attached and a consecrated cemetery. Confession and communion were the first things offered to a new hospital guest after he or she had been received and made comfortable. Hospital statutes echo the Benedictine Rule in prescribing the proper, reverent attitude for receiving guests as well as prayers and burial services for the deceased. Doctors did not appear in most hospitals until quite late, and the primary form of physical care was adequate nutrition. Regulations specify in considerable detail the amount and sorts of food to be given to various categories of poor and sick.[11]

While outright donations of property to support this care dominated gifts to charitable institutions early in the twelfth century, from the late century onward testamentary bequests increased in popularity, particularly in southern Europe. The church's doctrine of penance and its organization exerted the principal influence on will making and on the character of charitable provisions.

Most wills in this period were rendered on the person's deathbed, with priests in attendance; the presence of the clergy strongly influenced the out-come. The priest's duty was to remind the testator of the needs of the parish and its poor; often the priest drew up the will himself. If a notary drew it up, the priest was required to be present or to be provided with a list of the alms given by the dying person, for he was partially responsible for the execution of the eleemosynary terms of the will.[12] Through this clerical presence the church's newly elaborated penitential system came to shape charitable giving. The statutes of synods such as that of Rodez in 1289, instructed priests of the diocese to recommend almsgiving as a substitute for penance to the sick and dying (Martène and Durand 1717, col. 702B). Charity could thus fulfill peniten-tial obligations. The close association of penance with the increasing use of wills made bequests to pious and charitable causes practically a duty by the fourteenth century (Adam 1964, p. 93).

Ecclesiastical pressures were not alone in determining the patterns of chari-table giving. Notaries also played a part. If the priest were not present (and it is difficult to tell from the testaments whether he was), the notary reminded the testator which pious and charitable causes in his parish or region to consider in his bequests.

The character of medieval wills was thus highly conventual and uniform, even ritualized and formulaic. Frequently the testaments drawn up by one no-tary in a given register contain lists of pious and charitable bequests which are identical in the order of institutions named, in the wording of the bequests, and even in the amounts bequeathed to given institutions (Roberts 1973, p. 6). In many regions even the prologues or *harangas* are reduced to formulas like the following, which were fairly consistent from one notary to another:

> Since no one living in the flesh can escape the terrible judgement of the super-nal judge before whom we all must give account of our own actions, and since nothing is more certain than death and nothing more uncertain than the hour of death, I therefore. . . . [13]

It does not follow, however, that testamentary charity was entirely mechani-cal, driven by external pressures, and devoid of personal and social meaning. Medieval testaments were essentially religious documents, and genuine piety underlay the conventional forms.[14] The parallel development of will making and the church's penitential system made charitable gifts more personal; the need to do penance for sins committed linked almsgiving to testators' individ-ual problems of conscience.[15] The fundamental impetus behind charitable giv-ing was the desire for salvation. Individuals felt deeply the need to account for their lives before the Final Judge, who would judge them not on their statements of piety but on their charity toward the poor and unfortunate. This account was supported by the intercession of their families and the recipients of their charity. Wills were a practical expression of the need to do good works and provide prayers for the good of one's soul. The ritualistic aspects of wills taken as a group signify not indifference but rather social cohesion. "In traditional societies social rituals are the underlying and living skeletons of the body corporate, not the fossils of life long since passed away. The formulaic character of most late medieval wills offers evidence not of shallowness, but of overwhelming social consensus in religious convictions and priorities" (Duffy 1992, p. 355).

It is important to consider the phenomenon of funeral "doles" in this light. These bequests left money, food, and clothing to poor persons who assembled for a distribution on the day of the testator's death or who attended the funeral and were instructed and expected to pray for his or her soul. These are among the most often criticized practices of medieval charity, maligned for being indiscriminate, haphazard, ineffectual, and even harmful, for paying no attention to the material or psychological needs of the recipient.[16] It is, however, the reciprocal nature of these bequests which merits our attention. At the base of medieval pious foundations—churches, monasteries, hospitals, and other charitable institutions—lay the notion of continual intercession for the living and the dead. We have seen this ongoing prayer in the confraternities or spiritual associations of hospitals and leperhouses. The need for intercession also underlay testamentary charity. Often recipients were expressly instructed to pray for the soul of the beneficiary; at other times the obligation of prayers was implicit (Thompson 1965, p. 194). This is particularly the case when poor recipients of shirts and tunics were required to participate, clad in their new garments, in the funeral rites of their benefactor. Charity in this context became a sort of reciprocal aid: the poor had some of their material needs satisfied, and by their intercession, they fulfilled the spiritual needs of the testator (Roberts 1973, p. 15). The poor were consciously chosen for this role because their prayers were thought to carry special weight with Christ, who had identified with them (Duffy 1992, p. 360).

Because the recipients of charity had an obligation to intercede, testators were not entirely undiscriminating. The notion that prayers of the living for the dead could shorten their trials in Purgatory depended on the idea of shared merit within a mystical community of Christians (Duffy 1992, pp. 364–65). The prayers of recipients of charity were worthless if they themselves were in a state of sin and thus not members of this mystical community. Making wills on their deathbeds, medieval Christians showed their grasp of this doctrine by specifying the "poor beggars of Christ," the "shame-faced poor of Christ," "the indigent poor of Christ," and the "poor of Christ in the hospitals" as the recipients of their alms. These were to be chosen by the testator's heirs or executors. If the testator did not know personally the individuals destined to receive his generosity, then his executor did and used some criteria such as genuine need and good moral character in the selection process (Roberts 1973, p. 17).

Medieval testators did make choices about the recipients of their charity, and a number of options were open to them. Even the practice of giving small amounts of money to nearly every local pious and charitable foundation and some that were distant has been described as a consciously chosen strategy.[17] Medieval testators left charitable bequests of money, bedding, clothing, candles, grain, and other commodities to a broad range of institutions, such as the leprosaries and hospitals treated above and regular municipal and parish services which will be discussed below.[18] Often hospitals and distributions were founded by testamentary bequests. In their direct gifts to various categories of poor people with no intermediary save their executors, testators were perhaps most generous and spontaneous and their gifts more individualized. In giving clothing to the poor, dowries to poor girls, money and supplies to poor orphans and women, to the "shame-faced poor," and to prisoners, they appeared to value the immediate impact of these gifts above the longer-term effect of institutional charity (Coulet 1978, p. 234). In many such cases of direct charity, the testators had no part in choosing the recipients of their alms; in others, however, they did select certain groups of needy people or specific individuals to receive their charity. Even in bequests to the poor in general, many testators tended to limit these poor people to the inhabitants of their own domains or their fellow parishioners or to the poor of certain streets or quarters of their town if they were townspeople, thus showing a sense of community identity and responsibility. Within the confines of domain, parish, and town, testators distinguished several different categories of people to be aided: distressed gentlefolk, poor women of marriageable age, women in childbirth lying in the hospitals, widows, poor orphans, poor debtors, and poor priests. Wills often display charity on a more personal level, making provisions for the wife and children of the testator, for poor women of marriageable age, and for poor priests of the family. Often, bequests were only to devolve on other categories of poor when legitimate heirs died out or failed to appear (Roberts 1973, pp. 18–19).

The Charity of Corporate Bodies

Medieval charity was not only an individual but also a corporate enterprise. Embedded in community life, charity was an important ingredient in the cement that bound Christian society together. This role is evident from the reciprocal nature of charitable acts and the service and spiritual communities in hospitals and leperhouses. Caritative bonding is nowhere clearer than in the pious and charitable confraternities that originated and flourished in the high Middle Ages. Local organizations founded for purposes of mutual aid and communal devotion, confraternities are a form of human alliance that persists across many eras and cultures.

These pious associations formed under the impetus of the new evangelical spirituality. They appropriated older traditions of mutual aid in rural and urban communities; those traditions reinforced ties of family, neighborhood, and community at particular points of the agricultural or liturgical year or on the occasion of death or famine. Onto these gatherings evangelical spirituality grafted assistance to the poor, Christianizing the events and changing their function. Distributions to the poor at funerals and at feast days became the primary function of many of these community events. In particular, meals at Pentecost were an aspect of the devotion to the Holy Spirit which stressed the apostolic ideal of sharing, community of property, and the duty of Christians toward their neighbors. Numerous confraternities of lay people sprang up in France in the thirteenth century; their activities included administering hospitals and charitable distributions.[19] These strong lay traditions of mutual assistance contributed to the laicization of charitable institutions in the high Middle Ages.

With the twelfth-century spiritual revival lay men and women were inspired to lead valid spiritual lives following the communal, apostolic model. The results were numerous groups and doctrines, such as the Waldensians and the Humiliati, that were eventually declared heretical. In the thirteenth century lay attempts at a communal Christian life became closely associated with the spirituality of the newly founded Franciscan and Dominican orders. These mendicant friars themselves led lives devoted to poverty and preaching. They attempted to channel this lay impulse into orthodox paths. Charity had a special place in this spiritual environment, for the friars encouraged pious and well-to-do laymen to form associations devoted to helping the poor (Little 1988, pp. 78–79; see also Little 1978).

Pious confraternities formed for a variety of purposes in the thirteenth century and afterward, but most had some common elements appropriated from older monastic forms of spiritual association or confraternity: penance and pious practices, mutual aid, and some form of ritual or liturgical aid to the poor. The mutual aid given by members of a confraternity to each other was both spiritual and material in nature. The spiritual service of offering masses and prayers for the souls of their fellows was paramount. Both members of the confraternity and the recipients of their alms performed this service. Members could count on proper burial, aid in time of sickness, and sometimes assistance during legal difficulties. Officers of the confraternity would spread the word if a member was sick and would enjoin the others to visit. Needy members received assistance without having to beg for food (Roberts 1977, pp. 224–317; Little 1988, pp. 75–76).

Most confraternities offered a communal meal or distribution of food on the association's feast day. Giving food is a classic and highly visible form of charity. Sharing food, particularly in the form of meals with their sacramental quality, involves the poor in a moral and religious community and symbolizes more forcefully the human bonds that generate compassion. Many medieval confraternities, however, were specifically devoted to charitable activities beyond these yearly distributions to the poor. In some confraternities of Bergamo, officers were supposed to proceed through the city searching out the poor, the imprisoned, widows, and other needy folk and distribute alms to them. In others members made weekly contributions which were distributed to the poor (Little 1988, pp. 79–80). In mid-thirteenth-century Cremona confraternities were founded to bring alms to the distressed gentlefolk who were ashamed to beg, to orphans, widows, hermits, the sick, and the lame (Ricci 1983, p. 169). In towns of the Rouergue, confraternities dedicated to Saint James maintained hospitals for pilgrims and regular distributions of food to the poor (Roberts 1977, pp. 241–43).

These charitable confraternities were not independent of the larger community. While they received spiritual guidance from the clergy and mendicant friars, they were often subject to surveillance and regulation by municipal authorities. There was a close community of interest between confraternities and town governments. Their governing structures were similar, and officers of confraternities often advanced to seats on town councils. Their terms expired, they were again entrusted with the administration of confraternities.[20] Town authorities sought increasing control over these associations both as a means of social control and a resource for urban social welfare. In thirteenth-century Rodez, the consuls could force members of confraternities to pay their dues so that resources would be sufficient for the yearly "charity" or distribution of food to the poor. As we have seen, canon lawyers argued, albeit in an ecclesiastical context, that public authorities could enforce obligations to contribute to public charity.

The Charity of Civil Society

The close connection between municipal authorities and confraternities illuminates the place and meaning of charity in medieval public life and the role of secular governments in poor relief. During the expansive high Middle Ages, town governments in Europe assumed control of charitable institutions and functions. Considered an attribute of political and administrative power for town governments as it was for kings and princes,[21] the responsibility for ensuring the welfare of the community was nevertheless deeply embedded in the notion and reality of a Christian community. Pious activities had political ends. The mixture of administrative and religious elements in municipal poor relief illustrates the complex nature of medieval charity.

The process whereby municipal authorities came to control charitable institutions was in some cases smooth and in others marked by extended legal struggles. Charitable activities directed toward the community or the parish were a source of community solidarity. They also provided a kind of laboratory for emerging communal governments where villagers developed their ability to manage communal property. In the villages around Béziers, for example, the administration of charitable institutions preceded formal government. In the early twelfth century, care of the poor was the function of the church. In these villages, parishioners participated in the administration of church property designated for this purpose. By the mid-twelfth century, each large village possessed and ran a hospital and a leperhouse. Communal governments emerged later in the century. In the thirteenth century the charitable institutions depended on municipalities rather than the church for direction and financial support.[22]

The consular governments of southern France fulfilled their obligation to care for members of the community in a variety of ways. Assuming the formerly episcopal mantle of "protector of the poor," they sometimes "acted for the love of God" in remitting taxes for those without sufficient property to pay them, paying burial fees, shielding the poor from ecclesiastical exactions, and distributing to them the commodities such as grain, wine, and oil which they had confiscated because of violations of market regulations (Roberts 1977, pp. 398–404).

They ensured the welfare of all citizens by their surveillance and maintenance of public works such as roads and bridges; this activity was considered a pious and charitable work in the medieval era.

By assuming administrative control over charitable institutions such as hospitals and leperhouses, town authorities guaranteed that these institutions would continue to function for the welfare of the community. In many urban communities the consuls were responsible for the material support and functioning of these houses. They channeled the charitable gifts and bequests of individuals to their destinations, collected taxes to support municipal charity and made expenditures for food and other supplies and provided special pittances for the sick on holidays. They administered property, appointed rectors or administrators and received accountings from them, exercised control over who could enter the house both as staff and as inmates, and promulgated rules governing the internal life of the charitable community.[23]

In the fourteenth century in southern France there was a second wave of hospital foundations. Established largely by testamentary bequest for the usual pious motives—love of God, redemption of sins, and the salvation of souls of the founder and his kin—these institutions were placed directly under the control of municipal authorities. As canon lawyers articulated episcopal rights over diocesan hospitals, however, older municipal hospitals were often the subject of protracted struggles between the consuls and ecclesiastical authorities over who had the right to control the resources and the personnel of the institution.[24]

In many southern European towns collections of food and clothing for the poor and distributions of bread to the poor came under the aegis of the consular governments. These social services had probably originated in parish churches, and they remained tied to the religious calendar and location. Municipal distributions of bread, for example, were made at the door of a church on major religious feast days such as Pentecost, Ascension, Assumption, and All Saints

Day. Charitable collections appeared in the thirteenth century alongside those for liturgical purposes (fabric and lighting) and were equally specialized. In large towns regular collections were made for clothing for the poor, for the shame-faced poor, for poor women of marriageable age, and for the torch carried when communion was taken to the sick. By the fourteenth century consuls administered them, auditing their accounts and assigning revenues to them. Similar institutions appeared in the towns of northern France and Flanders in the same period; however, these *tables des pauvres* or *tables du Saint Esprit* operated at the parish level, independent of the *échevinages* or municipal governments (Roberts 1977, pp. 407–12).

Charitable distributions, or "charities" (also called *helemosynas* or alms) were a common and regular feature of medieval urban life. Private and funeral distributions, confraternal distributions at the annual feast, and parish alms may have been at the origins of municipal distributions which emerged in the late twelfth and thirteenth centuries. Even small towns had as many as four or five regular distributions. They were supported by rents, levies of bread or grain, and donations. Account books show the consuls to have been scrupulous in keeping track of these revenues and debts to the charities. They could also divert these revenues to other more pressing purposes, such as fortifications, when the need arose. Within the joint framework of religious motivation and civic needs, municipal authorities were capable of managing the collective almsgiving of the Christian community. They could levy contributions, pursue debtors, and hire assistance for the actual work of baking and distributing bread—in short they marshaled the people and resources necessary to sustain regular social services. Such activities dispel the myth that medieval charity was unsystematic and ineffectual and that the laity participated vicariously. These distributions offered assistance to individuals and families in temporary difficulties when work was scarce, wage earners ill and crops poor; many came in the spring and helped the entire community bridge the gap between one harvest and the next (Roberts 1977, pp. 410–39).

As town governments extended their control over all institutions that had potential for poor relief and social control, they also came to control large urban confraternities for which charity was not the primary purpose. Sometimes consuls intervened to ensure that the resources of the confraternity were used for the proper charitable purposes. In other cases, confraternities were established with the consent of the secular authorities who kept watch over their charitable functions and over the social and political peace of the community (Roberts 1977, pp. 440–58).

The economic expansion of the thirteenth century enabled municipal authorities to wrest control over older charitable institutions from lay and ecclesiastical authorities and to impose their direction on emerging new ones. With the growth of urban communities and the concentration of population within their walls, more people needed services, and charitable institutions had to be well organized. Communities needed to protect their members from disease and disorder and to channel resources from the well and well-off to the sick and needy. Urban governments administered charitable institutions to control resources, to protect and care for citizens, to care for and control marginal elements in society—in short, to maintain health, order, and Christian harmony in the community.

The combination of religious ideals and economic expansion in the high Middle Ages gave rise to a type of charity in which both spiritual and social, private and public needs converged. The poor and sick members of the community of the faithful benefited from this synergy.

The Late Middle Ages: Unraveling the High Medieval Synthesis

The flowering of charity in the high Middle Ages was a phenomenon of an expanding economy. The amount of assistance for the poor was proportional not to the amount of misery to be assuaged but rather to the degree of prosperity (Caille 1978, p. 266). The contracting, crisis-ridden economy of the late Middle Ages profoundly reoriented both the theory and practice of charity throughout Western Christendom.[25] This period, from the late thirteenth through the early fifteenth centuries, witnessed scarcities and brutal famines, recurring episodes of the bubonic plague, and frequent wars that included the major conflict of the Hundred Years War. This was an era of high mortality, severe demographic dislocation, and increased migration. Together these contributed to the disintegration of the seignorial system. Rural areas suffered severe disruption as peasants abandoned their villages and migrated to the towns. The landed upper classes likewise suffered economic difficulties. The demographic crises destroyed social bonds and patterns of mutual aid. Wars increased violence and crime and created a climate of distrust and fear. The ensuing collapse of social and spiritual values tore the fabric of society in many directions. Evidence of this disorder included endemic brigandage whose perpetrators came from all social classes, peasant uprisings, popular revolts both urban and rural, and attacks against groups such as lepers and Jews who were increasingly seen as outsiders (Heers 1970, pp. 97–120).

Charitable institutions, practices, and attitudes felt the reverberations of these upheavals. The traditional charity of individual and institutional alms was overwhelmed by the new social needs brought about by such fundamental changes. The result was a period of somewhat contradictory tendencies. Many institutions drifted away from their original charitable mission while many new ones were established. Traditional almsgiving persisted although numerous individuals directed their alms in a more discriminatory and self-interested fashion. As urban governments moved to organize charitable services, they introduced more rational and business-like procedures. This intervention aimed to guarantee the effectiveness of charity. Ironically, according to some historians, it weakened the religious and spiritual dimensions of charitable giving through its bureaucratic methods (Mollat 1978, pp. 401, 406). As the social function of charity became increasingly important, the balance of religious and administrative concerns which characterized the high Middle Ages shifted. The evangelical conception of charity with its inclusive attitude toward all the needy began to wane. The discriminating model, with its concern for wise allocation of limited resources, seemed a better guide for giving in a difficult and uncertain era.[26]

Hospitals intended to receive pilgrims, travelers, and townspeople could not contain the flood of uprooted peasants. This institutional crisis had several additional components. There were too many small hospitals, the administration was often inadequate and abuses were common. The costs of administration were high and often inhibited the flow of aid to the poor. Many hospitals declined when they became mere sources of income for absentee clerics or retirement homes for the relatively comfortable members of a community.[27] In addition, their clerical staff and revenues became increasingly tied up in such liturgical functions as anniversary masses for patrons and donors. In a sense, the spiritual function of these houses diverged from their charitable purpose. Municipal authorities intervened to ensure adequate resources and services for the increasing needs of their communities; such actions made institutions more effective but also often embroiled them in jurisdictional disputes. Although bequests to hospitals continued,[28] these characteristics cannot have been comforting or inviting for potential donors whose concern was primarily the spiritual efficacy of their gifts. Nevertheless, alive to the pressing needs of their fellows, pious individuals founded numerous new hospitals and often entrusted their administration to municipal authorities.

Concerned groups of individuals likewise established new confraternities dedicated to the assistance of the poor, often specializing in particular groups such as poor girls and the shame-faced poor. Closely linked to these were the parish-based "tables of the poor," which were sources of distribution of food and clothing to the needy (Mollat 1986, pp. 273–74). Some confraternities, however, also drifted into liturgical preoccupations. In the early fourteenth century in the region around Fanjeaux in southern France, for example, confraternities dedicated to Saint Mary were maintaining hospitals, but by the end of the century purely religious and eucharistic concerns took over, and the reception and care of the poor declined (de Fortanier 1978, p. 163).

In their wills, some individuals became more discriminating about the recipients of their charity. They were increasingly concerned for a "good return" on charitable investment. Testators from England to Italy sought to exclude idle beggars from their funeral doles and restrict recipients to the poor of their own parish or town or to certain categories thought to be especially worthy of assistance.[29] Poor householders, poor girls of marriageable age and distressed gentlefolk or the shame-faced poor were all "respectable" folk who could be counted on to pray for the donor's soul. The well-being of these recipients, enhanced by charitable acts, strengthened the fabric of society.[30] Many testators in late-fourteenth-century central Italian towns appear to have abandoned the practice of disbursing their wealth among a myriad of pious and charitable foundations and instead concentrated their charity in larger amounts to single institutions or purposes such as dowering poor girls.

The economic and social crises which increased the number and complexity of social problems also heightened religious anxiety. Increasingly concerned for more certain ways to salvation, anxious men and women turned their pious impulses away from social problems toward a more inward, personal piety, toward heightened concerns with salvation, family, and ancestors. Expenditures on family memorials and decoration of churches, on what has been called "earthly remembrance," diverted resources that might otherwise have gone to the poor. Masses or paintings to adorn chapels seemed to Italian men and women a safer means to salvation than the prayers of the poor (Cohn 1992). The loss of economic security impelled English urban dwellers toward activities that secured status and income and away from civic and corporate activity (Rubin 1987, pp. 51–52).

Behind these changing attitudes toward charity lay a fundamental transformation in the nature of poverty and a consequent shift in attitudes toward the poor. By the late thirteenth century a permanent class of economically poor people had come into existence; their condition was exacerbated by the economic crises of the following century. Alongside the traditional poor who were humble, weak, or infirm, there emerged a new kind of poverty, that of ablebodied urban workers kept by low and uncertain wages on the brink of destitution. Working poverty was difficult for contemporaries to understand and for institutions, designed to care for the abject and disabled, to remedy. With a sense of their dignity and the value of their labor, these people readily became involved in the popular disturbances which spread across Europe in the late fourteenth and early fifteenth centuries. These uprisings, in which the poor were numerous and visible, helped focus attention on poverty and its related problems. The resulting preoccupation with destitution and poor relief became closely linked with the problem of suppressing vagrancy (Mollat 1986, 211–24, 271).

The late-medieval crises inspired government intervention of many sorts. Governments assumed control over poor relief or tried to assign responsibility clearly to other institutions. English laws in 1388 and 1391 attempted to enforce the ecclesiastical system of poor relief to the genuinely needy. Sixteenth-century legislation in England and Lyon outlawed vagrancy and required registration of the poor. The consuls of Lyon took over administration of the city's major hospital in the fifteenth century and in the 1520s established the Aumône General; this new government body assumed responsibility for poor relief, centralizing all alms to charitable institutions. English laws of 1531 obliged not priests but parishioners, whose contributions could be legally enforced, to be responsible for providing for the poor.[31] In addition to rationalizing the administration of charity, princely and municipal authorities regulated the poor themselves. Seeking to stabilize the work force, they fixed prices and wages and tried to suppress vagrancy and begging. In Portugal, France, and England, mid-century legislation prohibited the poor from leaving their jobs and obliged them to find work; vagabonds were expelled from cities and denied access to hospitals and alms.[32]

Everywhere authorities tried to distinguish the genuinely needy from the able bodied and to provide the needy with effective assistance. Small hospitals were merged or consolidated; the poor who were capable of supporting themselves were evicted so that the deserving would receive better care. The idle were required to work, and those who were permitted to beg wore special insignia. But giving alms to beggars as a means of poor relief came to appear ineffective and undesirable, and governments undertook new initiatives. On the theory that loans to the deserving poor were better than alms, fifteenth-century Italian cities established *monti di pietà*, public pawnshops that gave credit at nonusurious rates.[33] Governments and confraternities in northern French and Italian towns developed token systems to control how much assistance was given to whom. The tokens were given to the worthy poor, selected on the basis of need, who exchanged them for distributions of various forms of aid.[34]

As poverty became a social problem rather than a spiritual opportunity, attitudes toward the poor and poverty were transformed, becoming more complex and contradictory. Sharpened distinctions separated deserving and undeserving, industrious and idle, needy and able-bodied, "good" and "bad" poor. Large masses of anonymous beggars and paupers, some of whom were given to vandalism during popular disturbances, seemed alien and menacing. These uprisings and the increase in crime made the poor seem envious, and envy was a major sin in a society based on stability and order. Fear of crime and suspicion of idleness as well as experience with false beggars discredited poor supplicants of all types. Attitudes toward work, begging, and poverty began to change. People came to see work as having positive value, begging as an affront to human dignity, and poverty as detrimental to state and society. These ideas engendered a more fundamental criticism of begging. It was no longer regarded as a valid manifestation of spiritual poverty, and even the mendicant orders confronted growing criticism. Voluntary poverty lost its sacred character, and consequently even ordinary wretchedness was desanctified (Mollat 1986, pp. 231, 551–58).

This new vision undermined the reciprocity crucial to the evangelical practice of charity. One could not be certain that an unknown beggar, perhaps not even humble, would render up truly effective intercessory prayers—or any at all. By the late fourteenth century the notion of the poor as dangerous had begun to supplant the image of the pauper as the chosen of God and the symbol of Christ (Mollat 1986, p. 226). As these developments called into question the ability and willingness of some poor to perform their expected and traditional role in the charitable relationship, their perceived role in Christian communities, from a spiritual as well as a social perspective, was increasingly negative and marginal. Motives of the nameless, transient poor—a group apart from most communities in imagination as well as fact—became suspect; a harder vision emerged of the poor as curse rather than Christ, as deceitful and dangerous to the stability of urban society.

Conclusion

It is tempting to conclude that social and economic problems became so acute as to overwhelm the capabilities of medieval charity, leading to disillusionment and flight. To be sure, the synergy of economic and religious forces that characterized the expansive high Middle Ages could not endure a period of economic crisis. Evangelical charity and the institutions it produced were not adequate for dealing with unemployment and uprootedness on a large scale. For a variety of reasons, attitudes toward charity turned away from the expansive and inclusive evangelical approach of the central Middle Ages. The discriminating model of charity had more appeal in the later period, because it was better suited to an increasingly complex and troubled society where charitable aid was more institutionalized, resources more limited, and social control a more pronounced concern.

Medieval charity, however, never intended to eliminate or solve social problems. Medieval people had no social theory of poverty, and they did not expect to change the social order; following Saint Paul, they believed that the poor would always be among them. In the final balance, the personal meanings inherent in the medieval charitable impulse (salvation, care of family, neighbors, and lineage) outweighed the social ones. The idea of Christian community caring for its members did not die out; it simply contracted its boundaries to exclude strangers and their economic problems.

Two views of the most deserving recipients of charity coexisted in the high Middle Ages. The homeless poor, the destitute beggar, the wandering stranger were all visible symbols of Christ and the redemption promised to the charitable. Less visible but with equal claim to alms were the humble neighbor, the honorable citizen fallen in status, the secret, ashamed, and domiciled poor. Of these categories only the latter, an older and more traditional group, survived intact the trials of the fourteenth century. The retreat from evangelical charity was unmistakable. But medieval people never chose between conflicting views of poverty and charity; they bequeathed them side by side to the early modern era.

The institutional evolution was also unmistakable. Throughout the high Middle Ages the institutions created by evangelical impulses and activities were, in their policies of reception, hospitality, and distribution, open to all the distressed. Both charitable establishments and the poor whom they assisted increasingly came under the watchful and discriminating eye of municipal authorities. Growing regulation of existing charity, the hallmark of the late Middle Ages, went hand in hand with the desire to husband limited resources for the truly needy, to discipline the able bodied and thus to discriminate among recipients.

From institutions founded in an evangelical mode grew secular public assistance programs which became divorced in part from personal religious charity. Guided by the principles formulated by twelfth- and thirteenth-century canon lawyers, early modern governments developed medieval institutions into secular systems of poor relief, which, though more efficient, lacked the characteristic spiritual and social reciprocity of the medieval donor-recipient relationship. The secularization of charity was the product not only of such "modern" phenomena as Renaissance humanism and the Reformation but also of a long medieval evolution.

Notes

1. Mollat (1986), pp. 38–40. Mollat's work provides the best synthesis and summary in English of many developments in the history of medieval poverty and charity.

2. A.D. Aveyron, 66H, no. 1 and no. 1bis. Roberts (1977), pp. 344–45. For indulgences granted in 1255 to the faithful who contributed to the care of the poor in the newly established hospital in Colmar, see Adam (1982), pp. 61–62.

3. See, for example, Webb and Webb (1927), pp. 4–5; and Jordan (1959), pp. 17, 146–47.

4. Cited in Tierney (1958–59, p. 363). According to Tierney, this view could have been the basis for "a severely punitive system of poor relief." Ibid.

5. Tierney (1958–59), p. 368. Among the interesting issues raised in these discussions was that of the nature of the food which should be given to the needy; rich foods were thought by some to be as bad for the poor as coarse foods were for the rich. An Anglo-Norman commentator stressed that a beggar's ability to work with his hands should earn him correction rather than alms and that the test of ability to work should be applied even to strangers. In addition he raised further problems with Ambrose's hierarchy of desert. Of two needy men, a close relative of bad character and a righteous outsider, who had a prior claim to an almsgiver's resources? One should help the just first, but unaided, the starving unjust man would die and go to Hell. If assisted he might repent, while the unaided just man would die and go to Heaven, so perhaps then one

ought to aid the unjust. With the feeling that this was not exactly the correct conclusion, the perplexed canonist abandoned the issue (pp. 367–68).

6. Tierney (1959), p. 96. This bull was the foundation of all hospital law in the later Middle Ages.

7. Mollat (1978), "Conclusion," and Caille (1978), p. 394. On the medieval society's psychological adaptation to the profit economy, see Little (1978), pp. 19–41.

8. For a study of hospital rules, see Le Grand (1901).

9. For the religious character of hospitals, see Imbert (1947); and Roberts (1977), pp. 139–223. Numerous twelfth-century donors provided resources to maintain the priests and the lighting in the chapel attached to the leprosarium of Saint Thomas of Trasgeig near Millau. One of the residents, a priest himself, made generous donations of money, land, cattle, and liturgical vestments, books, and chalices in exchange for which the community agreed to celebrate commemorative masses yearly for his soul and those of his parents (Roberts 1977, pp. 331–32).

10. Roberts (1977), pp. 217–18, 278–79; A.D. Aveyron, 61H 1, no. 2 (1194); Société des Lettres de l'Aveyron, Archives de Sévérac, LII, no. 8 (1305). In Alsatian hospitals, young and well-off townspeople, moved by religious devotion, often chose to enter hospitals as pensioners and do the hard, daily work of running the establishment. Adam (1982), pp. 126–30.

11. Roberts (1977), pp. 190–94, 301–303. See also Caille (1978), p. 275; and Caille (1977). Hospitals attached to cathedral chapters which maintained schools were an exception to the norm of largely palliative and spiritual care. The cathedral hospital of Laon possessed in the thirteenth century a medical staff consisting of druggists, "bleeders," and physicians; the chapter's physician-canons drew on the resources of a library rich in treatises on both theoretical and practical medicine. Saint-Denis (1983), pp. 108–14.

12. Adam (1964), pp. 91–93. See also the chapter on testaments in the statutes of the 1289 synod of Rodez in Martène and Durand (1717), IV, col. 733D.

13. Archives Départementales de l'Aveyron E.966, fol. 18v: The 1342 will of Dorde de Bonasnonas, butcher of the Bourg of Rodez, begins with this standard prologue: "Cum nemo in carne positus valet terribile iudicium superni iudicis evitare coram quo omnis sumus de nostris propriis actibus rediturus rationem et quia nichil certior morte nec incertior hora mortis, idcirco ego. . . . "

See also Coulet (1978), p. 231.

14. Duffy (1992), p. 355. Thompson (1965) notes that although average Londoners were conventionally pious, "there may well have been a genuine, though quiet devotion beneath the conventional forms" (p. 194).

15. Mundy (1955), p. 208. In the Rouergue in 1286, Hugo Landorra, lord of the castle of Salmiech, made a will in which he bequeathed among other generous charitable bequests, two shillings to the poor women and distressed gentle folk of the parishes of Salmiech and Artuivo in reparation for what he had won there by gambling; his heirs were to use the money to repay the persons from whom he had won it, or their heirs (Paris, Bibliothèque Nationale, Collection Doat, vol. 41, fol. 63).

16. These views are best expressed in Jordan (1959), pp. 17, 146–47.

17. Cohn (1992) describes this pattern as the "mendicant strategy of self-denial" that testators used following the advice of mendicant preachers about dispersing their wealth and thus severing ties to worldly gains and possessions (p. 17). Miller (1993) notes, however, that in Verona this "mendicant pattern" of spreading donations out among a multiplicity of pious institutions appeared in the twelfth century, well before the mendicants (p. 108. n. 41). Donors were hedging their bets, giving small donations to reproduce almsgiving and in their wills making their final dispersal of alms. This strategy was possible because of the rapidly expanding economy.

18. See Roberts (1977), pp. 459–508, and Roberts (1973), pp. 6–16. Also Coulet (1978), pp. 231–34; Thompson (1965), *passim*.

19. Chiffoleau (1978), pp. 70–79. These meals had more than a liturgical function, for they mobilized scarce food resources and aided the needy at moments of the year (Easter, Pentecost, etc.) between harvests when supplies were dwindling. The abundance of these distributions in the spring is explained by the need to foster solidarity and social equilibrium in a time of scarcity.

20. As the chapters in this volume by Ross and Jones demonstrate, there exists in many societies a close connection between charitable associations and political power.

21. Mollat, ed. (1974), p. 25. In the town of Millau, the consuls swore to be loyal to and to serve the poor as well as the rich members of the community. Roberts (1977), p. 401.

22. Gramain (1978), pp. 111–30, esp. p. 124. In the small fortified Rouergue town of Najac, the town government or consulate appears to have taken form during the construction of a church which had been imposed in the mid-thirteenth century upon the community as penance for heresy. Town accounts emerged from this effort and soon came to detail the consuls' involvement in the administration of charity. Roberts (1977), pp. 414–25.

Consular control of charitable institutions, while generalized in the Midi, was not absolute. In cities like Avignon and Aix-en-Provence with a strong papal or episcopal presence, nearly all charitable activity was tied to ecclesiastical society. The situation did not begin to change until the fourteenth century. See Chiffoleau (1978) and Coulet (1978), pp. 59–87, 213–38.

23. Roberts (1977), pp. 224–316, 383–85, 350–79. The magistrates of Alsatian cities played a major role in establishing hospitals in the thirteenth century and an increasing role in their administration. By the late Middle Ages most hospitals were governed entirely by town councils. Adam (1964), pp. 39, 54–79, 125.

24. A good example is the Hospital of the Passage in Rodez. Consuls struggled intermittently for over fifty years in the late thirteenth and early fourteenth centuries with episcopal authorities over the right to supervise the staff and the rector. Roberts (1977), pp. 260–304.

25. See Rubin (1987); Rubin's thesis is that the economic reversals of the fourteenth century brought about a weakening of the spirit of charity.

26. The instability and uncertainty of this period altered, in Mary Douglas's terms, medieval society's ability to envision the long term and thus to sustain an inclusionary, communitarian position on poverty. The long-term view was undergirded in the earlier period by the limitless horizons of economic expansion, the solidarity of consolidating social communities, and the evangelical optimism of a flourishing faith.

27. The twelfth-century communities of brothers and sisters serving the poor in Alsatian hospitals became in the thirteenth century confraternities of pensioners; they defended their own interests to the detriment of religious life and charitable services. Similarly, hospitals specialized in the thirteenth century in the care of foundlings and orphans later became boarding homes for the illegitimate offspring of the wealthy. Adam (1982), pp. 146, 216–17.

28. Hildesheimer and Gut (1992), p. 18. The authors note that in the beginning of the fifteenth century 60 percent of testators in Paris still left bequests to hospitals and that this relatively high percentage held for the rest of France.

29. Duffy (1992) pp. 262–65. Duffy cites examples of this phenomenon for the fifteenth and sixteenth centuries, suggesting that a better understanding of doctrine encouraged people to be more concerned about the quality of the recipient, the condition of whose soul determined the efficacy of the intercession. He notes, however, that "the norm

probably remained a general and undiscriminating distribution, so far as the means of the deceased allowed."

30. Trexler (1973) argues that bequests in favor of the shamed poor and poor girls of marriageable age were a good way to appear penitent and pious in one's will while reserving, through executorial discretion, most of one's wealth for needy family members (pp. 64–109). Only extensive studies of probate records, as he suggests, can prove this hypothesis.

31. Tierney (1959), pp. 113, 128–29. For Lyon, see N. Davis (1968) p. 242.

32. Mollat (1986), p. 202. In 1330, the city gates of Strasbourg were closed at night to keep beggars out; beggars who tarried too long in the city were mutilated. Authorities expelled beggars in 1391, and prohibited the able bodied from begging in 1409 and 1411. Adam (1982), pp. 249–53.

33. Mollat, *Poor in the Middle Ages*, pp. 272–93. For the regulation of beggars in fifteenth-century Strasbourg, see Adam, *Charité . . . en Alsace*, pp. 250–51.

34. Courtenay (1972), pp. 275–95. Tokens, according to Courtenay, played a significant role in the "monetization" as well as the centralization and secularization of charity which characterized the late Middle Ages.

3 | Philosophical Ideas of Charity
Some Historical Reflections

J. B. Schneewind

Pity would be no more
If we did not make somebody Poor;
And Mercy no more could be
If all were as happy as we.[1]

W E ARE PULLED toward charity by two calls. On one side we hear the cry of needs, often desperate, that would otherwise go unmet, and of desires that would otherwise be unfulfilled. On another side we hear an insistence on the importance of being concerned about the well-being of people with whom we have no personal connection. We are exhorted to extend our care beyond self, family, and friends to some larger community. The relation between the two calls is perplexing. Admittedly recipients need the help given by donors; do donors no less need the occasion to have and express this particular concern? It is sometimes thought so. Hence St. John Chrysostom says that "the rich have to *thank the poor* for the chance of alms-giving."[2] More commonly it has been thought that the poor should feel gratitude. Kant, however, suggests a different perspective:

> If men were strictly just, there might be no poor, in whose regard we think to display this merit of beneficence and give alms. Alms-giving is a form of kindliness associated with pride and costing no trouble. . . . Men are demeaned by it. It would be better to think out some other way of assisting poverty.[3]

Charity, answering the first call, resembles justice in being a virtue concerned with the distribution of goods. Responding to the second call it concerns the spiritual or moral condition of each individual. The medievals were much exercised about the latter concern. Modern philosophers have not ignored it, but when they have considered charity—and it has not been a major topic of investigation—they have tended to center their discussion on its relation to justice.

There have been and still are societies in which charity is not an issue. The preliterate societies investigated by anthropologists such as Marcel Mauss and C. A. Gregory give us cases in point (Mauss 1990; Gregory 1982). In these societies there is accumulation of material objects by one person or family or clan, and transfer of these objects to other persons, without contractual repayment in kind or in money. The recipients will typically give the objects away to yet others, and eventually the initial donor will be a recipient; but none of this is charity as we think of it. The donors are not securely and predictably better off than the recipients, and the point of the giving is not to provide material assistance to the recipients. The whole cycle of giving and receiving is viewed as a way of securing honor, prestige, or recognized social standing; and the practice serves to reinforce solidarity and the sense of interdependence of the members of the community.[4]

It is thus a contingent fact that charity has such an important place in modern Western understandings of morality. Varying ways of structuring wealth, work, and access to resources create different social spaces within which the concept can come to operate. They alone, however, do not account for the ways in which we explain to ourselves and others the kinds of responses we have to those in severe need. Charity does not appear in the lists of virtues the ancient Greek and Roman philosophers give, and the subject itself receives at best marginal treatment. Jewish and Christian teaching is largely responsible for the difference between our ways of thinking about the needy and ancient Greco-Roman ways. The emergence of religious ideas of charity is treated elsewhere in this volume. I take up the story at the point at which the dominance of the Roman Catholic view, as that was elaborated by St. Thomas, was being challenged. The fragmentation of "Christendom" caused by the religious reformation did not lead directly to efforts to work out wholly nonreligious theories of morality. No one hoping for any public impact could fail to acknowledge the importance of God for morality, let alone present himself as an atheist. Post-reformation thought about charity was therefore still largely religious. But it was so with a difference.

For obvious reasons a serious history of thought about charity would be inseparable from a history of thought about property. Jordan reminds us that for many Protestants (as of course for Catholics) property was viewed as a trust, assigned to its possessors by God so that they could carry out his purposes on earth.[5] This is Calvin's direct teaching.[6] It will be useful to review it briefly so that we can have in mind a major version of the position from which more modern views departed.

In a section of the *Institutes* which Calvin says is about "the precepts of love" (III. X.5) he tells us that "we are the stewards of everything God has conferred on us by which we are able to help our neighbor, and are required to render account of our stewardship. Moreover, the only right stewardship is that which is tested by the rule of love" (III.VII.5). This is part of his insistence that only selflessness will bring us salvation. Calvin holds that the scriptural command to esteem others above ourselves is one which we cannot naturally fulfill. Because of our fallen nature, we are wholly selfish, so we must empty the mind of what are now its natural feelings in order to act as we ought (III.VII.4). Only unmerited grace can enable us to do this. If grace is given, we will love our neighbors regardless of their merits or their charms. And this love will result in concrete aid.[7] What matters, Calvin stresses, is not works of love alone, but the motive that gives rise to them: "he who merely performs all the duties of love does not fulfill them, even though he overlooks none; but he, rather, fulfills them who does this from a sincere feeling of love" (III.VII.7).[8]

As with St. Thomas, the doctrine of property as stewardship is associated not only with views about God's purposes in setting us amid material goods but also with a doctrine about the providential ordering of social and economic differences. Calvin thinks the things of this world were put here for our use. Though we are to think of ourselves as only pilgrims (III. X.1), we are not to be ascetic. God made things beautiful and delicious and enjoyable so that we should not be limited to a bare minimal existence. "He meant not only to provide for necessity but also for delight and good cheer" (III. X.2). He also created social hierarchy. Each person is placed in a special station in life, like a sentry at his post, and each station has its definite and limited responsibilities. The resources at the disposal of each of us are also providentially ordained. The rich must learn how to use their wealth modestly, moderately, and generously, while the poor "should know how to bear poverty peacably and patiently" (III. X.4). We must do no less than our calling requires of us; but it should console everyone, Calvin thinks, to bear in mind that we are not expected to do more (III.XI.6).

The doctrine of the calling makes it easier to understand how Calvin can put so much stress on the motivation of the individual donor. Acting within the limits of our calling, we need not worry about the overall success of our charitable endeavors, provided of course that they are sincere. We also need not worry about whether, and how, one's own efforts fit in with those of others. It is central to Calvin's view that God's providence is constantly exercised. With that in mind, all one need do is act lovingly to carry out the (charitable) duties of one's station. The consequences are in God's hands.

Broadly speaking St. Thomas and Calvin share the belief that property is only possible under conditions which entail that ownership involves social responsibility, in particular responsibility for those who are poor and needy. The conditions are that God made material goods for the well-being of everyone alike, and that ownership is the best instrument for increasing those goods and thereby increasing everyone's well-being. On such a view charity as we understand it is a necessary obligation arising from even moderate wealth. As a new understanding of property emerged, new views of charity had also to be formed.

New conceptions of property arose with new conceptions of rights. To see how these developed, we must look at the line of thought initiated by two thinkers, both devout Protestants who agreed that the principles of morality and politics should be explained in ways that made no use of revealed religion and as little appeal to natural religion as was feasible. The primary concerns of Grotius and Pufendorf were with law, and largely with international law. Within this set of concerns, however, they made room for charity; but they gave it a more fully secularized interpretation than it had previously received.

Hugo Grotius brought into modern secular discourse a new way of viewing individual human rights.[9] Instead of seeing basic rights as coming to someone because the person occupies a position in a complex social structure, he took them to be qualities belonging to each of us simply as individuals. What rights do is to make it possible for us to have or do something. Sometimes the quality is fully present, or is, as Grotius says, "perfect"; sometimes it is only incompletely present, or "imperfect." Perfect rights are modeled on the rights arising from contracts, such as the rights conferred by credit or by ownership, or the rights of a master over a slave. These rights can be specified with considerable precision, and give rise to correspondingly precise duties. Justice, strictly speaking, is concerned with these rights. There is another equally important domain, concerned with "those virtues which have as their purpose to do good to others, as generosity, compassion, and foresight in matters of government." Here too there are rights, but they are "imperfect." Their possessors are "worthy of" certain kinds of treatment: for instance, a beggar is worthy of, or has an imperfect right to, alms.[10]

In making these distinctions, Grotius is attempting to replace the Aristotelian notion of general justice with a more precise and limited notion. He contrasts justice properly with what he labels love. The way he spells out the differences between strict justice and love makes his point clear.

Justice allows perfect rights to be protected by the use of force, but love does not permit the enforcement of imperfect rights.[11] In strict justice, for instance, it is permissible to kill someone who is about to strike you or who is robbing you. A creditor may lawfully exact the last penny from a poor and needy debtor, and in doing so do "nothing contrary to his right according to a strict interpretation." But, Grotius says, there are rules of love as well as rules of law, and they tell us that such a creditor is guilty of heartlessness (III.xiii.iv, p. 759). The contrast between rules of love or the law of love, and rules or laws of strict justice, is noted in several places. Perhaps the most striking is the discussion of whether a government may deliver an innocent citizen into the hands of an enemy in order to prevent the ruin of the state. All that we learn from the older writers on this subject, Grotius thinks, is that the citizen is not bound to give himself up for this purpose. But, he adds, "it does not follow also that love permits him to do otherwise. For there are many duties which are not in the domain of justice properly speaking, but in that of affection, which are not only discharged amid praise . . . but cannot even be omitted without blame."[12]

It is, I think, quite significant that what Grotius contrasts to justice is the virtue of love. The contrast is not, as it is in St. Thomas, with the traditional virtues, prudence, temperance, and courage. Grotius has little to say about these virtues, but he makes a definite place for the virtue of love as a wholly natural way in which we are related to others. The law of love cannot yield the precise rights which characterize the realm of expletive justice. But love is to be counted on in ordinary human transactions. It is not an infused theological virtue, ordered to our supernatural good. It is not treated as relating us first to God in friendship and only then to humans.[13] And Grotius does not treat charitable love as impossible for those not given the special grace of God. By treating Christian love in this naturalistic way, Grotius takes the first step toward transforming it into benevolence.

Grotius says little about works of charity as such, but in considering the origins and limits of property he gives an important discussion of cases of necessity which bears directly on our concerns. God initially "conferred upon the human race a general right over things of a lower nature." As industry and knowledge increased, spurred by dissatisfaction with a life sustained only by what nature yields, dissension arose, and natural fairness was not observed in dividing goods. Community ownership, as conferred by God, was no longer adequate. So it became necessary that there should be "a kind of agreement," either express or tacit, about who would own what. The simplest settlement was that each should own what he then possessed (II.ii.ii, pp. 186–90). And from then on, there are perfect rights to private property, conferring on each the absolute mastery over what is his own. Or nearly absolute: there are some cases in which one person may have a right over something which another already possesses. These are cases of necessity, and they permit infringement of property rights because of the "intention . . . of those who first introduced individual ownership." They intended "to depart as little as possible from natural equity." Hence this intention must be used in interpreting positive laws. It follows, Grotius thinks, that "in direst need the primitive right of user revives, as if community of ownership had remained." For example, when fire breaks out and threatens my house if your attached house catches fire, I may destroy your house.

The principle governing cases of necessity is explicitly denied to be "that the owner of a thing is bound by the rule of love to give to him who lacks." Dire necessity grounds a claim of justice, not of charity. Its basis is that those who instituted property would have insisted that the exception for necessity be made before they would have agreed to set up the system (II.ii.ii, pp. 193–94). It is thus clear that for Grotius, aside from exceptional cases of necessity, property is not directly connected with social responsibilities. Even your ownership of more than you need for your family does not entail any strict obligation on you to help the needy. This view reflects Grotius's position about the point of society: "society has in view this object, that through community of resource and effort each individual be safeguarded in the possession of what belongs to him" (I.ii.5). For him it is strict justice that enables society to function as it should. The law of love does not represent the real meaning of society. The contrast with the position of St. Thomas is striking. For him the social order of justice operates within a deeper order of love, and the significance of the order of justice can be understood only if it is seen as the condition for the fullest possible earthly expression of love. In this life that will not be a very full expression, because the command to love God and neighbor cannot be wholly obeyed here (IIaIIae 44, 6). But it is in the order of the special love called *caritas* that the highest value comes closest to realization in this world.[14]

Grotius's most influential follower was Samuel Pufendorf, author of several widely read works on natural law.[15] Accepting and clarifying the Grotian distinction between perfect and imperfect rights, and adding to it a more definite connection with duties, he elaborated also on the application of these ideas. The domain of imperfect duties is, he says, that "universal justice" which covers all our obligations outside the domain of strict justice.[16] As examples Pufendorf gives coming to someone's aid "with counsel, goods, or personal assistance," or performing a service of "piety, respect, gratitude, or generosity" where one is indebted in some way to the person thus aided. In carrying out these imperfect duties, the point is only to give to the possessor of the imperfect right some good or other. This is to be done "without observing whether the service furnished is equal to, or less than, that which was the reason for the obligation" (L.I.vii, 7–9, pp. 118–21). It is not to be done, however, without taking note of some pertinent distinctions among recipients. Not only are family and national ties relevant, merit is so as well (L.III.iii.15, pp. 373–74). With this, Pufendorf builds into his theory what had long been recognized in practice, a distinction between deserving and undeserving poor. If a man is in desperate straits due to his own fault—his "sluggishness and negligence"—he is less deserving of aid than one who is destitute through no fault of his own. Without this proviso, Pufendorf says, "a right is apparently given to lazy scoundrels . . . to appropriate . . . by force what has been secured by the labour of others." It is to be left up to the property owner to decide who is deserving, and who not (L.II.iv.6, p. 304). Perfect rights and duties, by contrast, typically arise from contract, and require the precise carrying out of the terms of the contract.[17] Thus precision as well as enforceability mark perfect rights and duties, unenforceability, imprecision, and consequent need for the agent's discretion mark the imperfect.

Pufendorf explains the distinction of kinds of rights in a way that is pertinent to our concerns. Among the laws of nature there are some which must be observed if society is to exist at all, and others whose observance conduces to "an improved existence." Perfect rights and duties take their character from the first kind of law, imperfect from the second. In their different functions, imperfect and perfect rights and duties supplement one another. Men have many needs which can be satisfied only if others help. But love, or the feeling of humanity, would not normally prompt people to give all the help others need, and anyway it is embarrassing to be always asking for assistance. Contract steps in to serve the purpose. It enables us to get what we need by paying for it in goods or services (L.III.iv.1, p. 379).

Although society cannot exist without strict justice, the imperfect duties of love have special claims to our attention. They alone can give rise to merit. Two aspects of merit are relevant. First, performance of imperfect duties deserves a return of gratitude, while the performance of perfect duties does not. We have considerable leeway in what we should do to show gratitude, but the general obligation to do something is not to be ignored (L.III.iii. 16–17, pp. 374–78). Second, there is the religious aspect of merit, "the efficacy of which, as some would claim," Pufendorf adds cautiously, "will be found to avail even against God," presumably to balance our sins. We acquire merit only when we do something not strictly owed to another (L. I.ix.5, pp. 138–40; cf. III.iii.15, p. 373). On both counts, what Pufendorf calls the works of love must be done from the appropriate loving motive: not from recognition of a perfect duty, for in that case I would not be giving anything that is really mine to give; and not from private interest, "for as soon as a kindness is done for private advantage, it loses forthwith its designation and essence" (L.III.iv.1, p. 380). The works of justice, however, being compellable, need not spring from any form of love. Pufendorf shows the importance of this when he says that works of love win the hearts of others, and therefore provide for a kind of social solidarity which cannot be created by acts which will be exacted by force if not done voluntarily (L.III.iv.6, p. 386).

Pufendorf does not isolate property as strongly from social responsibility as Grotius does.[18] He considers property to have been instituted by agreement, and sees the point of the institution as the avoidance of quarrels and the increase of industry (II.vi.5, p. 301; cf. IV.iv, pp. 532ff.). With Grotius Pufendorf takes property rights to be perfect rights. But in his discussion of cases of necessity an important difference emerges. For Pufendorf the duties of humanity or love are continuous with the duties of strict justice. Natural law itself says only that help to the needy is to be given out of the virtue of humanity, under an imperfect obligation. But "nothing prevents this imperfect obligation from being strengthened by civil law into a perfect one," and in fact, Pufendorf adds, precisely that took place among the Jews (II.vi.5, p. 302). He argues that it is not a Grotian tacit reservation in the original agreement about property that allows force to be used to take property in a case of necessity where the owner will not give it out of love. It has to do with the nature of imperfect rights. They exist so that a person who grants what is asked may "show that his mind is intent upon voluntarily doing his duty, and at the same time possesses the means to bind others to him by his kindness." But this is less important than saving a life, and if someone is so hard-hearted that he refuses to act in an emergency, he forfeits his chance to display generosity: "whoever refuses to show humanity should lose his property as well as his merit" (II.vi.6, p. 305).

Pufendorf presents the whole body of natural law as a means to increase human sociability—a need for one another's company which goes far beyond desires for material assistance. His treatment of necessity shows how seriously he takes this. He does not believe that societies will ever be wholly dominated by humanity or love, but the goal is to increase sociability as much as possible. If performance of imperfect duties, including duties to aid the needy, is not required for the existence of society, it represents the highest flowering of human capacities. Pufendorf departs strikingly from Grotius in this effort to show that the Christian doctrine of love as the point of social life can be put without effective loss into secular terms.

No discussion of thought about property and charity during the seventeenth century would be complete without a discussion of John Locke's views. Yet these are so complex, and so hotly debated, that nothing resembling even an adequate summary is possible here.[19]

Locke faced a situation in which radical challenges to the justifiability of property were answered by extreme claims about the absolute right of property owners to do as they wish with their own. We can get some idea of the challenges from the writings of the great leader of the mid-seventeenth-century Digger (or "True Leveller") movement, Gerrard Winstanley. Seeing the poor faced with starvation while vast tracts of land went untilled, he denied that the system of property could be justified as it stood. All original acquisition, he argued, had come about through foul play and force, and no length of unholy and immoral possession, whatever its legal status, could justify ancestral proceedings so that they would result in contemporary rights. If the dispossessed could plant the land and cut timber from the forests, there would be enough and to spare for all to live; but the system of property prevents this, and thereby forces people into beggary and other forms of unwarranted dependency. " 'And is not this a slavery,' " he has "the people" asking,

> that though there be land enough in England to maintain ten times as many people as are in it, yet some must beg ... or work in hard drudgery ... or starve or steal ... the subjects (so called) have not their birthright freedom granted them from their brethren, who hold it from them by club law, but not by righteousness. (In Hill, ed. 1973, p. 282)

Winstanley's basic idea is that there could be enough for all, so that there need be no poverty, but that the distribution of property prevents this. Consequently he believes that the claims of the destitute are claims of justice and not claims of charity. Against these claims, he passionately believes, no existing system of ownership can rightly stand. Winstanley was one of the first, and certainly not the last, to assert that poverty results not from divine ordinance or individual sin and idleness but from social and economic structures made by humans and capable of being changed by humans. Grotian reasoning would not protect the rights of present owners if this were correct. The poor could argue that no one in the condition of natural equity would have agreed to the kind of distribution that currently exists, nor, consequently, to the legalization of the procedures of acquisition and exchange that led up to it. And on Pufendorfian grounds it would seem that seizure of land from the hard-hearted, to prevent mass starvation, would be justifiable.

Locke was well aware of the force of economic considerations of the kind to which Winstanley appealed. Holding, as was commonplace, that God created material goods for the necessities and comforts of humans, he argued that property rights could only be rights to the use of things, not to their substance. The use of things is to be directed by God's commands, which are given us quite clearly. We are not entitled to make others starve, or to take advantage of them when they are destitute. God, Locke declares in a centrally important passage,

> has given no one of his Children such a Property, in his peculiar Portion of the things of this World, but that he has given his needy Brother a Right to the Surplusage of his Goods; so that it cannot justly be denied him, when his pressing Wants call for it. . . . As *Justice* gives every Man a Title to the produce of his honest Industry, and the fair Acquisitions of his Ancestors descended to him; so *Charity* gives every Man a Title to so much out of another's plenty, as will keep him from extreme want.[20]

Property rights must respect this basic constraint. And the economic aspect of the functioning of property rights is always present in Locke's thinking.[21] This is evident in the proviso that we may acquire property, in a state of nature, by "mixing our labor" with things, only if as much and as good is still available for others. It is evident also in Locke's justification of acquisition beyond what is of immediate use, through the value set on gold or on diamonds and other pebbles which do not spoil over time. For the basic justification is that a system of property in which unused wealth can be accumulated will be much more productive than any alternative system, so that everyone will benefit more by accepting it than by rejecting it. Consequently such a system of property is permitted by God's intentions for the use of material goods, and especially of that basic good, the land:

> he who appropriates land to himself by his labour, does not lessen but increases the common stock of mankind. For the provisions serving to the support of humane life, produced by one acre of inclosed and cultivated land, are . . . ten times more, than those, which are yielded by an acre of Land . . . lyeing wast in common. And therefore he, that incloses Land and has a greater plenty of the conveniencys of life from ten acres, than he could have had from an hundred left to Nature, may truly be said, to give ninety acres to Mankind.

For Locke, then, whatever the complexities of his doctrine, property rights are not cut loose from social responsibilities. One is not to force others to work by the threat of starvation, and one is to bring up one's children not to be grasping about goods, but to be generous and giving.[22] Our rights are basically instrumentalities, serving to bring about the good for all humans as God intended it to be brought about. Even in exercising our rights we must keep God's general purpose in view. The distance between the rights that determine justice and those that determine charity is decreasing. Locke does not think, as Pufendorf does, that the point of society is the increase of sociability.[23] He is concerned with the increase of benefits to everyone in society. Justice still has its own origin and function. But the need to accommodate the claims of love has moved him a step closer to a utilitarian theory of the justification of property and of the responsibilities that accompany ownership.[24]

The natural law writers focused on legal problems. Precise and enforceable perfect rights, and the laws involved in them, got most of their attention. In this domain, if people obey the law, it does not matter why. Hence the lawyers paid relatively little attention to motives. Critics thought they were thereby leaving out the central concern of morality proper. Christian morality is basically a morality of love. Christ's summary of the law in the love commandment shows that law should be derivable from love. Various opponents of the Grotian natural lawyers accordingly tried to explain justice and the statutes that specify it in terms of the expression of love. Jean Domat, for example, an important legal theorist of the late seventeenth century, codified French law in terms of two requirements. God and neighbor are to be loved, and human law should serve to form communities of loving persons. The most basic requirements of justice "command only the effects of mutual love," and particular laws should express love reciprocally owed.[25] Leibniz defines justice as "the charity of the wise." The wise agent knows the amount of perfection or good that each action would bring about, and is moved solely by enlightened love of good. Virtuous agents, therefore, act as much like God as is humanly possible, bringing about all the good they can. On this basis Leibniz proposed a different systematization of law.[26] But neither he nor Domat tried to work out a detailed view of morality.

British moral philosophers paid considerably more attention to love-based morality. Frances Hutcheson, a Presbyterian minister, propounded a theory basing all morality on benevolent love, and Joseph Butler, an Anglican, pointed out difficulties it runs into. David Hume, presenting one of the first fully secular views of morality, offered a new way of seeing the relations between love and justice. The main lines of the debates can be put without following all their intricacies.

For Hutcheson morality is not simply a matter of behavior; it concerns motive first of all. We approve of benevolence, and therefore of benevolent actions.

We neither approve nor disapprove of self-interested action, recognizing its inevitability and expecting it to be kept within bounds. But benevolence is, for him, the whole of virtue; and benevolence is Christian love, given a name that might enable morality to be freed from sectarian disputes. The greater the benevolence from which we act, the greater the approval we elicit. If everyone acted from love, there would be no need for laws backed by threats of punishment to obligate people to behave properly. Hutcheson sees that kind of obligation, despite its centrality in the Pufendorfian system, not as the core of morality, but as a remedy for human defect.[27]

Rights, indeed, Hutcheson recognizes. Benevolence, he says, seeks the greatest happiness of the greatest number—a phrase that Bentham later made famous—and so when we see that if we allowed everyone to do or own something the result would tend to the good, we say people have a right to it. Perfect rights are those whose universal violation "would make human Life intolerable." Imperfect rights are those whose violation "would not necessarily make men miserable." We do not set penalties for violation of imperfect rights because to do so would cause more harm than good, and "deprive men of the greatest pleasure in actions of kindness, humanity, gratitude."[28] Hutcheson thus tries to respond to both calls to charity: its response to the needs of others and its expression of our personal concern for them.

Bishop Butler had no wish to deprecate charity, and in fact he added considerably to the arguments Hutcheson had given against the view that all voluntary action is necessarily selfish. But he saw in the morality we all accept a complexity that he thought had escaped Hutcheson. We approve of helping some people rather than others even if the total amount of benevolence shown is the same. We do not think it right that someone should take property from one person to give to another who would get more good from it. Thus we do not disapprove of injustice simply because it produces less good than justice. Benevolence, therefore, cannot be "the whole of virtue." God, he added, may be concerned only with the well-being of everyone alike; but we are not God, and conscience shows that he has set down rules that we are to obey, even if we cannot see the good that comes of obedience. Morality has two domains, for Butler, and they are strikingly like those defined by Pufendorf in terms of perfect and imperfect duties.[29]

Like Butler and Hutcheson, David Hume intended his moral theory to accommodate the patterns of ordinary approval and disapproval. He refused, however, to attribute any religious significance to them. Morality arises, he argues, as a natural response to ordinary human needs and feelings. Like Hutcheson, he thought benevolence an important part of our make-up. But he accepted the force of Butler's arguments against the claim that virtue involves nothing more. His profoundest philosophical move was to transform the Pufendorfian law-based theory of perfect and imperfect rights, which depends on a divine lawgiver, into a theory of different kinds of virtue, which need no such external source.[30]

One kind of virtue, of which justice is the prototype, arises from commerce and the need for security of property. As long as we lived only in small family groups or face-to-face societies, there was no need for it. But as we come to deal with strangers over long periods of time, it becomes important to have security for our transactions. In such circumstances, a system of property laws which are reliably obeyed produces an enormous increase in the well-being of every-one in society, even those worst-off. Hence the virtue of justice requires strict adherence to the property laws that happen to hold in one's own society. And these may require us to act in ways that in some instances do nothing to increase happiness. It is only adherence to the whole system or institution of justice that improves our condition; justice remains a virtue even when it requires us to thwart benevolence in particular cases. Hume nowhere ties possession of prop-erty to social responsibility, and he makes no room for cases of necessity that would allow using one person's property to help another.[31]

Virtues of the second kind, of which parental affection and kindness to those in need are examples, lead us to try to do good each time they come into play. Here no rules or laws are involved. Exercising these virtues, we express our benevolent feelings toward particular people or small groups, if not toward society or humankind as a whole. Although the term "philanthropy" was com-ing into use in the eighteenth century, Hume would have had no use for it, be-lieving that there is no such thing as the love of mankind in the abstract. But with Pufendorf, though in wholly different ways, he constructs a domain of mo-rality which responds to the less extensive kindly impulses that we all feel.[32] Hume also works out a counterpart to the Pufendorfian idea that the perfect duties are indispensable for the existence of society (*Treatise* III.II.ii, p. 491). Vir-tues like justice function in one kind of group, virtues like generosity and pa-rental love in other kinds. We all need the personal relations governed by the virtues of affection as well as commercial arrangements governed by justice. Both bring about good; but benevolence is the dominant motive only in one.

It would be hard to find two moral theories more deeply opposed than those of Hume and Kant; yet they have many points of contact. Like Hume, Kant aimed at replacing the natural law picture of morality as dependent on an ex-ternal lawgiver with a new picture in which humans are wholly self-governing. And like Hume he too tried to find a way in which duties of justice and duties of love could occupy different but equally significant places in our lives. Raised as Hume had been on the vocabulary of perfect and imperfect duties, he re-verted to it at various points in his work. Only toward the end of his career did he come to anything like a satisfactory accommodation of it.

In his first major work on ethics Kant seems to deny that natural feeling has any proper role in moral motivation. There is a single moral law, he argues, telling us to act only in ways that we could rationally will to be permissible for everyone; and we ought to obey the law out of respect for it as the moral law.[33] The complexities inherent in his initial statement emerge in a later work in which he shows how his basic principle can be applied. There he distinguishes perfect duties requiring compliance with law from imperfect duties that arise because the principle of morality requires us to have certain ends or goals. One end we are required to have is the well-being of others. Since we cannot ourselves will that everyone may ignore all the ends of others, we must ourselves will that we not ignore all such ends. And this entails that we must make some ends of some other people our own. But morality does not say which ends, or which people. Because of the principled lack of detail imposed by this requirement, it matches Pufendorf's imperfect duties. Like them, moreover, it is also unenforceable; our compliance with it makes us praiseworthy; and though the motive at first will be a purely rational concern for the good of others, this may in time be transformed into or accompanied by a feeling of love for those we aid.[34] But for Kant the duties of virtue, as he calls those involving mandatory ends, are no less and no more important than the duties of law, as he calls those requiring only external compliance. As with Hume, the two kinds of duties operate within different aspects of human life, neither of which can be omitted.

Kant's views about perfect and imperfect duties give us most of his thought about the care of our neighbor. He says little about charity as such, and the reason may lie in his attitude toward it, which is plainly revealed in a marginal note from about 1772:

> Many people take pleasure in doing good actions but therefore do not want to stand under obligations toward others. If one comes to them submissively they will do everything. They do not want to subject themselves to the rightful in people, but to view such simply as the object of their goodheartedness. It is not all one under what title I get something. One must not give me, merely because of my request, what belongs to me. (Kant 1974, vol. 19, p. 145, #6736)

This attitude is not a result of Kant's view of property. Property, for Kant, is essential for moral personality, and the whole institution of ownership can take place only within civil society. The justification of the institution of property rests, therefore, not on its usefulness, but on its direct relation to our being moral agents. And while ownership as such carries no direct responsibility for the well-being of the less fortunate, the moral personality which it supports does have such responsibilities, though they cannot be precisely specified.[35] In the realm of politics, Kant allows that the sovereign within a properly constituted state has the right to use public money for the support of the indigent, and of abandoned children or children who would otherwise be left to die.[36] The money, he thinks, should not be donated by the citizens, but taken by taxation, because this is a matter of the right of the state. Questions have been raised as to whether the assertion of such a right is compatible with Kant's contractarian view of the state, but he plainly thinks it is. The general will of the people, he says, has formed a society, and for the purpose of maintaining itself permanently has agreed to allow the state to support "those members . . . who are not able to support themselves." There may be an argument buried here, to the effect that the social contract would have to include an agreement to support the indigent since otherwise the permanence of society would be threatened. If so, Kant would seem to be making support of the poor into a necessary condition of the continuation of society, thus assimilating it to Pufendorf's perfect duties. This would be consistent with the belief recorded in the lecture notes that relief of the poor is a matter of justice, not of magnanimity; but whether it is Kant's own intention is hard to tell.

I have gone on at great length about the distinction between perfect and imperfect duties because it provided the main framework for discussing charity from early modern times until the beginning of the nineteenth century. The review may suggest a question. It is not hard to see why the distinction seemed useful for so long. It enabled those who used it to handle a number of points that cannot be avoided in any thorough treatment of the general topic of helping others—that charity combines obligation and discretion, for instance, in ways that many other duties do not. But there is, I think, a deeper question about the appeal of the distinction, one relating to the question of why so useful a conceptual tool should lose its hold after the end of the eighteenth century.[37]

The answer, I believe, has to do with a new way of looking at charity itself. However the distinction between perfect and imperfect duties was spelled out, it enshrined the assumption that the need for charity is as permanent as the moral principles that instruct us about it. This assumption itself came into question in the nineteenth century. It was not a matter of doubting whether people would always need the help of others, in unpredictable ways, and therefore of questioning whether helpful dispositions would always be considered virtuous. The charity whose necessity came into question was that which deals with severe needs arising from basic economic and political inequalities. The reason for the stability of the distinction between perfect and imperfect duties in earlier centuries may be related to this issue.

We can see the connection by considering a point suggested by Hume's famous remarks about the circumstances of justice.[38] Justice, he argues, obtains moral approval because it is useful. And it is useful because of the concurrence of several factors. One is the transferability of things people need from one possessor to another. If no goods could be transferred, no commerce could arise, and no contracts could be made, so no justice would be needed. A second is our limited generosity. We give happily to family and friends, but otherwise we tend, on the whole, to put our own interests first. If we were infinitely benevolent, we would give others whatever they needed, regardless of cost to ourselves, and justice would, again, be pointless. A third factor is the relative scarcity of commodities. If there were either so much in the way of goods that no one would ever be needy, or so little in the way of commodities that no division of them could sustain us, justice could have no use.

It is this last claim that is suggestive. St. Thomas brings up a comparable idea in connection with individual charity. Reminding us that each must give to the poor, he adds that "those who suffer want are so numerous and they cannot all be supplied out of one stock, and this is why it is left to each individual to decide how to manage his property in such a way as to supply the wants of the suffering."[39] Thomas's idea is that the duty of charity must be exercised at the individual's discretion because none of us has resources enough to take care of all the claims of need that are made on us. Individual discretion is the only formula available for decision making.

Let us move this to the social level. Suppose there is enough in the way of goods to sustain many, or most, but not all the members of a society, and that, as it happens, some members of that society have far more than they need for sustenance, while large numbers have significantly less. Suppose that even an equal division would not provide sustenance for all. It is still true that if those who have more than enough (the rich) give to some of the others (the poor) then *some* of the poor will be helped, even though not all of them can be helped. Now there are no salient and evident ways in which some of the poor can be picked out for aid: none, at least, which are as precise and as widely accepted as the marks by which transactions under justice are indicated.[40] The poor are poor because they do not possess enough under the strict rights of justice to provide themselves with the necessities of life. So unless the poor are to be ignored altogether by the rich, some other way must be found for selecting those who are to receive.

Charity understood as an imperfect duty seems to provide such a selection procedure (if that term is not too strong). A belief that everyone has duties of love, which cannot be enforced and which cannot be precisely specified, produces social action by which some of the poor are helped, in a situation where that is possible although it is not possible to help all the poor. If it is widely believed that there is not enough to go around, and would not be were property to undergo radical redistribution, then justice cannot cover the claims of everyone. Some claims *must* be treated differently, and an imperfect duty of benevolence seems to give a way for deciding what that treatment will be.

A doctrine which treats charity as one of the imperfect rights or duties, then, might be a moral response to genuine material scarcity which is unavoidable at the time given the technology available. But if there is no such scarcity, or if scarcity could be removed by redistribution of the resources of production, an interpretation of charity as an imperfect duty might be simply an ideological defense of an unjust division of property which itself produces the very poverty which the exercise of that imperfect duty is meant to alleviate. Kant's position is perceptive. He sees a permanent place for duties of love—but he does not wish to include among them charity, in the sense of relief of desperate need. That sort of charity should be replaced by justice. The nineteenth century was a period of increasing debate about whether alternative schemes of property distribution could or would conduce more to social well-being than the existing one. It is little wonder that the distinction between perfect and imperfect duties should have remained socially important while the eradication of poverty seemed a merely utopian hope, and that it came into question when the possibility seemed within grasp.

I have tried to indicate the major steps by which the Christian doctrine of love or charity was transformed into a secular view about the centrality of the production of benefits for everyone in society. Grotius treated love as simply a human feeling or motive which could be relied on in ordinary life, independent of infusion or grace. Pufendorf agreed, but insisted nonetheless that the growth of a form of neighborly love was the real point of society, beyond the aim of protecting each person's "own." Locke held that God meant society to bring about an increase of benefits, not least material benefits, for everyone in the society. Hutcheson and Hume came even closer to utilitarianism, agreeing that it is the beneficial results due to some character traits that—directly or indirectly—account for our considering them virtues. From here it was only a short step to the utilitarian view, which none of the earlier writers held, that an individual could determine what it would be right or obligatory to do by calculating the utilities of the available options. Toward the end of the eighteenth century Paley, Bentham, and Godwin took that step. The two major forms of opposition to it were spelled out at about the same time, in the work of Kant and of Thomas Reid.

With these developments, moral philosophy took a decisively new turn, abandoning, for a variety of reasons, the vocabulary of natural rights and duties, and developing a new set of problems. But it was not mainly because of changes in philosophical ways of discussing what people ought to do that discussions of charity and how to help the poor were so different in the nineteenth century from what they had been earlier. Two other developments had much more to do with the way the discussions developed.

First, changes in society and the economy became increasingly visible as population increased markedly, literacy spread, and urban poverty became an increasingly unavoidable problem. To interpret and influence these changes a spate of theoretical writings appeared, many of them directly concerned with the problems of poverty, many more broadly theoretical but with important bearings on charity. Although there were always some who thought that society should do nothing in an organized way about poverty, the general weight of opinion was that society had to do something about it—if only to prevent revolution.[41] The question therefore was not so much whether something was to be done by society: the question was what. Writings on population, political economy, and political reform, far more than theoretical philosophical treatments, carried the weight in these arguments. Is there a tendency for population to outstrip resources, and if so what, if anything, can be done about it? Is there an "iron law of wages" which guarantees that some will always be paid substantially less than others? Will relief sap the desire to work and breed a population of permanent indigents? English discussions of poverty from the 1790s centered for four decades on reform of the Elizabethan poor law, and the changes of the 1830s did not end the debates. Malthus, Adam Smith, Ricardo, Cobbett, and later Dickens and other novelists, contributed more to these discussions than moral philosophy did. Bentham indeed was a mighty voice but though he brought his doctrinaire utilitarianism to bear on the problem, he was no more specifically a philosopher when writing about the poor law than he was when he wrote about penal institutions (it is a little hard sometimes to tell whether Bentham is dealing with paupers or criminals). (See Bahmueller 1981.)

My first point might thus be put by saying that with the rise of claims to have accurate knowledge bearing on the question of what would or would not work to help the poor, the center of gravity shifted decisively away from discussion of moral principle to discussions of allegedly scientific facts. The second reason for the change of focus is equally important, and not unrelated to belief in a new science of society. Claims were vociferously made, at first in England and in France, later in Germany, that the whole existing system of property relations was immoral and unnecessarily harmful. Anarchism, socialism, and various forms of communism were proposed, all of them holding that the poor were not sinfully idle objects of imperfect duty, owing gratitude to benefactors, but victims of the injustice of the basic structure of society and the economy, to whom great wrongs were being done and strict restitution owed. These were of course hardly majority views; but, often in conjunction with political action, they helped generate serious reconsideration of the problem of poverty. Specifically, they intensified the concentration on economic and demographic issues, because the safest way to attack the extremists was not to criticize their moral outlooks but to argue that their plans violated "societal laws" or were otherwise hopelessly impracticable.

We can see the change from treating the poor as objects of charity to treating them as victims of injustice by looking briefly at two of the early British utilitarians, Paley and Godwin. In 1785 Paley produced his *Principles of Moral and Political Philosophy*, used as a standard university text for the next four decades. Godwin's *Enquiry Concerning Political Justice*, first published in 1793, served for a short time as the paradigm of the anarchical and immoral horrors into which pure utilitarianism leads, and was then forgotten.

Paley justifies property by an argument like that used by the natural law writers: it "increases the produce of the earth," preserves it, prevents quarrels, and increases the conveniences of life by fostering the division of labor and the arts.[42] Hence we may conclude that "even the poorest and the worst provided, in countries where property and the consequences of property prevails, are in a better situation, with respect to . . . the necessaries of life, than *any* are in places where most things remain in common" (III. I.1–2). Justice, which relates largely to property, and other equally determinate duties form one branch of morality. Charity is the first of our "indeterminate" duties. It is defined, not, Paley says, in its ordinary sense of bounty to the poor, but more compendiously as "the promoting of the happiness of our inferiors." Prudence teaches us how to behave toward superiors, politeness toward equals, while "virtue and religion" have charity—and subordinates—as their chief province (III.II.i). We are to act kindly to our servants and dependents, and must not assume that men in "low and ordinary stations" are not affected by benefits, that is, are not grateful: they are (III.II.ii). As long as the abominable institution of slavery persists, we should be kind to our slaves (III.II.iii).[43] If the laws of the land or our profession put some of the poor under our protection, we must do our best for them. The country gentleman serving as magistrate must oversee the poor law officers to ensure that they genuinely help the poor, and the lawyer can do the poor a special kindness by preventing them from pressing their rights at law (III.II.iv). Paley argues also that God instilled pity in our nature for the purpose of moving us to relieve need with "pecuniary bounty" (III.II.v). Gratitude for these good offices is of course to be expected (III.II.xi).

Godwin's tone, like Kant's, brings us to the threshold of another world. He holds that everyone has a right to "that, the exclusive possession of which being awarded to him, a greater sum of benefit or pleasure will result, than could have arisen from its being otherwise appropriated." But he thinks the present distribution of property does not at all reflect this principle. Strict justice would require massive redistribution; but those who defend the present state of affairs treat the issue not as the debt of justice it is, but as a matter of generosity. And the effect of this "accommodating doctrine"

> is, to place the supply of our wants in the disposal of a few, enabling them to make a show of generosity with what is not truly their own, and to purchase the submission of the poor by the payment of a debt. Theirs is a system of clemency and charity, instead of a system of justice. It fills the rich with unreasonable pride . . . and the poor with servility. (Godwin 1971, Bk. VIII, ch. 1)

Godwin's claim, in short, is that charity as "bounty to the poor" should be replaced by justice. The old assumptions, still visible in Paley, about superiors and inferiors, and about a society tied together by benefit and gratitude, are gone.

There were those who argued, against even much less drastic claims about the need for social change than Godwin's, that if society made effective provision for the poor it would do away with the need for individual charity; and then where would Christians find an opportunity to express the love that saves? To this Bentham replied at length, and to good effect. (See Bahmueller 1981, ch. 4.) Rather than cite so familiar an author, however, I cite another, to indicate that the same worries about what would happen if justice replaced charity were being felt in Germany. Here is Hegel:

> Poverty . . . has a subjective side which demands similarly subjective aid, aris-
> ing . . . from love and sympathy. This is the place where morality finds plenty
> to do despite all public organization. . . . Casual almsgivingand casual endow-
> ments . . . are supplemented by public almsgiving, hospitals, streetlighting,
> and so forth. There is still quite enough left over and above these things for
> charity to do on its own account. A false view is implied both when charity
> insists on having this poor relief reserved solely to private sympathy . . . , and
> also when it feels injured or mortified by universal regulations and ordinances
> which are *obligatory.* (Hegel 1942, §242 and note, p. 149)

Godwin took up Winstanley's challenge to the existing order in the name of the poor. His stance was one which later thinkers developed at greater length, with greater sophistication if not greater passion, and to much greater effect. It seems to me that the question posed by Kant, Godwin, and these others is at the core of much present discussion of charity and philanthropy. Must we say that there will always be a need for spontaneous charity in the treatment of those in desperate need, or is the only way of successfully dealing with the problem one which requires what have traditionally been seen as the tools of justice?

Notes

1. William Blake, "The Human Abstract."
2. Cited in Hands (1968), p. 159, n.68.
3. *Moralphilosophie Collins*, in Kant (1974), vol. 27, pp. 455–56.
4. See Mauss (1990), pp. 17–18; Gregory (1982), pp. 42–43; and also Titmuss (1971), p. 72. It is also important to bear in mind that these are not societies with a market economy. Exchange of goods generally, and not only in the cases of these large gifts, has dif-
ferent social meanings from those it has in market or commercial societies.
5. Jordan (1959), p. 152, 168; and cf. the whole of ch. VI. He also stresses the considerable social pressures on the wealthy to give generously: honor paid to donors, scorn
and contempt shown to those who did not give. His thesis is that there was an enormous
outpouring of private charity during the sixteenth and seventeenth centuries, doing far
more than the government could have done to help the destitute, and that this outpouring
was motivated by generosity and social concern on the part of the rich. Although he notes
the fear of the unemployed and the worries about social instability, he nowhere suggests
that such concerns played a major part in motivating donations. I do not find the rosy
picture he gives of the motivations of the wealthy to be wholly credible.
6. References given in the text are to Book, Chapter, and section of *Institutes of the Christian Religion* (Calvin 1961).

7. He does suggest that members of "the same household of faith" will be preferred objects of charity (III.VII.6).

8. The way men can get themselves to do this, Calvin says, is to "put themselves in the place of him whom they see in need of their assistance, and pity his ill fortune as if they themselves experienced and bore it, so that they may be impelled by a feeling of mercy and humaneness to go to his aid just as to their own" (III,VII.7). Hume's doctrine of sympathy shows how this notion can be reworked in wholly secular terms.

9. For what follows about Grotius I am much indebted to Tuck (1979). Tuck traces the development of the "subjective" conception of an individual right back to medieval canon lawyers, through a series of other religious writers. Critics argue that Tuck over-states the case for Grotius's originality. Original or not, he was certainly the main force in spreading the idea and winning it acceptance.

10. *Laws of War and Peace* (Grotius 1925), I.i.iv–viii, pp. 35–37. The Grotian distinction between perfect and imperfect rights, which Pufendorf later elaborated into a theory of perfect and imperfect duties as well, is not the same as the Stoic distinction of kinds of morally significant acts that Cicero sometimes made in terms of more and less perfect. Cicero was translating the Stoics' Greek terms, *katorthomata* and *kathekonta*. The former referred to acts done by the perfectly wise man, which were accordingly perfectly good and right. The latter referred to acts which could be done both by the wise and by the rest of us, and which, although not possessing the highest value, were appropriate. Cicero uses the Latin phrase *officium perfectum* in referring to the former and *officium medium* in referring to the latter (*de Officiis* I.8). But for the Grotians perfect duties are as incumbent on everyone as imperfect, and there are numerous other ways in which the distinction is not the same as the one Cicero draws.

11. I do not think this is a matter of definition in Grotius. He argues the point indi-rectly in connection with his argument to show that war is permissible. "Right reason . . . and the nature of society . . . do not prohibit all use of force, but only that use of force which is in conflict with society, that is, which attempts to take away the rights of another. For society has in view this object, that through community of resource and effort each individual be safeguarded in the possession of what belongs to him" (I.ii.5, p. 53). This says that force may be used to protect the rights which are central to society. The rights exist prior to, and are the justification of, the use of force. They justify use of force because they indicate the ends of nature, that is, God's purposes in creating us with the nature we have, a nature which includes possession of rights. Cf. I.ii.4, p. 52.

12. Grotius, II.xxv.iii.2–3, pp. 579–80. See also I.ii.viii.10, p. 75, the reference to "the law of well-ordered love"; and II.xii.ix.2, p. 347, where it is said that if you are selling grain, and you know that many ships bringing grain are shortly coming, but your pur-chaser does not know this, you cannot omit informing him "without violating the rule of love. Yet such an omission is not unjust, that is, not inconsistent with the right of the one with whom the contract is made." Tuck does not discuss the role of love in Grotius, except to say that Grotius advocates using a "principle of charity" in deciding what sorts of rights people might yield up by contract. I agree that this kind of interpretive principle is proposed (see below), but I think that more is involved. For a somewhat different view, see the masterly article by Haakonssen (1985), which concentrates on expletive justice. On his view, Grotius excludes the other virtues from the realm of natural law.

13. As St. Thomas holds, *Summa Theologiae*, IIaIIae Q. 23.1.

14. For a modern account see Messner (1949), §53, pp. 231–35. "The order of justice is only part of the social order. . . . charity by its essence places the final seal upon the order of justice. . . . justice has its deepest root in charity and receives from charity its in-most life. . . . "

15. *On the Law of Nature and of Nations* (Pufendorf 1934); indicated as "L" and cited in the text. See Schneewind (1987), from which much of the following material is drawn.

16. By asserting that there is a domain of universal justice beyond that of strict or expletive justice, Pufendorf is distancing himself from Grotius and bringing the imperfect duties into closer connection with the perfect.

17. But there are some natural rights that precede any contractual relations.

18. There are important differences between Grotius and Pufendorf about the condition prior to the institution of property agreements between people. Grotius believes that in a state of nature all things belong to everyone in common, in such a way that everyone has an equal right to the part of the common he wants. Pufendorf thinks that in a state of nature everything is common in a negative sense: no one has any right to anything. Though each takes what he or she needs, possession is not yet property. Property only comes about through agreement. For Grotius the contract involved in establishing property within society is an agreement that each shall keep what he already has, that is, what is already his own property, taken by right from the common.

19. MacPherson (1962) touched off a major debate which is still heard. See Dunn (1984) for an excellent brief account; and on property more particularly, see Tully (1980), a controversial work to which I am much indebted.

20. *Two Treatises of Government* (Locke 1963), I.42; see also II.5.

21. For what follows, see Locke's second *Treatise*, chapter V, "Of Property."

22. See the first *Treatise*, §42, and the brief citations given by Tully (1980), p. 176.

23. The connection between individual rights and benefits to society in Pufendorf is complicated. But the gist of his view can be put crudely in this way: the exercise of rights is in the long run for the benefit of all, and God sees to it that things will work out for that benefit if rights are exercised and respected. But humans do not know enough to figure out either the extent of their rights or the exceptions to them simply by calculating what is for the good of the whole. For us rights must be absolute guideposts.

24. Locke admired Pufendorf and recommended his books for the education of the elite. He did not similarly recommend Richard Cumberland, often described as the first utilitarian. Cumberland held that the basic law of morality is to promote the good of all rational creatures, and that rights are guideposts, indicated by God, showing us the best way to do this. Cumberland drew conservative conclusions about property, thinking that because of limits on our ability to foresee consequences and the great risks involved in change, the present distribution is the best we could attain. Locke rejects Cumberland's untrammeled appeal to consequences as the ground of all rights.

25. *Traité des lois*, 1689, I.3–8; IV.5. In Domat (1828).

26. Leibniz, p. 83.

27. Hutcheson, *Inquiry*, VII.1, pp. 269–70.

28. *Inq.* VII.vi, pp. 278–81.

29. Butler's short "Dissertation on Virtue" brilliantly summarizes his ethical views; for the quotations see §8. For God's position, see *Sermons*, 12.31 and the important note. Butler is here struggling to reconcile the dictates of conscience with the love commandment that says that love is the whole of the law. References are to the *Works* (Butler 1900).

30. For a fuller account see Schneewind (1990).

31. For Hume on justice, see *Treatise of Human Nature* (Hume 1983). Istvan Hont and Michael Ignatieff (1983) argue that Adam Smith's *Wealth of Nations* was intended to reply to St. Thomas's claims about the right of necessity, by showing that a society organized as Smith indicates in his treatise would allow of absolute property rights, since all would be far better off than in any other sort of society. The authors also suggest that Smith is continuing Hume's project in arguing as he does.

32. For these virtues, see *Treatise* Book III, Part III.

33. See Section II of the *Foundations of the Metaphysics of Morals* (Kant 1959). The work was first published in 1785.

34. See *The Metaphysics of Morals* (Kant 1991), pp. 187–98.

35. For what follows in this paragraph, see Kant (1991), pp. 136–37.

36. He also thinks the state should support a church, that is, a formal institution for worship (but that the state should not and indeed cannot have anything to do with religion, which is a purely inner condition).

37. Although the distinction was not nearly as widely used in the nineteenth century as it had been earlier, it continued to shape the thought of less original writers, for example, William Paley, *Principles of Moral and Political Philosophy*, 1785, who is discussed briefly below, and the American Francis Wayland, whose widely used *Elements of Moral Science*, 1835, Book Second, divides duties into those of reciprocity and those of benevolence, and in the section on "The Law of Benevolence" provides a compendium of the commonplaces on the topic of charity. Occasionally the distinction finds a place in the work of major figures: for example, J. S. Mill, *Utilitarianism*, 1863, Ch. V, where duties of justice are portrayed as perfect in contrast to others which are imperfect; and see also Franz Brentano, *The Foundation and Construction of Ethics*, drawn from lectures given between 1876 and 1894, Part V, Sec. v, where the breakdown of the distinction between duties of justice and duties of love is seen as cause for grave concern. Charity and other classes of helping actions are discussed by two other major British Victorian moral philosophers, William Whewell and Henry Sidgwick, but not under the heading of "imperfect duties."

38. See *Treatise* III.ii.ii., esp. p. 494.

39. *Summa Theologiae* IIa IIae, 66.7.

40. The distinction between deserving and undeserving poor is an attempt to supply such marks.

41. Fear of physical attack by the poor was alleviated by the rise of a police force, but the political power of the poor was not to be underestimated. Even without enfranchisement, which came late, the poor were to be reckoned with; and a desire to get them on one's side was a motive working on many politicians. Mack Walker has suggested to me that one of Bismarck's aims in instituting programs of social welfare was to "dish the radicals," showing that conservatives (good Christian conservatives) could do better for the poor than socialists and liberals.

42. References to Paley are all to his *Principles of Moral and Political Philosophy*, 1785, of which there are many editions—but no recent ones.

43. Paley is strongly opposed to it but thinks it should be abolished gradually.

4 | The Philanthropic Perspective after a Hundred Years

Alan Ryan

Introduction

MY SUBJECT HAS two aspects: philosophical and historical. Philosophically, I suggest that turn-of-the-century arguments about philanthropy can still illuminate conventional moral philosophy. Historically, I sketch some ways in which philosophers a hundred years ago contributed to the discussion of philanthropy. To put it differently, this is an essay in the history of ideas with a moral. It focuses on the turn of the nineteenth and twentieth centuries for an obvious reason. Both in Britain and the United States there was a brief period when moral philosophers who worked in the academy also took a fairly prominent part in forming the public view of philanthropic activity. In Britain, the Charity Organization Society was run on a daily basis by C. S. Loch[1] and Mrs. Helen Bosanquet, but Mrs. Bosanquet's brother-in-law the Idealist philosopher Bernard was a political theorist whose distinctive, if slightly unnerving, view of the duties of the better-off toward the poverty-stricken provided the ideological backbone of the Society.[2] In the United States, nobody of comparable philosophical distinction played an active part in the doings of the American COS, but John Dewey was a vigorous participant in the settlement house movement, as was his Michigan friend, the economist C. F. Adams, among others.[3] And as in Britain, there was a good deal of overlap between the participants in the American COS and the settlement movement.

The settlement house was perhaps the most distinctive material embodiment of late-nineteenth-century moral philosophy; London's Toynbee Hall, named in memory of the saintly young economic historian Arnold Toynbee—the uncle of the much less saintly, much more famous, and much longer-lived world historian—was the prototype and the example on which the American movement modeled itself. As an enterprise founded by the radical Church of England clergyman, Canon Samuel Barnett,[4] Toynbee Hall was naturally very different in aim and organization from its American successors such as Jane Addams's Hull House and Lillian Wald's Henry Street Settlement in New York; but here I want only to suggest that what they had in common was their status as an exemplary outlet for the moral energies and anxieties of highly educated middle-class reformers, and as a focus for certain values that English and

American reformers shared, rather than as a physical locus for particular activities. My purpose in rehearsing this story is not primarily historical. Indeed, as history this essay is parasitic on the historical work acknowledged in my notes. I wish rather to point a moral: that the late-nineteenth-century British Idealists and the young John Dewey held views that are permanently valuable in thinking about philanthropy. In the course of the paper I hope to explain why.

Justice and Charity: Philosophical Issues

The insistence of late-nineteenth-century philanthropists that charitable action did more good to the giver than to the receiver responded very directly to the anxieties of upper-middle-class young men and women; but it also responded to a curious passage in English moral philosophy. This was the way in which the most philosophically compelling theory of morality developed in the nineteenth century—utilitarianism—created two deep difficulties for its adherents. The first was that it made it important to draw a clear line between *justice* and *charity* and at the same time made it harder to do so. The second was still more alarming; utilitarianism claimed to be uniquely scientific in its approach to morality, but utilitarians found it hard to explain how we are moved to do what we believe we ought to do. It thus seemed to be well equipped to explain why we have duties, badly equipped to explain why we (mostly) fulfill them. A philanthropist tempted by utilitarianism would thus have found herself or himself in a tight corner: unsure whether philanthropic action was dictated by justice or by charity, and unsure what the motivation was out of which she or he was to act.

I do not mean to exaggerate the extent to which reformers wait upon philosophical clarification before taking action. I do mean to suggest that activities like those that engaged the energies of nineteenth-century volunteers had a peculiarly articulate moral theory behind them—one that stressed the motivation of the volunteers and their relations with their clients, and that by the same token emphasized the difference between this kind of voluntary and unofficial charitable work and welfare programs implemented by government. Not all moral theories would make so much of the difference; not all moral theories would concentrate so hard on issues of motivation. The more crudely benevolent might think that all that matters is whether the miseries of the poor are relieved, paying attention neither to the agency by which the good is done nor to the frame of mind in which the agency operates or the beneficiaries receive its benefits. Utilitarianism was notably ill equipped to provide what the reformers wanted.

The prehistory of this tension between philanthropic action and its philosophical justification does not do much to explain why the tension arose in the first place. The concept of philanthropy played no particular role in a philosophical context until the third quarter of the nineteenth century. Activities of a philanthropic sort had for centuries been common enough, of course: foundling hospitals, charity schools, societies for the improvement of the morals of the servant classes, all have a very long history. Late-nineteenth-century reformers continued such activities among servants, poor children, fallen women, and the like, and many of the organizations they established continue to operate today. Criticism of their work has almost as continuous a history. Among the targets of Mandeville's early eighteenth-century satires, charitable ventures of this sort were prominent, for reasons that twentieth-century critics of the welfare state would find familiar. Yet "philanthropy," whether considered as the state of mind of disinterested love of humanity at large, or considered as charitable activity devoted to the relief of poverty, ill health, and misery without government sponsorship or support, was not a subject of *philosophical* discussion.

There was much discussion of the plight of the poor, of parish relief, and a great deal of argument about the virtues of the poor at the level of the modern popular newspaper's discussion of people on welfare; but there was no philosophical discussion of "philanthropy." An explanation of this absence might be that there was no room for such a discussion and no call for it. What one might call the intellectual or conceptual space later occupied by the idea of "philanthropy" was then occupied by terms like "benevolence" or "sympathy," while philanthropy as an institutional practice—the creation of the functional equivalent of a welfare state by private initiative—lay a long way in the future.

One thing that connected early modern writers with their late-nineteenth-century successors was the question of *property*. Whether the property rights of owners pro tem invariably outweighed the needs of the poor had been discussed throughout the Middle Ages; in the seventeenth and eighteenth centuries it was again discussed by John Locke, Adam Smith, David Hume, and many less distinguished writers. On the whole, arguments started from the assumption that the poor could only be expected to respect the possessions of the rich so long as it was tolerably obvious that over the long run the poor themselves benefited from the sanctity of property. The details of discussion reflected the fact that the discussion took place in an agrarian society. The question of when property rights had to give way to the needs of the poor arose, not against a background of industrial or commercial un- or underemployment as we know it, but against the background of the failure of a harvest and general dearth. Hume was squarely in the mainstream when he suggested that whatever one thought of the sanctity of property rights, a government faced with famine had no choice but to "break open the granaries." Similarly when Locke discussed the question of what price a seller may charge for goods that are temporarily scarce, it was food he had in mind, and the guiding principle he offered was that one may not raise prices to the point of extortion.

None of this suggested a need for the characteristic activities of late-nineteenth-century philanthropy. Ordinary, everyday hardship was a matter for the family to deal with as best it could. Where this failed, poverty in England was coped with by "parish relief," given on whatever terms the locality could afford; as to old age, the otherwise unprovided-for elderly could hope to be looked after in almshouses when family provision failed. The better-off might visit the sick and the infirm elderly, especially where there were preexisting ties to superannuated servants or farm workers. Readers of late-eighteenth- and early-nineteenth-century English novels will recall any number of occasions when unwilling daughters are dragged off on their dutiful rounds by their mothers. Any idea that the state, or individuals in the state's place, had some continuous general obligation to work for the welfare of the badly-off played little role. Until the late nineteenth century, the able-bodied unemployed were an object of fear and suspicion rather than compassion, and were vulnerable to some savage, but apparently not very frequently enforced, Tudor legislation against "sturdy beggars" and vagabonds. Curiosity about their condition is reflected in works of fiction, but not in anything resembling protosocial science. The dysfunctional family doubtless existed in large numbers, but it was not known under that label.

This is not to say that issues of justice were other than perennial; it was the institutional focus on the daily lives of the poor that we take for granted that was so strikingly absent. Hume and his contemporaries took a considerable interest in the question whether there existed a duty to be concerned for other people's welfare. "Benevolence" was a large and important issue in the moral philosophy of writers like Bishop Butler; and its cousin, sympathy, played an equally important role in the work of Smith and Hume. It would have seemed obvious to everyone until the rise of what we now call utilitarianism that a sentiment such as "rational benevolence" was needed to close the gap between our tendency to seek our own welfare at the expense of others and the duty to consider their welfare impartially with our own.

Eighteenth-century moralists suggested, plausibly enough, that as individuals we do well to cultivate benevolence in ourselves. Those who take pleasure in the well-being of other people fare better than the envious. Notice that this is a self-centered argument. It does not call attention to the obvious truth that a society of benevolent persons will prosper more than one riddled with envy and backbiting. It calls attention to the less obvious truth that taking pleasure in other people's welfare is a reliable source of private happiness. They, after all, will constantly be trying to live happy existences, and if we sympathize with their aspirations, their happiness will make us happy too. There was no suggestion that it took much effort to cultivate benevolence; human beings were supposed to be endowed with enough fellow-feeling to share the pain of others in distress and therefore to have adequate motives to relieve that distress. In the middle of the seventeenth century, Thomas Hobbes argued that in the absence of government, men would fall into a "warre of alle against alle," but even he took it for granted that once there was political stability, peace and prosperity would nourish the kindly emotions. Even though we were ready in extreme cases to sacrifice others for our own welfare, in non-extreme situations our natural dislike of other people's distress would sustain charitable action.

It is a striking feature of utilitarianism, as it was developed by Jeremy Bentham and further refined by John Stuart Mill, that it makes the competition between a care for ourselves and a care for others very much starker than it had been in earlier moral philosophy. Whether this was because the rise of economics as a discipline had begun to infect moral philosophy, or simply an effect of a new desire for scientific precision in ethical reasoning it is hard to say. Nonetheless, the result was to exaggerate the difficulties of acting morally. Utilitarianism in its new scientific guise relied on the axiom that our natural inclination is to maximize our *own* welfare to argue that the moral good must be the maximization of the welfare of all sentient beings. Mill's *Utilitarianism* provides the best-known version of just this claim.[5] What even so sophisticated a thinker as Mill never quite recognized was that the argument sets up a tension between what we *must* psychologically seek—our own welfare—and what we *ought* morally to seek—the general welfare—and that this tension is only partially relaxed by his account of how we come to make the pursuit of the welfare of others part of our own welfare. Indeed one oddity of Mill's essay *Utilitarianism* is that Mill deals with the problem of altruistic, other-directed desires several times over, as though he sensed that each argument was inadequate but hoped that several inadequate arguments might add up to one adequate one.

Sometimes Mill suggested that *habit* will allow us to prefer the greater good for others to our own lesser good; sometimes he suggested that what the vulgar would explain in that way is better explained by the lesser good having become the greater by association; and sometimes it seems that the *object* we pursue has been changed. If the pursuit of an ideal perfection of character gives us pleasure, doing what we *ought* is the reliable route to pleasure. *Natural* benevolence was not something that Mill much relied on; *trained* benevolence was rather more in the forefront of his mind, and he emphasized quite fiercely the need to socialize children into taking the interests of other people seriously.

I don't mean to exaggerate; Mill was, by our standards, somewhat blithely confident in the socialization process. He had little doubt *that* we could get children to grow up ready to behave as they ought. The difficulty was a philosophical one. Mill knew that children were brought up, or "socialized" into behaving like decent morally serious people. The difficulty was to explain how the process worked. And Mill's explanations had a tendency to undermine their own credibility, just because they were too numerous and too complicated. Many of his readers thought that this elaborate machinery did no justice to the simplicity of their moral sentiments; but whatever gloss one puts on it, it was a fair complaint against utilitarianism that it made it needlessly difficult to account for the everyday phenomena that sustain social and individual life—such as ordinary kindness, spontaneous good nature, unaccountable outbreaks of fellow-feeling.

What is less generally noticed is that it was not only Millian utilitarianism that ran into such difficulties. Comtean positivism followed the same route as utilitarianism. The term "altruism" acquired its modern sense only in the mid-nineteenth century, but an emphasis on it expressed—as it did in the work of Auguste Comte who coined the term—the same view that morality made sense against a background of natural egoism. One thus had the same alarming spectacle of an attempt to transform a wholly selfish natural endowment into a wholly unselfish moral nature. Comte indeed went much further than Mill in creating an ethics of absolute self-sacrifice. Mill had some sense of the logical absurdity of an ethics of altruism. If *all* of us wish only to do what will make other people happy, nobody has any reason to wish to do anything in particular. *Some* self-centered wishes for our *own* happiness have to provide a foundation for benevolence to work with. Mill deplored what he thought was the tendency of Comte's moral theory to reduce society to the state of an armed camp, where utter self-sacrifice was the order of the day. Comte's devotees seemed not to mind, and generally shrugged off Mill's attacks. In securing their loyalty, Comte had an advantage over Mill inasmuch as he provided an entire religion—"Positivism"—with a Positivist Church included, to accompany his demands.

Utilitarianism and the Supererogatory

If late-nineteenth-century moral philosophy was left with the problem of filling the hole that Mill had carved out between our duties and our inclinations, Mill recognized that he also faced another problem. Utilitarianism had a difficult time drawing a persuasive line between the demands of charity and those of justice. The line had been deliberately erased by William Godwin (discussed by J. B. Schneewind in his chapter in this volume) in one of the first modern works of utilitarian political philosophy, his *Political Justice* of 1792. Eccentric though Godwin was, his argument was hard to evade. Alarmingly, Godwin erased the distinction between justice and charity by abolishing the category of charity; in his account of utilitarianism, every action was either just or unjust. There was no such thing as an innocently optional action that we might either perform or not as we chose, let alone a good deed that we could without injustice not perform. This rigorism is not unique to utilitarianism; some religious moralities have held that what God does not prescribe He proscribes. But it is a surprisingly plausible implication of utilitarianism.

Utilitarianism is a theory that has come in many versions, but the basic idea is that morality requires us to promote happiness, and generally that actions are better the more happiness they promote—allowance being made for the kinds of happiness in question, as well as for the utility involved in their causes and their effects. Godwin's *Political Justice* declared that justice required that every act should be judged by its optimific quality. Unless we did what was for the best we acted unjustly. This meant, for instance, that property rights must always be subordinated to "best use" considerations; nothing is "ours" if it would do more good in someone else's control. Since the notion of charity depends on the thought that we perhaps *should* but certainly do not *have to* part with what is *ours* to the needy, any theory that dissolves the idea that something can be ours to do with as we like dissolves the distinction between charity and justice. More shockingly to his readers, Godwin insisted that marital and sexual relations also ought to be scrutinized in the light of impartial justice. If utility would be increased by my partner leaving me for you, I should let her go without regret and without jealousy, even though I might feel a few uncontrollable pangs of unhappiness. Godwin's devastating question was "what has the adjective 'my' to do with eternal justice?"

Now, it may be said that Godwin allowed room for philanthropy, strictly speaking, since he believed devoutly that justice must spring from the heart as well as the mind; we must *feel* the claims of general utility before we act on it. Indeed, one might say that this is rather to abolish justice than charity, since it makes so much of our motives for action, as accounts of justice characteristically do not. The point remains that Godwin's account does not find room for charity in the usual sense, where that is understood as gratuitously doing for others what they have no *right* to have done for them. In Godwin, whatever would promote utility is the object of a right; conversely, I can have no right to do or to possess anything if my doing it or having it fails to maximize utility. There is no room for charity, when what others call charity is swallowed up within justice. If what is momentarily in my possession will do more good in your hands, it is already, as it were, "yours" rather than mine; to effect the transfer is not to behave particularly well, but to arrange matters so that things are more nearly as they should be.

Mill felt the threat of this all-embracing moral rigorism and reacted in a complicated fashion. He saw the danger of leaving no room between the obligatory and the supererogatory. For one thing, if there was no room for nonobligatory goodness, each of us would be threatened by a total loss of moral liberty. If it was unjust for us not to do always the best we could, and we continued to think of the demands of justice as particularly exigent demands, it seemed that a wholesale moral police could be imposed in the name of justice. Mill had denounced the tendency of society to enforce rules of conduct based on the mere "likings and dislikings of the majority" in his essay *On Liberty*. The rules of all-embracing justice, however, would be the dictates of a rational morality, and not mere likings and dislikings. This would be the world according to Comte. In Comte's universe a *pouvoir spirituel* was to secure our compliance with our duty, and one can readily imagine a utilitarian version of the same moral authority—not in the ambitions of Godwin, since Godwin thought that the right of each person to act on his or her own judgment was absolute; but in the hands of someone with Bentham's passion for detail and deafness to the value of liberty, it was all too easy to imagine. Appropriately enough, Mill denounced the idea that duty was to swallow up all freedom of choice in his essay on *Auguste Comte and Positivism* rather than in the essay *On Liberty*. There he observes that it was true as a matter of logic that we must meet our obligations, but added that if these were so defined that we are always obliged to do what maximizes the total welfare of all sentient beings, there could be no room for freedom of choice, except in the uninteresting case where two different courses of action yield identical results, and we could flip a coin to choose between them.

Once this difficulty was out in the open, it became part of the permanent stock of philosophical debate, and in recent years it has been peculiarly prominent. The view that utilitarianism is excessively demanding in just this way underlay Bernard Williams's attack on utilitarianism in his exchange with Jack Smart in their *Utilitarianism For and Against*, and many of his dismissive comments elsewhere.[6] Finding ways round this problem has been one motive driving the recent work of John Rawls and Tim Scanlon. Mill's own contribution was interesting. One of Mill's thoughts was that we do have stronger obligations to other people than earlier moral theories had thought; another was that these obligations become more stringent as society develops. As society becomes more tightly organized, we have more effect on each other; as knowledge grows, we understand each other better; we also better understand the nature of duty, and all these things increase the obligations upon us. It was there that Mill turned the argument on its head. Just because these ties were now so stringent, an adequate moral theory must find ways to stop them crushing us.

Mill had an argument against Comte's insistence on *vivre pour autrui* as the test of moral duty. Mill insisted that as the ties of obligation bind more tightly now than formerly, so we needed a doctrine of liberty and a doctrine of the supererogatory more than formerly. The "liberticide" quality of Comte's thought was encapsulated not only in his passion for quasi-Catholic hierarchies and doctrines, but in his moral philosophy. Mill saw the strength of the other side's case so clearly that he was all the more anxious to have defenses against it. In terms of our topic, this implied that room had to be preserved for what the term "philanthropy" covers, that is, for supererogatory activities done for the benefit of others. The difficulty was that on one interpretation utilitarianism left no room for supererogatory action, and on another its individualism left it unclear why people should feel the ties of common affection and common purpose that philanthropy supposes. Mill's Idealist critics never gave him credit for being so clear about the problem; but even if they had, they would not have thought he had found a solution.

Interestingly enough, Idealism met the need, not by establishing a persuasive line between justice and charity, but by looking at moral character rather than utilitarian consequences. They then stressed the importance of the charitable motive in the moral life, and as one might say thereby finessed the issue of how to distinguish justice and charity. Whereas utilitarianism was tempted to dissolve charity into justice, Idealism made philanthropic motivation a substantial part of the virtuous character. To the extent that Idealism dealt in the usual conceptual distinctions, it actually tended to place philanthropy in the category of the demands of justice—it was so central an expression of our membership of a human community that a failure to acknowledge it was a violation of the terms of social association.

Idealism and Pragmatism

English Idealism and its American cousin, the Idealism sliding into Pragmatism of Dewey's early moral philosophy, was not only better equipped to tackle the questions that arise in a philanthropic venture than the utilitarianism that preceded it, it was better equipped than most of the ethical theory that succeeded it. Idealism, and especially its Pragmatist offshoot united a concern for charity work that began in a distinctively Christian framework with ideas that arose more naturally in a secular framework, and provided a persuasive picture both of the motivation to charitable activity and of why such places as settlement houses were an appropriate environment in which to engage in philanthropic activity. The story is not complicated, but it has a certain charm.

To see what the Idealists and their American counterparts relied on, we must take a very brief detour through the ideas of G. W. F. Hegel. In the twentieth century, Hegel has become a byword for obscure portentousness, but he was read with ease and pleasure in the late nineteenth century by readers more used to the spiritual vocabulary of Christian preachers and controversialists than analytical philosophers in the twentieth century have been. Hegel complained, and in this he was followed by the English Idealists and by the Pragmatist Dewey, that most moral philosophy, (and this is as true of utilitarianism as it is of most theories), placed too much weight on decision making by isolated individuals. It was as though the only situation of any interest to the moral philosopher is one in which moral agents are engaged in inquiry into what their duty is on some particular occasion. Idealism was more inclined to see individual moral agents in the middle of a world of other moral agents, and in this, too, it was followed by Pragmatists.

Idealism, however, relied on a metaphysical picture of the world that held no attractions for a naturalistic thinker such as Dewey or Mill. Its attractiveness to committed Christians was a more complicated matter. Hegel held that human intellectual and moral history is intelligible in a historical and evolutionary perspective only when it is understood as the autobiography of *Geist* or Spirit. Unlike the God of Judeo-Christian tradition, however, the Spirit or Mind that animates the world is not something detachable from it. This naturally raises puzzles about quite what the relationship is between the world and Spirit. Hegel's views could be pressed in two very different directions, in what one might call the transcendental and the sociological directions. The first turns Hegel's philosophy into an account of the spiritual reality underlying moral discourse, and so emphasizes its affinities to traditional religion. The second, and for us here the one that matters more, turns Hegel's account into a broadly sociological account of the development of morality. Morality, on this view, is a *community* possession in which the individual participates by learning how to see himself or herself as a moral agent. The moral good is therefore from the beginning a shared good, and the individual's life has value to the individual to the extent that it is a shared value. An individual moral agent is thus not exactly the same creature as the biological individual that first appears on the scene in childbirth and childhood. He or she learns how to be moral by the same process as that by which he or she learns how to become an individual person, that is by learning the way of life of the community into which he or she has been born. The foundation of morality is therefore "my station and its duties."

We may well be called on to do more than our station and its duties require, and in modern, mobile societies we surely shall be; but we can only know what that "more" is and know how to do it in the company of others. We are not isolated individuals staring at the demands of duty on the one hand and the impulses of our psyche on the other and wondering how to balance them; nor are we forced to start all moral arguments from scratch. If that was our state, it would be hopeless. We may be pitched into situations that have a nasty resemblance to this isolated condition—we may be thrown among people whose moral values we do not share and do not understand, perhaps, or be forced to deal with such people for whatever reason, or we may find ourselves somehow out of touch with our own former resources and hard put to it to know where to start again. But these are not the standard conditions, and we know that they are difficult just because they contrast so sharply with the standard conditions.

It is now not hard to see why Green and Bosanquet and a host of other Idealist philosophers in the last third of the nineteenth century, should have thought that it was possible to write about charity and philanthropy in the way they did, and how they managed to do so without spending all their time in nitpicking conceptual analysis or anxious attempts to rewrite the distinction between charity and justice. In Bosanquet's case, the connection with charitable work was of the very tightest. Bosanquet gave up his fellowship at University College, Oxford, in order to live near London and engage in social work himself. In none of this did he suggest that he engaged in something supererogatory; it was an expression of citizenship, not an expression of an individual kindliness of temperament, and although it was owed as a duty to those who were to benefit, it was also owed as a duty to himself. Nor was this an unusual view. Green and his earnest disciple Arnold Toynbee insisted that the upper classes owed charitable good works to the lower classes, and especially to the outcast classes. Any attempt to say that this was confusing justice and charity would, rightly, have been dismissed as a failure to see the point. It was a duty, though not one a state could enforce. The poor had a right to such assistance, though once again not such as a state could usefully enforce. By the same token, they claimed that the upper classes owed such charitable activity to *themselves* as well as to the obvious beneficiaries of it. It was a route, perhaps the most effective route, to finding their own best selves.[7]

A more traditionally Christian strand in these views was provided by Toynbee's claim that the better-off needed to go among the destitute and the ignorant and confess that they had *sinned* against them. I am sure that, psychologically, many young men were driven to work in places like Toynbee Hall by the sensation that their education, and their ability to make something of their lives had been given to them at the expense of the outcast, and thus by something like a sense of sin. It was not a sentiment that stood up to orthodox economic analysis; the roughest parts of the East End of London were also places of large immigrant populations, whose plight was both temporary and largely caused by pogroms in Eastern Europe rather than unrestrained capitalism in Britain. Nor were the unrespectable poor likely to have created much surplus value for their superiors to appropriate. There was a sentiment here that had nothing much to do with economics, in fact, and a lot to do with what subsequently agitated Dewey, namely, a society in which sharp splits and separations between social classes were commonplace. The "sin" that Toynbee wanted to expiate was that of having lost touch with the poor, having nothing to say to them, not knowing how to share the riches of upper-middle-class culture with them. This was very much Jane Addams's sentiment when she opened Hull House, and wiping out the occasion for it was a central element in Dewey's political philosophy all his life.

To explain this in any great detail would require a careful account of the nature and genesis of the characteristic moral anxieties of upper-middle-class young people like Jane Addams in the United States and the pupils of Green and Bosanquet in 1870s and 1880s Oxford. That would make an engrossing book. Still, it seems clear that one element of that anxiety was the declining hold of formal religious allegiances on educated young people. They felt their lives would be meaningless if they were not devoted to "service," but the service had to be secular and immediate, and yet to have the same moral flavor as if it were motivated by the faith of their pastors. We must not exaggerate, of course; Toynbee Hall's founder was an Anglican clergyman, Canon Samuel Barnett. Those who felt that they could not believe in a *literal* Christianity were no less inclined to subscribe to Christian ideals, and found it no hardship to use the old words with new meanings.

Some of the anxious sense of duty to be done, and poor people to be served, had simpler sources. These were the years of the most rapid social and economic transformation that Britain and the United States ever underwent. The comfortable classes were sharply conscious of the buffeting to which the uneducated, the unskilled, the poorly paid, and the sick were subjected. The brief story of their debt to Idealist moral philosophy as a device for making sense of themselves and their aspirations and anxieties is that the debt was both sociological and logical. The logical point is this. Although Green and Bosanquet, as well as my own favorite among the Idealists, D. G. Ritchie,[8] took very different views of the logical relationship between the whole that possessed ultimate reality and in which we could ultimately reconcile the contradictions of everyday experience, and the perceptions of the individuals that each of us empirically turns out to be, none of them refused the challenge to show that both sides of the equation had a reality and a seriousness that the philosopher ought to elicit. That is, the standing temptation of a quietist was to insist that Reality was good, and all the apparent chaos and misery only "good misunderstood." This was the use of Idealism for what William James termed a "moral holiday." No reformer could be tempted by it. If there was some ultimate reality that was untainted by the visible chaos of 1880s London and Chicago, it was not 1880s Britain or 1880s Illinois. The miseries, poverty, moral discomforts of individuals counted in the balance. And they looked for a remedy. Green was more of an individualist than Bosanquet, and Ritchie more eager than either to reconcile Fabianism and some form of natural rights-based socialism; but all held that individual moral ambitions had to be reflected in a community life. In other words, the social critic or the grumbling dockworker might well be right in maintaining that things were radically amiss. Mere complaint has no place in an Idealist universe, but criticism certainly has.

In day-to-day policy, the crux comes when we must decide whether to side with the individual who complains that the community is letting him down in some way or to trust the leaders of the community when they claim that the complaining individual is a malcontent and troublemaker. There can be no algorithm to read off an answer, but the demand of moral logic is that the two poles must balance. The payoff in discussions of charity is the thought that we mutually belong to one another, and that what holds the moral world together is a life that reflects this truth. This is a view hostile both to revolutionism and to hierarchy, though perhaps more to all versions of the former than to certain versions of the latter. One cannot imagine a revolution without sharp splits between insurrectionaries and old guard, but one can imagine a hierarchy built on mutual trust and regard. Once we reach this point, we can see why the dichotomy between justice and charity had ceased to be so alarming—although we are all tied to one another, we are tied by something other than enforceable obligations, and although charity in the sense of absolutely gratuitous kindness makes little sense in such a schema, the fact that what we owe one another is mutual regard and respect above all else promptly brings back the supererogatory virtues. Justice in such a moral theory is no longer a formal and demanding virtue to be distinguished from the less formal and more optional virtue of charity. This refusal of old sharp distinctions is one more way in which idealism and Dewey's Pragmatism are deeply akin to one another.

In utilitarian accounts of ethics other than Godwin's, the line between justice and charity has to be strict, because utilitarianism is so entangled in the distinction between what we feel like doing and what we have to do. Morality is understood as imposing obligations that override our own wishes. In Idealist ethics, what we *want* and what we *should do* come much closer together. Another way to see the same point is to see that for utilitarianism the starting point is human selfishness, understood as an essentially *natural* tendency to want what is in our interests rather than other people's. The Idealists did not think that wants were in quite that sense "natural." They did not deny, what the Pragmatists made so much more of, the fact that we are born as biological individuals, and all our lives see the world from the perspective of our *embodied* selves; but they thought we shared in something superbiological. Because Dewey defined his Pragmatism in contradiction to the idealism he had abandoned, it is necessary to be scrupulous about *not* saying that we share in a "superbiological" world; Dewey was emphatic that everything that could be explained could be explained naturalistically. "Supernaturalism" was invariably a term of abuse, and "superbiological" would probably attract the same opprobrium.

All the same, Dewey and the Idealists shared the view that morality sprang from our membership in a community. If the network of communication that holds a community together is not something supernatural, it is at any rate something super-individual. Dewey's view was that individual moral agents became such when they learned how to make sense of their own lives by using the community's resources. To derive anything very concrete about the merits and demerits of the community's resources from this rather abstract first move is obviously not easy. Once more, however, idealism and Pragmatism made similar moves. Hegel's philosophy had relied heavily on the idea that intellectual and cultural life was propelled by the discovery and elimination of contradictions in thought and action; Dewey's thoughts on "growth" were not dissimilar. Communication and self-expression had a tendency to become richer, deeper, and fuller, but only if obstacles were detected and removed.

Just as important, Dewey and the Idealists agreed that no desire was truly satisfying if it could not be "re-endorsed" as something other than the satisfaction of a mere want. Morality was a matter of self-development and self-discovery. Finding out what we "really" want is the same thing as finding out what we ought to do, for it is finding out who we wish to be, what sort of person we want to become. Wants and inclinations were thus moralized from the very beginning. While the "demands" of morality are certainly demands, it does not follow that they must be felt to be demanding. If we feel them so, and feel that they are at odds with what we want, that implies only we have not yet managed to avail ourselves of all our society's resources to sustain us in our membership. Properly socialized adults—in a properly functioning society—want to do what they ought to want to do, and find it satisfying to do it. Once again, a little caution is required. To put the matter thus and to leave it at that may suggest that all failures lie with individuals who fail to understand themselves and their society or whose habits are at odds with decent behavior. This is quite wrong. Both Dewey and the Idealists insisted that this sort of talk reinstated the view of morality that they deplored—that of the isolated individual facing dictates he or she could not live up to. Their analysis was more apt to spread the blame more widely; it was because whole communities got into a tangle that their members felt themselves unable to act decently. Certainly, it was true that the individuals were unable to act decently, which was to that degree a fault in them, but it was not so to speak an absolute truth about them or an intrinsic fault in them.

Implications

Sociologically, this vision focuses the attention on how a given society lives up or fails to live up to the ideal of a functioning moral community in which the common good is actualized in everyday life. When Green wrote his lecture on *Liberal Legislation and Freedom of Contract* in 1881, it shocked his contemporaries. It was not the political conclusions that seemed alarming. Green was less of a socialist than J. S. Mill, and had little of Mill's capacity for losing his temper with the complacency of the possessing classes. Mill, famously, thought working-class calls for revolution were silly and unrealistic, but he had no *moral* difficulty with calls for the revolutionary overthrow of the existing order. The existing order was a tissue of injustices and irrationalities, but it was not beyond the reach of rationally directed reform, and its follies were in need of careful analysis more than violent assault. But there was certainly no immorality in thinking the system should be swept away, and Mill always had something of a liking for the French taste for revolt. Green was altogether unsusceptible to the charms of insurrection. It is hopeless trying to decide whether Green's idealism mirrored his longing for social seamlessness or vice versa, but it is clear that the two meshed in his mind, and that nobody of such a temperament could have had a taste for insurrectionary politics. Nonetheless, what Green's readers learned was that the rights of property were not sacrosanct but conditional on service, that it was perfectly proper for a state to override the wishes of individuals who wished, in particular, to open pubs (or on the other side of the bar counter to buy excessive quantities of strong drink). The moral whole needed repair and restoration, not destruction; but Green was quite clear that the social fabric of mid-Victorian Britain was very far from being a smooth and seamless expression of the moral aspirations of everyone born within the British Isles. What alarmed Green's readers was the implication that the everyday economic activities of the British middle classes might be so much less respectable than they had thought.

According to Green, the working man who was beset by the temptation of the gin palace on the street corner was not a free man but something scarcely better than a slave. There was little actual and present in his life to call him to remembrance of what his better self might be. Low wages, boring work, the risk of unemployment, and excessively large families conspired to lure him into a world in which the narcotizing effects of booze and the raucous bonhomie of his fellow workers were a temporary respite from the misery of existence. His wife and children suffered the ill effects of this condition; if she was his drinking companion, the children went neglected; if she wasn't, wife and children were all emotionally starved. What made Green a radical was his insistence that our failure to share in a common work of self-development and self-fulfillment was an indictment of the social order. Because Green was much closer, morally speaking, to ordinary middle-class sentiment than Mill had ever been, he caused more pain, if less anger, than Mill. Green's view that property owners who stood pat upon the rights of property and freedom of contract were causing their fellows to sink into squalor and vice hit British opinion in its most vulnerable regions. It implied that the respectable created the "undeserving poor" whose behavior they so deplored. Here was the other face of the sense of "sin" that Arnold Toynbee wanted to be rid of. It was not straightforwardly true that the possessing classes reduced the poor to misery by exploiting them, but it might be true that in going about their everyday business of making money in a laissez-faire economy they were creating an environment that made a decent life for the propertiless less possible rather than more.

It is a contentious philosophical claim that the *logic* of ethics implies that we should be able to re-endorse our wants; it is a contentious thought that we should be able to feel that our characters were what we would have created if we had been their creators. It is an equally contentious philosophical claim that these doctrines do much to explain the nature of morality duties or our understanding of it. It is a plausible sociological proposition that the self-confidence of the British mercantile, administrative, and political elites rested on a naive confidence that their desires and their moral convictions were such as any soundly brought up person would have had, and that their characters were such as anyone of sound judgment would have wished to instill in their offspring. The thought that the characters of the undeserving poor were not a natural affliction or something perversely self-created, but a predictable effect of the conditions in which the urban poor lived, *and* that those conditions were the predictable effect of the existence of the respectable and deserving classes was a decided blow to their moral confidence.

If they had had other views about the relations between property and the general welfare, they might have been less embarrassed. But they did not; they thought their rights as owners reflected the benefits they conferred on the British people as a whole. For reasons that may not have one simple explanation, British opinion has never quite thought that the rights of property were built on natural and prepolitical right, or that society is best understood as a quasi-contractual arrangement between essentially independent property holders. The common law had never treated property or person in that way, and British politics had never suggested that the legitimacy of the British state rested on such contractual foundations. Where contractual notions played a part in political debate, they were tied in with the thought that social groups, such as commons, lords, and clergy, had a title based on long tradition, to enforce an implicit—necessarily implicit—agreement about how the body politic might remain a harmonious and functional body.

Locke's claim that we are born free and equal and only become obliged by our consents freely given never became a majority view. How the British invented laissez-faire while disbelieving in Locke is an interesting and complicated story, but one upshot of it was that Green had plenty of purchase when he argued that property rights were justified only to the degree that they promoted the common good, and that freedom of contract was not an absolute but an ideal, and one that implied a good deal about the contracting parties that no one could seriously believe at the time Green died in 1882.

The question necessarily arises whether Green was at odds with his contemporaries. I think not, although I think he marked one end of a spectrum of intellectual and moral possibilities. Consider Bernard Bosanquet; he was a conservative in politics and found the world less radically at odds with itself than did Green, as readers of his *Philosophical Theory of the State* can see. Nonetheless, his commitment to much the same philosophy meant that he had to accept more of the same sociology than one might suppose. Indeed, in *The Ethics of Compassion* Professor Gertrude Himmelfarb insists that Green and the COS shared one worldview. This may be right, but it blurs the differences between Bosanquet and Green, considered as moral philosophers. Bosanquet had a less optimistic view of the potentiality of the common man than Green, and was less ready to lift the topic of social work to the elevated level implied in Green's vision of a community of fellow citizens modeling their lives on those of Christ's apostles.

Nonetheless, the COS was not an implausible implementation of the Idealist moral vision. To a later age, the COS has looked altogether too like an organized procession of Lady Bountiful figures handing out a combination of minimal relief and moral exhortation to the poor of East End London. In fact, this was what it was at pains not to be. The very idea of a charity *organization* society shows something of the temper of the people who ran it. What they mostly wanted was to do as much good as possible with the resources that could be brought to the inner city poor of their day; generally, they thought that it was extremely important that those resources should in the first place be provided by the family or friends of the needy so that the recipients of help were motivated to put themselves on their own feet. Certainly, they talked for the first twenty years of their existence of the "deserving poor," but that had rather different overtones from the ones a later age has tended to hear.[9] The thought was rather that some of the poor were more plausible targets of assistance because they had more aptitude for self-help than others.

It was a moral view that the English working class itself subscribed to without any embarrassment. A line has always been drawn between the respectable and the unrespectable without any great censoriousness, but with a perfect consciousness that what it entails is that it is a waste of time and effort to try to help the excessively unrespectable. No matter what their circumstances, they would make a mess of their lives, and would assuredly end up on the dole, in jail, or in the river. "Respectability" has overtones of that great English activity, keeping up appearances, but the thought behind even that activity might be less obnoxious than we usually think. Only someone with the desire to look like a full member of the community would have the energy and foresight to get employed, stay in work, and try to improve himself. People who want to keep up appearances at least have some inkling of what it is they are trying to seem; they are "capable of assistance."

The ladies who did good works for the COS were given quite fierce instructions about how to treat the targets of their efforts. They were always to knock on the door before entering a house, they were always to address the women of the house as Mrs., they were to say and do nothing that implied moral, social, or economic superiority on their part. Those who gave them that advice knew why they were giving it; it was not because they would achieve an egalitarian relationship with the working-class families they were visiting—all hands agreed that the working classes yelled a good deal and addressed one another by their Christian names if not by nicknames of any degree of indelicacy. The COS understood that working-class women knew that ladies spoke nicely to each other, and that working-class women would wish real ladies to treat them as ladies too. The work the visitors did was not elaborate, certainly not by the standards of a later day. The COS was not itself a charity but a society for organizing charity; that is, its aim was to understand the size of the problem, to help charities of which there were many dozen in the cities of Britain, to spend their money wisely. "Method not muddle" was the slogan. In fact, branches of the COS seem always to have found themselves raising money too, but the point I want to make here is how far the attitude toward the giving of charity, that is, toward philanthropic activity, exemplified the Idealist position.

That is, there was no attempt to turn the distinction between the deserving and the undeserving poor into a distinction between those for whom assistance was required as a matter of justice and those for whom it was at best a matter of benevolence. Such a distinction would, of course, nowadays mark the line between persons with entitlements and those without. The distinction the COS was concerned with lay between those whose characters were such that a bit of help would lift them back into the community of the working poor—in practice, what this meant was that help would stave off starvation during periods of unusually deep or long drawn out economic depression when even the most diligent might be thrown out of work or unable to find a new employer—and those whose characters were such that even with such assistance they would probably be unable to help themselves. Again, the attempt to maintain moral egalitarianism in the face of an unquestioned class distinction suggested ways in which the tension between the ideas of justice and charity could be handled. The better-off owed a duty of assistance to the worst-off, but only to those who would thereby be helped to rejoin the moral community to whose maintenance all ought to contribute. To the degree that it was owed, one might say it was a demand of justice, to the degree to which it was a duty of the advantaged to the disadvantaged one might say it was a duty of charity. More important, one might say that it expressed a commitment to an ethic of "fellowship" or "membership" within which that distinction is blurred or dropped.

Settlements

If the COS was one characteristic product of the time and its ethos, another was the settlement house movement. I want to say one or two slightly cryptic and certainly overbrief things about this, as a way of suggesting the affinities between the idealism of Green and the developing Pragmatism of Dewey, and thus to suggest that the social climate of Britain and the United States was—and perhaps still is—more similar than one might think. The first and most famous of the English settlement houses was Toynbee Hall, created in the East End of London in 1884. It was—like its successors such as Balliol Hall and Wadham Hall—a difficult place to describe. It was not intended as a place where charity was dispensed, or social work activities took place, but where the East End poor could see a better life in action. Henry Street grew out of Lillian Wald's work on the medical needs of her Lower East Side neighbors, and Hull House provided most of the benefits of a social services department. There was thus a good deal of difference between Toynbee Hall and Hull House and the Henry Street Settlement. The idea behind Toynbee Hall was that young men from Oxford and Cambridge should come and live in the Hall for periods of a year or two, and should occupy themselves with community service during their spare time. They were not to abandon their regular work, but they were to combine it with social work in the neighborhood and running the educational program of the Hall. Hull House and Henry Street were much more nearly social welfare departments organized by gifted volunteers. Within a few years of its foundation, Hull House had a dispensary, a school, and a shelter for young women thrown out by their families for sexual indiscretions. Henry Street specialized in home nursing, and eventually spun off more specialized local institutions including a community hospital. The obvious explanation for such differences lies in the greater provision of such services as free hospitals and people's dispensaries already in place in Britain, rather than in any large difference in the ethos of the reformers involved. One might, perhaps, think that the fact that the two best-known American settlements were founded by women was also important. It certainly made a difference to Hull House that Jane Addams was so uncensoriously disposed to take in single mothers whose families had thrown them into the street, to shelter battered women, and to provide midwifery services in emergencies. But, then, Canon Samuel Barnett's wife Henrietta was a formidable reforming force in her own right as well, and the quasicollege of Toynbee Hall was only one item in the Barnetts' work for Whitechapel.

The educational program of Toynbee Hall was one of the *similarities* with Jane Addams's Hull House—one social service was to provide a liberal education for those who ordinarily would not get it. Dewey, Michelson, Veblen, and Albion Small lectured at Hull House, and Henry Sidgwick, Lord Haldane, Leslie Stephen, and Mrs. Humphrey Ward lectured at Toynbee Hall. Still, even there there were differences, too. What Chicago needed and Jane Addams provided was an emphasis on remembering the culture of the countries from which something like half her clientele had emigrated; in East End London, the emphasis fell rather on displaying to the newcomers the riches of Shakespeare and Wordsworth. Nor did Hull House set out to democratize the privileged young men of the nearby university; Hull House was founded before John D. Rockefeller's expensive new University of Chicago, the young men scarcely existed, and they did not form a social class with the class consciousness of their English counterparts. Jane Addams was, to be sure, an exact American counterpart to these Oxford and Cambridge young men, but there was no analogous figure to T. H. Green working in an institution analogous to Balliol.

All the same, the morality underlying the experiment was very much the same both sides of the Atlantic. It was a morality in which the word "democracy" played a large role, perhaps surprisingly so, since Green died in 1882, two years before the third great Reform Act of the nineteenth century finally enfranchised just about every adult British male, though not—until 1928—their mothers, wives, and daughters. Alongside the word democracy the word "civilize" was prominent. To say that as soon as Dewey found his own voice, it was raised to defend democracy—and to explicate in the course of defending it what democracy was and why we were willy-nilly committed to it—is not exactly to break new ground. Whatever else Dewey is known for, it is for *Democracy and Education*. More interestingly, however, in the years before Dewey found his own voice, the voice he used was Green's.

It is almost impossible to date the changes in Dewey's moral theory with any precision. The outer limits can be drawn, however. Until about 1892, Green seems to hold his own as an inspiration, and after about 1895 he has become tarred with the brush of "untenable dualisms." That is, Dewey came to think that Green's contrast between the Ideal self in which we aim to participate and the everyday selves we are stuck with was too sharp; it was also too reminiscent of the sin-obsessed distinction between our bad empirical selves and the Christ-like virtue to which we ought to aspire that marred the Congregationalism of Dewey's childhood. I don't want to place too much weight on this. Jane Addams had an affinity for Tolstoy, even though it did not entirely survive a visit to his estate; Lillian Wald came out of a Christian household through public health nursing into a close relationship with the British Fabian Society and numbers of Labour politicians including Ramsay MacDonald. To suppose one could explain either of these personal histories by appeal to the philosophy of Green or Dewey would be silly. The point is rather different. An ideal of "social service" had a philosophical basis before there were "Departments of Social Services," and a natural environment in which that ideal could flourish was provided by the settlement.

What had made Green attractive to Dewey was not only that he offered a way of reconciling a thinned-out Christianity and a moral philosophy that found its values where it could, but that he was a democrat and an egalitarian. Indeed, Green was only as much of a Christian as he could square with his democratic allegiances. The settlement house was a place where the search for an egalitarian moral life could be pursued. In England, it was more obviously aimed at the upper-class young men who would become politicians and administrators—and they did; the future Lord Beveridge was warden of Toynbee Hall and Clement Attlee was for four years a resident there. In America, it meant that charitable work was not to be aimed only at alleviating the horrors of unemployment during the long depressions at the end of the nineteenth century. It meant that a complicated work of integrating immigrants into American society had to go hand in hand with the work of raising their consciousness of their own cultural resources. Practical matters weren't to be neglected; Toynbee Hall helped the dockers and the match girls in the famous strikes of the late 1880s, and Jane Addams took on the Chicago political machine on many occasions from the mid-1890s. Lillian Wald fought Tammany Hall, in neither case with much success. But the settlement house was an end in itself, not a base from which to launch a political movement.

Is this a face of charity? I think it is. It is sometimes a face of charity in a slightly roundabout way; just as the COS emphasized that it wasn't itself a charity, so Hull House emphasized that it was not an organization and not a charity either. None of which prevented Hull House from getting into the business of vocational education, language teaching, and health care, and ending up as a miniature welfare state implanted in Halsted Street. By the time this happened, a lot else had also happened, so that even more than before, talk of the "deserving poor" was inappropriate. But Dewey, for one, believed that his experience of Hull House and Henry Street had made a great difference to his entire theory of education. Lillian Wald in turn took a proprietary interest in the impact of Dewey's work on Russian education (Wald 1933, pp. 255, 269). The way settlements worked was by stressing the continuity of settlement and society, and this impelled Dewey to stress—it was his leitmotif—the continuity of classroom and society. What might have become "charity" in the Lady Bountiful sense turned out to be an exercise in transmitting a culture's sense of its own resources and problems. This was Dewey's definition of education. This is a slightly paradoxical ending: Bernard Bosanquet *stopped* teaching in order to engage in social work, while Dewey turned philosophy into the theory of education, and thought of education as social work in its largest and best sense. As for the distinction between justice and charity, along with many other "bright line" conceptual distinctions that appeal to lawyers and philosophers it had become one more piece of intellectual apparatus that we might or might not find useful in particular applications. Given the holistic and "growth"-oriented moral theory that Dewey was busy creating at the time, it was more than likely that he, at least, would not find it useful.

Notes

1. Charles Stewart Loch was born in 1849 and died in 1923; he was a pupil of T. H. Green at Balliol in the early 1870s and served as secretary of the Charity Organization Society for thirty-nine years from 1875. Characteristically, he rather disapproved of the social welfare legislation that the Liberal government of 1906–1915 introduced to Britain; it was too bureaucratic and relied too little on the initiative and sense of responsibility of the poor themselves.

2. Bosanquet was born in 1848 and died in 1923; he was a contemporary of Loch's at Balliol in the early 1870s. His half-brother Charles, who died in 1875, was Loch's predecessor as secretary to the COS from its inception in 1869. Although Bosanquet was a pupil of T. H. Green at Balliol, his best-known contribution to political theory, *The Philosophical Theory of the State* (London, 1898) was more hospitable to a rather German conservative collectivism than Green's work ever was. His biographer in the *Dictionary of National Biog-*

raphy (A. D. Lindsay) emphasizes Bosanquet's liking for Plato—no German, but a defender of a conservative form of collectivism.

3. The best account of the American settlement movement is M. Carson (1990); Himmelfarb (1991) is an excellent general history of English philanthropy from the 1870s to the First World War. For the various leading figures in the British COS, see their entries in *Dictionary of National Biography*.

4. Barnett was born in 1844 and died in 1913; unusually, he was neither a student of T. H. Green, nor an alumnus of Balliol, but of Wadham College, Oxford. For two decades, he was vicar of St. Jude's, Whitechapel, a parish his bishop described as "the worst in the diocese, inhabited mainly by criminals," and devoted all his adult life to improving the education, health, and housing of the East End working classes. Toynbee Hall occupied only a small corner of his astonishing energies, but he was immensely assisted by his wife, Dame Henrietta Barnett (1851–1936), herself a leading social reformer, and the friend and ally of Octavia Hill (1838–1912), the leading light in the campaign to improve the housing of the London poor, and founder of the COS.

5. There are innumerable editions of *Utilitarianism*; my introduction to *Mill and Bentham: Utilitarianism and Other Works* (Ryan 1987) emphasizes the point made in this paragraph.

6. Smart and Williams (1971); see also Williams (1987).

7. Meacham (1987) provides a useful history of Toynbee Hall's first years. His chapter 2 (pp. 24–61) is aptly titled "Connection and the Education of Best Selves."

8. Ritchie (1853–1903) was a Scot, the son of a minister, whose early training took place at Edinburgh University, before he went on to Balliol, where he was friendly with Green and Arnold Toynbee. Unusually, Ritchie moved to the socialist, or at any rate the Fabian, left, rather than the informal and nonparty political world of philanthropy.

9. This is spelled out quite persuasively in Himmelfarb (1991).

5 | Charity, Justice, and the Idea of Moral Progress

Allen Buchanan

The Expansion of the Realm of Justice and the Nature of Charity

> We . . . have an impulse to benevolence, but not to righteousness. This impulse makes a man merciful and charitable to his neighbor, so that he makes restitution for an injustice of which he is quite unconscious; though unconscious of it only because he does not properly examine his position. Although we may be entirely within our rights, according to the laws of the land and the rules of our social structure, we may nevertheless be participating in general injustice, and in giving to an unfortunate man we do not give him a gratuity but only help to return to him that of which the general injustice of our system has deprived him. (Immanuel Kant, *Lectures on Ethics*)

> We may not withhold from any one what is due him [as a matter of justice]; having complied with this condition, we can be charitable with our surplus. (Immanuel Kant, *Lectures on Ethics*)

In the first passage Kant states that we sometimes—perhaps usually—draw the line between justice and charity incorrectly, and that we make this mistake because we fail to be sufficiently self-critical. In the second passage he claims that once the line is drawn properly, justice takes absolute precedence over charity. If, as the first passage says, correcting our error requires expanding the realm of justice into what we had believed was the domain of charity, and if, as the second passage says, we may direct our efforts to charity only when doing so does not interfere with discharging all our obligations of justice, a disturbing question immediately arises: If a more accurate view of "our position" warrants a significant expansion of the realm of justice, what room for charity remains in the moral life?

In this essay I intend to take both of Kant's remarks seriously. First I will summarize the traditional wisdom about how justice and charity are distinguished one from another. Next I will identify several transformations in our moral thinking that can lead us to redraw the boundary between charity and justice, and to redraw it in such a way that what was thought to be a matter of charity comes to be recognized as a matter of justice. Then I will argue that *moral progress,* to a large extent, consists of the expansion of the realm of justice into what we previously believed to be the domain of charity.

Developing this thesis that moral progress consists (or mainly consists) of an expansion of the realm of justice will be my principal aim. A secondary goal will be to determine what, if anything, is left of the domain of charity, after the course of moral progress has been fully traversed.

Pursuing this line of inquiry may require a fundamental revision in our understanding of the nature of charity. If moral progress means the expansion of the realm of justice, does it follow that charity is merely a *remedial* and *temporary* virtue, a kind of second-best way station along the path of moral progress, an inferior destination with which we must be satisfied only until a more perfect moral condition is reached? My hope is that our exploration of this question will be a better understanding of the role of both justice and charity in the moral life.

The Traditional Distinctions between Charity and Justice

At least in the Western tradition of ethical theory, three contrasts are commonly drawn between charity and justice.[1] First, duties of charity are said to be imperfect, duties of justice perfect. Perfect duties are determinate both with regard to the content of what is required and with regard to the identity of who is the object of the duty. Imperfect duties are indeterminate in both respects: Both the kind and amount of aid he or she renders and the choice of a recipient are left to the discretion of the individual. Thus you and I have a duty to aid the poor, but how we render aid, how much aid we render, and to whom among the poor we render aid is a matter of our choice. In contrast, if, as a matter of justice, I have a duty to transfer some of my goods, principles of justice specify the kind and amount of the goods to be transferred and the identity of the individual or individuals to whom the goods are owed.

Second, it is often said that the fulfillment of duties of charity is a strictly voluntary matter, but that duties of justice may be and in some cases rightly are enforced. Justice supplies a warrant for coercion that would not be appropriate in the case of charity.

Third, at least in modern Western ethical theory, justice is thought to be a matter of rights; charity is not. If a duty is a duty of justice, then there is a correlative right. With duties of charity there are no correlative rights. Thus if I have a duty of justice, there is some definite individual (or, on some accounts, some definite group of individuals) to whom I *owe* that duty. Part of what is involved in saying that someone has a right that is the correlative of my duty is this: If I fail to fulfill my duty, I have not only done wrong—I have *wronged* someone, namely, that individual or those individuals whose right is correlative to my duty. To say that I have wronged someone implies that restitution, compensation, or at least special apologies are due to him or her.

These three contrasts are not unrelated. If my duties of charity are imperfect, that is, indeterminate as to content and recipient, then it would seem to follow that no one in particular has a right to anything in particular from me as a consequence of my having these duties. Moreover, this same indeterminacy is thought to make enforcement of duties of charity inappropriate, since only those duties whose content is definite are suitable objects of enforcement. In fact, the relationship between the three contrasts seems straightforward: It is the indeterminacy (imperfection) of duties of charity that is the primary feature, the one that explains the other two. Indeterminacy implies both the lack of correlative rights and the inappropriateness of enforcement.

Expanding the Scope of Positive Duties of Justice

Perhaps the most obvious way in which the line we draw between charity and justice can change—and has changed—is by the recognition there are general *positive* duties of justice where before only duties of charity were acknowledged. In a number of main figures in the history of Western ethical theory there was a tendency to assume that general duties of justice are exclusively negative—duties to refrain from injuring, killing, taking the property of others by force or by fraud.[2] In other words, the rights which people in general have were thought to be exclusively negative: the right not to be killed, injured, robbed, defrauded, and so on.

With the exception of the most extreme libertarians, contemporary ethical theorists now generally acknowledge the existence of some general positive duties of justice (and hence correlative general positive rights).[3] The greater part of the disagreement among ethical theorists now turns on the nature of the moral basis of such positive rights and their extent. Positions range from the view that there are strongly egalitarian positive general rights to all productive assets, to the view that there is only a general right to a welfare "safety net" or decent minimum of basic goods and services.

There are three main factors that explain this widening of the realm of justice to include general positive rights. First, there has been a shift in the ways in which ethical theorists *justify* claims about the existence of rights. Or, more accurately, instead of simply announcing that certain rights are self-evident, or plain to the least reflection upon natural law or accessible by divine revelation, or included in the concept of a rational being, modern ethical theorists have attempted to ground statements about rights in secular moral arguments. These arguments are attempts to supply good reasons in support of statements about the existence of various rights, including positive general rights. Generally speaking, the reasons offered connect rights with certain ideals of human flourishing and attempt to demonstrate that the recognition of these rights is essential if these ideals are to be attained or even approximated. In some cases the arguments are utilitarian in the strict sense: Rights are justified as the best means for maximizing overall utility. But even in nonutilitarian or anti-utilitarian theories, such as that of John Rawls, rights are typically justified as socially recognized protections for important interests—the interests which persons have in liberty and in making their own choices, in material well-being, and in securing the conditions for meaningful participation in communities (Rawls 1971).

The crucial point is that once these forms of moral argument are adopted, it becomes difficult—without incurring the charge of arbitrariness—to limit arguments for rights to exclusively negative rights. The same sorts of considerations that ground negative rights also seem to support similar statements about at least some minimal negative rights of a general sort. For example, if it is true that a (negative) right to freedom from arbitrary arrest and seizure is necessary for being able to lead one's own life and flourish as a chooser of ends, it is also true that secure access to a minimum of the material means of life (shelter, food, etc.) is also necessary.

A second factor is suggested by Kant when he goes on to explain his remark (cited in the first passage above) about "the general injustice of our [social] system." That system is unjust because it puts the stamp of legitimacy upon fundamental inequities in access to resources.

> Although we may be entirely within our rights, according to the laws of the land and the rules of our social structure, we may nevertheless be participating in general injustice, and in giving to an unfortunate man we do not give him a gratuity but only help to return to him that of which the general injustice of our system has deprived him. *For if none of us withdrew to himself a greater share of the world's wealth than his neighbor, there would be no rich or poor. Even charity therefore is an act of duty imposed on us by the rights of others and the debt we owe them.* (Emphasis added)

It is worth noting that Kant is striking a very modern—and given the generally conservative character of his political philosophy—radical note. He describes the man to whom we owe a duty of justice (though we mistakenly see him as a recipient of our charity) as "unfortunate." The suggestion is that inequalities in access to resources are inequities because they are not deserved. In particular, some are fortunate to be born into wealthy families, others are unfortunate in this regard. In the vocabulary of modern economics: The *initial endowments* individuals bring to the market system are not earned; they are the resources that an individual can use in order to earn economic rewards. A system which allows the unequal—and unearned—distribution of initial endowments to determine whether or not an individual has reasonable opportunities for flourishing is exposed to the charge of injustice. Once the distribution of initial endowments is regarded as unearned and inequitable, and once the role of positive general rights in ameliorating this putative inequity is acknowledged, the case for extending the realm of justice beyond purely negative rights begins to become more compelling.

The third factor that encourages the extension of the realm of justice to include some positive general rights is the development of social institutions which allow the "perfecting" of imperfect duties to aid those in need. The most obvious of these institutions, of course, is the modern welfare state itself. Such institutions serve (1) to identify the appropriate recipients of aid, (2) to coordinate efforts to render aid effectively, (3) to assign determinate duties for which individuals can be held accountable in order to ensure that the aid is provided, and also (4) to provide assurance that the burden of aiding those in need is distributed fairly among the better off. In the case of the welfare state, some citizens, usually on the basis of need, but sometimes on the basis of assumed desert as well, are identified as appropriate recipients of aid, and other citizens (at least in principle the better-off) are assigned determinate and enforceable tax obligations (on the basis of their ability to pay) to fund the aid in question.

In the absence of institutions for collective beneficence, aid to others can only take the form of independent, uncoordinated, individual acts of charity. Since one individual cannot be expected to aid all of the poor, the idea that duties to aid are "imperfect" makes perfectly good sense: It is up to the individual to choose what sort of aid to provide, how much of it to give, and upon whom to bestow it. But once an effective institutional infrastructure is in place to "perfect" imperfect duties and once a sound ethical rationale is available for grounding positive general rights in the same sorts of considerations that are adduced to justify negative general rights, the path is clear for the first way of extending the realm of justice. Justice is now thought to include some general positive rights.

Indeed, the very recognition that it is feasible to create institutions that can perfect imperfect duties seems to bring with it an extension of our obligations, a widening of our moral horizons. For once it is seen that institutions for specifying, fairly distributing, and effectively enforcing positive duties can be created, it is hard to evade the conclusion that we have an obligation to lend our support to their creation.

Of course this is not to say that any individual's obligation to contribute to the creation of such institutions is absolute. Two qualifications generally seem eminently plausible. The first is that one is only obligated to contribute if doing so does not come at excessive cost to one's own basic interests or one's other legitimate commitments and obligations. The second is that one has reasonable assurance that others similarly able to contribute will do so, at least in cases in which lack of reciprocity on the part of others would put one at a significant disadvantage. Reliance upon the state can, under favorable circumstances, sat-

isfy both of these conditions. If the state fairly distributes the burden of contributing to the provision of welfare services for the needy and if the level of services provided is not too ambitious given the citizens' resources, then no one
individual will have to bear an excessive cost. And if the state effectively en-
forces the obligation to contribute to the provision of welfare services, then each
taxpayer will be assured that others are bearing their fair share as well (Buchanan 1984).

At this point a perplexing question arises: Is this meta-obligation—the obligation to help create the conditions under which the realm of justice can be
expanded to include positive general rights—itself an obligation *of justice*? I am
unsure both as to how to answer this question and as to the importance of answering it one way rather than another. But this much is clear: Whether or not
this meta-obligation is itself an obligation of justice, the mere recognition of it
reflects not only an important expansion of our thinking about justice, but also
a dramatic change in the way we conceive of the boundary between charity and
justice. For in recognizing that we have an obligation to create institutions
which will perfect imperfect duties, we acknowledge the boundary between
charity and justice is not fixed, but is subject to human choice and control. In
other words, what is a matter of justice and what is a matter of charity depends
upon the nature of our institutional resources, and the latter depend, within
constraints, of course, upon what resources we *choose* to devote to building appropriate institutions. In that sense, boundary between justice and charity is
seen to be an artifact—an artifact of our moral will. We can choose to expand
the realm of justice—and we can have compelling moral reasons for making
this choice.

The three factors just outlined provide a rational account of how our conception of the realm of justice can come to be enlarged to include some positive
general rights. In fact, not only most ethical theorists but also perhaps most citizens as well now assume there are some positive general rights. The least controversial among these are rights to a basic education, to at least some minimal
health care services, and perhaps the right to income support at least for those
unable to work or to find a job that meets their subsistence needs.

For the most part, however, at least until quite recently, the general assumption has been that our positive general obligations of justice are owed only to
our fellow citizens, not to human beings generally, including those who are citizens of other states. The most obvious direction for expansion of the realm of
justice along the dimension of positive duties—and yet perhaps at present the
most controversial—is the recognition of positive general obligations toward all
human beings, not just one's fellow citizens.

There are both practical and theoretical obstacles to such an extension. At
the practical level, international institutions for redistribution are largely lacking. At present there exists no institutional infrastructure capable of specifying,

fairly assigning, and effectively enforcing duties of aid on a global level. Moreover, there are quite reasonable fears of the concentration of power that would be required to create and operate such institutions.

At the theoretical level, there are two serious hurdles. First, the view that one has special—and much more demanding—obligations to one's fellow citizens than toward persons generally enjoys strong support, even if the reasons that are supposed to support it generally remain unclear. Second, it has proved difficult enough to come to a working consensus in one country as to the extent of general positive obligations. The task of achieving the needed international consensus on the content of a human right to welfare assistance is much more daunting.

My purpose, however, is not to enter the fray on the question of positive duties of justice extending across borders. Instead, I want to concentrate for the remainder of this essay on several additional, quite different, less obvious, but more momentous ways in which the way we draw the line between charity and justice can shift. I focus on these because they represent more fundamental changes in the boundary between charity and justice and require more profound transformations in our understanding of ourselves and of our moral relations to others.

Expanding Conceptions of the Community of Subjects of Justice

Most would agree that the emergence of the idea that there are *human rights*—rights which accrue to all human beings simply by virtue of their humanity, regardless of differences among one another—is a major milestone in the path of moral progress. What is less well understood is that this development represents two distinct shifts in moral understanding, both of which involve an expansion of the realm of justice into what had been conceived as the domain of charity.

The first and most obvious moral advance we associate with the idea of human rights is the long and bloody road toward *consistent application of the criterion for being fully human.* There was a time when many Europeans and Americans acknowledged that the realm of justice included certain rights that accrue to all human beings simply by virtue of their humanity, but denied that blacks were fully human. Similarly, European colonists hunted Australian aborigines and southern African Bushmen for sport, rationalizing these outrages by excluding their prey from the community of human beings. At most, blacks or aborigines were regarded as objects of charity in the most attenuated sense: They were not to be made to suffer unnecessarily, and those who chose to treat them humanely were thought to be deserving of praise for their exceptional generosity. Those who enslaved or killed them were not thought to be guilty of violating rights because the beings in question were not thought to possess rights. Conceptualizing—and actually treating—all human beings as subjects of justice obviously counts as moral progress if anything does.

What is less obvious is that a more fundamental conceptual development has to occur *before* the question of the consistent application of the criterion of humanity and hence of the doctrine of human rights can even be raised. I refer here, not to the emergence of the concept of a right itself (though that, of course, is of major importance). Instead, I have in mind the rejection of what I have elsewhere called the concept of *justice as self-interested reciprocity* or, more briefly, *the strategic concept of justice,* and its replacement with a radically different concept of justice.[4]

Justice as reciprocity is a view about what makes an individual a subject of justice. By a subject of justice I mean a being who has rights and to whom we owe correlative obligations. According to justice as reciprocity whether one is a subject of justice depends upon whether one has either or both of two *strategic properties*: the ability to make a net contribution to the good of others in a given framework of social cooperation and the ability to harm others. Several prominent ancient ethical theorists either endorse or mention the negative version of justice as reciprocity—the view that makes being a subject of justice depend upon the ability to harm. For example, Epicurus says that nonhuman animals are not subjects of justice because they are weaker than us and hence we have no need of refraining from harming them in exchange for their not harming us.[5] Glaucon, in *The Republic,* endorses a similar view:

> People say that injustice is by nature good to inflict but evil to suffer. Men taste both of its sides and learn that the evil of suffering it exceeds the good of inflicting it. Those unable to flee the one and take the other therefore decide it pays to make a pact neither to commit nor to suffer injustice. (Plato 1979, Bk. 2, sec. 359, p. 32)

For both Epicurus and Glaucon the recognition of others as subjects of justice is the result of a strategic bargain: We refrain from harming others on condition that they will not harm us. Only those with the capacity to harm are even eligible to be members of the community of justice. Hume suggests the same view when he speculates that creatures otherwise like us, but powerless to harm us, could at most hope to be treated charitably, but could not expect to be treated justly (Hume 1975, pp. 190–91). Finally, Hobbes is another obvious instance of this negative version of justice as reciprocity: He held that what we call principles of justice are simply articles of peace adopted by rationally self-interested individuals to escape a situation in which each is subject to being harmed by the other (Hobbes 1958, pp. 104–91).

The most rigorous and systematic expositor of justice as reciprocity, in this instance in the positive form, is the contemporary philosopher David Gauthier. According to Gauthier, only those capable of providing a net benefit to us are beings to whom we owe obligations of justice (D. Gauthier 1986, pp. 113–56).

What all versions of justice as reciprocity have in common is this: They make the possession of any rights whatsoever—even the most fundamental rights—depend exclusively upon whether one possesses the strategic properties of being able to benefit or harm others. The reason for focusing only on these strategic properties is simple. The recognition of rights is seen as the outcome of a rational bargain among purely self-interested individuals. Those who can neither harm us nor benefit us have nothing to bargain with and hence are excluded from membership in the class of subjects of justice.

It should now be clear why acceptance of the doctrine of human rights requires rejection of justice as reciprocity. Human rights are those that accrue to all human beings simply by virtue of their humanity, regardless of whether the individual is capable of harming us or providing a net benefit to us in a given cooperative scheme. The doctrine of human rights, which makes being a subject of justice dependent only on being a member of our species, is one among several possible alternatives to justice as reciprocity. According to some theories, it is not being human but merely being sentient—having the capacity for pleasure and pain—which makes one a subject of justice, a being with rights. According to Kantian theories, it is not sentience but rather the capacity for practical rationality that distinguishes subjects of justice.

In a sense the doctrine of human rights is a sort of place-holder for specifying a theory of the subjects of justice until what is essential to being human is identified. Which particular theory one gets depends upon whether one takes practical rationality, or that plus sentience, or both of these plus some other characteristic, to be peculiar to and morally important about human beings.

Elsewhere I have labeled "subject-centered" (or "nonstrategic") those theories of justice which reject justice as reciprocity (Buchanan 1990). What subject-centered theories have in common is that they reject the idea that an individual has rights only if she has the strategic properties of being able to harm or to benefit others. Instead, subject-centered theories pick out various nonstrategic properties of the subject, such as sentience or practical rationality, as the criteria for membership in the class of subjects of justice.

The rejection of justice as reciprocity expands the realm of justice profoundly. Unlike the recognition of positive general rights, which only extends new duties of justice toward those already recognized as subjects of justice, the shift to a subject-centered theory expands the very class of subjects of justice itself. Those who lack the ability to benefit or harm us are transformed from (at best) objects of charity to subjects of justice.

The doctrine of human rights, as a version of subject-centered justice, extends the most basic moral status to all human beings, regardless of the *power relations* that exist among them. The weak and the disabled as well as the strong and capable are recognized as having equal status: All have at least the most basic rights.

I will make no attempt here to provide a comprehensive account of the reasons for rejecting justice as reciprocity in favor of subject-centered justice, or, more specifically for accepting the doctrine of human rights. It is worth noting, however, that the most obvious reason for this shift is the growing sense that taking the perspective of justice (and the moral point of view more generally) *consists* in part in refusing to regard any mere difference in power as being in itself a relevant basis for treating people differently, at least in contexts in which their fundamental interests are at stake.

In other words, making membership in the class of subjects of justice depend upon sheer power simply misses the point about what justice is about. Justice is concerned fundamentally with impartiality, with the exclusion of morally arbitrary or irrelevant reasons from our justifications for acting and from our justifications for the legitimacy of institutions. And if anything is now generally thought to be morally irrelevant reason for treating two people differently, the mere fact that one happens to be more powerful than the other is.

Instead of developing further this intuitive criticism of justice as reciprocity, however, I want to focus on a less obvious, but in some ways more disturbing feature of all versions of justice as reciprocity: the inability even to make sense of questions about the *justice or injustice of frameworks for cooperation.*

The point is most readily grasped if we concentrate on the positive versions of justice as reciprocity. According to these views, whether one is a subject of justice (or at best an object of charity) depends upon whether one can make a net contribution in social cooperation. But social cooperation always occurs in some particular framework for cooperation or other. And whether one can be a net contributor in social cooperation depends not only upon one's own characteristics, one's abilities and skills, but upon the character of the framework of cooperation as well.

Having the strategic property of being a net contributor is *framework-relative* for this reason: Whether one can make a net contribution depends, not only upon what skills or abilities one has, but upon whether there is an appropriate "fit" between those skills and abilities and the tasks that constitute the cooperative framework in question. Different cooperative frameworks will enable the same person to be a net contributor or preclude her from being a net contributor, depending upon the "fit" between the tasks of cooperation that comprise the framework and the abilities and skills of the individual. For example, a person who is seriously myopic may not be able to be a net contributor in a Paleolithic big-game-hunting society but may be a net contributor in a modern society (in which corrective lenses are available). Similarly, being profoundly dyslexic may deprive one of the ability to be a net contributor in a cooperative framework that consists largely of sophisticated information-processing tasks requiring a high degree of literacy, but would be no hindrance to social contribution at all in a preliterate society (Wikler 1983). In this sense, *being a net contributor*—and hence, having any rights at all, according to justice as reciprocity—is a relational and indeed *socially relative* property.

Thus in order to know whether someone is a net contributor—and hence, on this view of justice, whether he or she has rights—we must *first* specify a cooperative framework. Any statement to the effect that an individual is a subject of justice is incomplete unless a cooperative framework is specified.

From this it follows that for justice as reciprocity the concept of justice only applies *within* cooperative frameworks. No sense can be made of the question of whether considerations of justice constrain our *choice of cooperative frameworks.* But clearly, at least in certain stages of human development and under certain conditions of resource availability, we *do* have a choice of cooperative frameworks, at least within certain limits, and which one we choose will determine which of us will be a net contributor and which will not. Choosing one sort of cooperative framework rather than another may result in more or fewer people being included as full participants in social cooperation. And as we shall see presently, whether one can be a fully participating member of the cooperative framework deeply affects the quality of one's life, one's social status, and the way others conceive of their moral relations toward one.

The choice of one cooperative framework rather than another, therefore, will promote the interests of some (those whose skills and abilities "fit" the framework) and operate to the detriment of others (those whose skills and abilities don't "fit"). Thus the choice of a cooperative framework can involve fundamental conflicts of interest. Which sort of framework of cooperation is chosen will determine the distribution of burdens and benefits not only *of* social cooperation, but of inclusion *in* or exclusion *from* social cooperation.

To reiterate: A disturbing feature of justice as reciprocity is that it can provide no guidance whatsoever as to the momentous choice of a framework of social cooperation. Yet such a choice—involving as it does a conflict of basic interests—seems to raise questions of justice of the most fundamental sort. To restrict questions of justice to whether those who are net contributors to a given cooperative framework are receiving their proper share of the burdens and benefits of cooperation while ignoring the profound effects on peoples' life-prospects of the choice of a cooperative framework seems arbitrary.

The Morality of Inclusion: Redrawing the Boundary between Charity and Justice *within* the Class of Subjects of Justice

We have already seen that the rejection as morally arbitrary of the criterion of power as a basis for membership in the class of subjects of justice marks one important step in the expansion of the realm of justice. The acknowledgment that it is arbitrary as well to ignore questions of justice concerning the choice of cooperative frameworks leads to yet another significant change in our conception of the boundary between justice and charity. This next stage of moral progress also expands the realm of justice into what had been regarded as the domain of charity. But, unlike the replacement of justice as reciprocity with subject-centered justice, this change does not involve expanding the class of subjects of justice to include individuals who previously were thought to have no rights whatsoever. Instead, it is a transformation in our thinking about relations of charity toward beings whom we already recognize as subjects of justice. I refer to the recent change from thinking of efforts to accommodate the special needs of disabled persons as a matter of *charity* to conceiving of it as a matter of *justice*—as not treating them generously, but rather simply according them their rights.

The current debate about "disability rights" is not, of course, a controversy about whether disabled persons are subjects of justice. The question is not whether they have the same basic human rights as those who are not disabled. Rather, it is whether they have a right to special provisions to increase their access to transportation, work environments, public amenities, and so on. Advocates of disability rights are not pleading for charity, they are demanding justice. It is worth noting that both sides to the debate usually assume that justice requires some special provisions for disabled persons, the main controversy being over the extent of these rights and the magnitude of costs which others must bear to implement them. To that extent the disability rights debate already marks a significant expansion of the realm of justice into what had been regarded as the domain of charity.

One way of looking at this particular expansion is to see it as the result of a growing acceptance of an enlarged notion of *equality of opportunity* as a principle of justice. A very limited notion of equality of opportunity requires only the removal of legal barriers to social positions (for example, racial laws barring members of certain groups from certain occupations or laws reserving certain positions for members of a hereditary aristocracy). A more expansive notion requires that informal barriers of prejudice (for example, racist hiring practices) also be abolished. Applied to the case of the disabled, an enlarged principle of equality of opportunity requires not only an end to barriers of prejudice against "cripples," the "abnormal," and so on (the analog of racial discrimination), but also special efforts to remove physical barriers that prevent disabled persons from having opportunities for employment, education, and recreation that are available as a matter of course to others.

Our discussion of the inability of justice as reciprocity to make sense of questions about the justice of choosing frameworks of cooperation supplies a different interpretation of the rhetoric of disability rights. What I am suggesting is that the recognition that the disabled have rights of access (rather than there being duties of charity toward them in this regard) can be seen as an extension of the concept of justice to our choices about the nature of frameworks for social cooperation. Viewed in this light, the disability rights movement raises a profound and disturbing question about the extent of our obligations of justice: Does justice require that we structure our society in ways that maximize inclusion—that ensure that more rather than fewer people can enjoy full participation in social cooperation? According to this interpretation, the most fundamental challenge of the disability rights movement is that it forces upon us the very question which justice as reciprocity deems not only unanswerable but senseless: What constraints does justice place on our choice of cooperative frameworks?

If this is the question, then answering it has implications that far exceed concerns about those now usually considered disabled. Once we take seriously what I have elsewhere called the morality of inclusion, we may come to see as injustices not only physical barriers to full participation such as stairways and street curbs, but also less obvious but more pervasive features of our society which exclude from important areas of life many people not now considered to be disabled (Buchanan 1993).

For example, there is considerable evidence that public education in this and many countries favors a certain constellation of cognitive skills while in effect devaluing others. (In its crudest form, this is the complaint that those who are predominantly "right-brained" are penalized by the standard curricula and evaluation techniques for educational advancement, while those who are predominantly "left-brained" are rewarded.) Similarly, it is sometimes predicted that a significant proportion of the population will simply be left behind in our collective march into the "information age" because they lack the necessary literacy and numeracy skills.

It is important to understand just what is at stake here. I have already emphasized that once we abandon justice as reciprocity, fundamental questions of justice inescapably arise concerning the choice of cooperative frameworks because of the deep and pervasive effects which this choice has on different individuals' ability to participate in social cooperation.

It is also worth emphasizing that to the extent that individuals are excluded from full participation in the dominant cooperative frameworks of their society they thereby are relegated to an inferior moral status, even if we all acknowledge that they are in other regards subjects of justice, and as such possess some basic rights. When the demands of social cooperation exceed the abilities of an individual and she is in consequence excluded from participation, she becomes an object of charity. As an object of charity her well-being and opportunities depend, not just upon the generosity of others, but also upon their choices as to what aid she is to be given and what conditions will be imposed on her receipt of that aid. This is the meaning of conceiving of our duties toward the excluded as duties of charity—as imperfect duties.

So far I have only concentrated on what is at stake in the choice of cooperative frameworks for those who will be excluded from full participation by a particular choice. It is also important to see what is at stake for those who could participate fully in a cooperative framework that would exclude large numbers of others but are forced to live in a more inclusive framework. A simple analogy may be helpful here. Consider a group of four hikers. Two are superb hikers; two are very poor hikers. If the two more able hikers are allowed to determine their own route, taking into account only their own abilities, they will be able to travel very far in the allotted time and to reach a distant peak that affords a magnificent view. If they must choose a route that is within the capacity of the two other hikers they will not be able to travel very far and will not be able to enjoy a magnificent view.

The purpose of this example is to emphasize the point made earlier that the choice of a cooperative scheme can involve fundamental conflicts of interest. Choosing the framework that maximizes inclusion may benefit greatly those who otherwise would have been excluded, but this may come at the price of reducing the prospects of those who could have flourished in a less inclusive framework. It is just this sort of conflict of interest that principles of justice are supposed to shed light upon. Yet for the most part theorists of justice have simply assumed a cooperative framework as given and then worried about how the burdens and benefits of cooperation are to be fairly distributed among those who are able to function as full participants in the framework.

My suggestion, then, is that a deeper understanding of what is at stake in the disability rights controversy reveals it to be a challenge, not only to our assumptions about whether certain duties are duties of charity or of justice, but to our very understanding of the *subject matter* of judgments of justice. More precisely, it involves a recognition that not only the character of the relations among persons within a cooperative framework but the choice of a cooperative framework itself is a matter of justice. Once we see that which sort of cooperative schemes we have is, within limits, a matter of human choice, *and* that this choice determines who is "disabled"—excluded from full participation and relegated to the status of an object of charity—the conclusion that this choice is a matter of justice seems inescapable. As Kant stated, once we examine our position we may conclude that what we thought was a matter of charity is a demand of justice. But we may also reluctantly conclude that justice requires more fundamental social changes than were ever contemplated in our most charitable moods.

The Right to Be Included in a Rights-Protecting Regime

The final expansion of the realm of justice I want to explore is quite independent of the preceding two shifts in the boundary between justice and charity. This expansion does not assume that justice extends to positive general rights, though it is compatible with that view. Nor does it require that justice requires efforts to choose cooperative frameworks on the basis of their inclusiveness, though it is consistent with that view as well. This final change in the boundary between charity and justice stems from the belief that the same reasons for acknowledging that all human beings have certain rights (whatever those rights are) also ground *a human right to membership in a rights-protecting regime*, guaranteed access to some political unit in which the power of society is wielded to uphold individuals' rights. For convenience we may label this the right to a regime of justice. Here I can only sketch the line of reasoning which leads from the recognition that all human beings have certain basic rights (regardless of their strategic capacities) to the conclusion that all have a right to a regime of justice.[6]

The plausibility of a right to inclusion in a regime of justice (once the step of recognizing human rights has been taken) becomes apparent once we consider how a subject-centered theory of justice grounds those duties that are the correlatives of human rights. To say that our duties not to kill or torture or rob others are correlatives of their rights not to be killed, tortured, and so on, is to say that these are not only duties *regarding* others but are duties *toward* them. To say that our duties are toward and not merely regarding them is to say that we are obligated to help ensure that all human beings receive this treatment *in virtue of the sorts of beings they are*. This much is entailed by adopting the perspective of a subject-centered theory of justice.

In other words, if, as subject-centered theories of justice such as the doctrine of human rights insist, it is the nature of human beings themselves which grounds the obligation not to treat them in certain ways, then what is of ultimate importance is that *they not be treated in those ways*, not merely that I (or you) do not treat them in those ways. But if this is so, then it looks as if the same sorts of considerations that ground claims about the existence of human rights also lends support to the conclusion that there is also an obligation to help ensure that they have access to a regime of justice in which those rights will be protected.

In contrast, if human rights were not subject-centered, if the sole basis of one's duties regarding others were, say, the command of God (that one not kill, torture, etc.), then we might have no reason to think that there is an obligation to contribute to ensuring their access to such a regime. Or, if, as the theorist of justice as reciprocity holds, the only basis of our ascription of rights to others were their capacity to make a net contribution to our well-being or to harm us, then again, there would be no basis for recognizing an obligation to facilitate access to a rights-protecting regime.

To summarize: Once the subject-centered perspective of the doctrine of human rights is adopted, there is something quite odd about holding that all persons have certain basic rights, while at the same time insisting that there is no obligation to contribute to establishing the conditions under which these rights will be implemented. My first conclusion, then, is that given a subject-centered view of justice, as opposed to justice as reciprocity or a divine-command view, there is at least a presumption that we have obligations to help foster arrangements for the enforcement of all individuals' rights. The burden of argument should be on anyone who would deny such an obligation.

Notice that nothing so far has been said about whether this obligation is the correlative of a *right* to access to a rights-protecting regime. What has been said so far is compatible with the thesis that we have an obligation of charity to ensure everyone access to a rights-protecting regime, but not an obligation of justice.

This is precisely the point we reached earlier when I noted that, once institutional resources exist for perfecting positive duties of charitable aid, we are under an obligation to develop the appropriate institutions. Notice also that our discussion of the perfecting of imperfect positive obligations to aid the needy also provides a key to rebutting an obvious objection against the claim that there is an obligation to ensure access for all to a rights-protecting regime. That objection was that such a duty would be impossibly demanding for an individual to fulfill.

The appropriate response to this objection, you will recall, was to recognize an obligation to contribute to the building of institutions which will specify concrete obligations, distribute them fairly, and enforce them effectively, without imposing undue burdens on anyone and without inflicting unacceptable restrictions on individual liberty. Once an institutional structure of this sort exists, the chief reason for not regarding obligations of charity as enforceable— namely, that they are too indeterminate—no longer applies. But once these obligations become determinate and enforceable, they no longer bear the distinguishing marks of duties of charity—and the way seems clear for regarding them as duties of justice. The same sort of argument can be marshaled to show that an obligation to help ensure that everyone has access to a regime of justice can give rise to specific duties of justice *if* the appropriate international institutions become available.

It would be absurd, of course, to claim that any individual had an obligation to ensure that everyone has access to a rights-protecting regime, just as it would be absurd to say that any individual has an obligation to feed all the hungry. And the idea of attempting to enforce such an obligation would be equally absurd. But the obligation in question in both cases ought not to be understood in that way. Instead it is simply the obligation to contribute, along with others, to establishing an international institutional infrastructure which will then make the enforcement of determinate obligations feasible.

In the case of the obligation to contribute to establishing conditions under which all have access to a rights-protecting regime, the institutional structures would no doubt be complex and exceedingly difficult to construct. Building them may be the work not of decades but of centuries. That work has already begun, however, in the efforts of institutions of international law to articulate a right of political sanctuary and a right to emigrate, and in the struggle to develop effective sanctions to levy against those who violate them. Indeed the effort to identify human rights abuses and to exert pressure for reform against those governments that allow or commit them is itself an important step toward ensuring that everyone has access to a rights-protecting regime.

In the case of the obligation to contribute toward institutions that will perfect our imperfect obligations to help the needy I expressed agnosticism about whether this was an obligation of charity or of justice. Similarly, it is not clear to me whether the obligation to contribute toward universal access to a rights-protecting regime is a matter of justice or of charity. However, I would like to offer one bit of evidence that many of us seem to be assuming that it is a matter of justice.

Consider a common reaction to the unspeakable horrors now being perpetrated in the former Yugoslavia. There is, as well there should be, serious debate about what sort of measures, at what cost, are called for in an attempt to stop the ethnocidal conflict. But there is also, I think, a pervasive feeling that to sit idly by—to leave millions of people to suffer violations of their most fundamental rights—is deeply wrong, even if it is not *we* who are violating those rights. To say that the self-reproach we feel as we do nothing is simply the recognition that we are being insufficiently *charitable* seems to ring false. Duties of justice seem to be at stake here.

The Obsolescence of Charity?

In this chapter I have traced several revolutionary changes in our understanding of moral relations, transformations leading to fundamental changes in the way we regard not only the boundary between justice and charity but the nature of both as well. I have also suggested that the idea of the expansion of the realm of justice into the domain of charity can be seen as a unifying theme in moral progress. That the needy no longer have to rely exclusively upon the uncoordinated, highly inefficient, and arbitrarily selective charitable acts of individuals, that being recognized as a subject of justice is not thought to depend upon one's relative power but upon one's fundamental status as a human being, that the humanity of all who are human is acknowledged, that society is beginning to take responsibility for designing institutions so as to include more individuals as full participants in social life, and that the international community is slowly working toward guaranteeing all individuals access to a political order that will protect their basic rights—these are major steps toward collective moral improvement. Each, as I have argued, represents a rethinking of the distinctions we make between justice and charity.

As was noted at the outset of our inquiry, this way of understanding the role of the concept of justice in moral progress naturally raises a disturbing question. If moral progress consists, at least in significant part, of the recognition—in belief and action—that what we thought were obligations of charity are demands of justice, does it follow that there would be no place at all for charity in a state of complete moral perfection?

Given the gross deficiencies of our present condition and of all of human history of which we have any knowledge, speculations about the nature of moral perfection may seem not only hubristic but even slightly obscene. It should be emphasized, however, that I have focused only on what I take to be the *conceptual* dimensions of moral progress—the changes in the way we understand membership in the community of subjects of justice, expansions of our conception of who is human, and the extension of our conception of the subject matter of judgments about justice to include the choice of frameworks for social cooperation in particular. Though these conceptual revolutions are necessary for moral progress, by themselves—considered simply as changes of belief rather than of conduct—they achieve no moral improvement whatsoever.

Nevertheless, we may well ponder where the forces of moral progress are pointing even while acknowledging how far we are and may always be from the final destination. Our question, then, is perfectly appropriate: What role if any would charity play in a world in which all of the conceptual revolutions discussed above were not only completed in cognition but expressed in individual action and in the shape of our institutions?

The first point to emphasize is that any *warranted* extension of the realm of justice must recognize that there are limits on what we owe others—must acknowledge that we each have only one life to live and that genuine sacrifices of self for the sake of others ought to be the exception rather than the norm in human affairs. None of the expansions of our conception of justice discussed above inevitably requires sacrifice of the self or denial of the prerogative to show special regard for one's own personal goals. So even if these changes were wholeheartedly and universally embraced—as none of them so far has been— there would still be room in the moral life for giving preference to ourselves and our personal goals, so long as the proper limits of the demands of justice are observed. But wherever there is still room to act on this preference for one's own interests and personal goals there is also the possibility for individuals, out of concern for others, voluntarily to subject the pursuit of their own interests and personal projects to further limitations than those required by justice. That is to say that there would still be room for charity even if we all "examined our own positions" and came to express in action the belief that what we once thought of as charity was indeed a matter of justice. Thus the idea that moral progress consists in large part in the expansion of the realm of justice poses no threat to the possibility of charity.

Notes

1. For a historical survey of the distinction, see J. B. Schneewind's chapter in this volume. For a critical examination of various ways in which the distinction is made, see Buchanan (1987).

2. See, for example, *The Theory of the Moral Sentiments* (Smith 1976), pp. 82-85. See also *The Metaphysical Elements of Justice* (Kant 1965), pp. 20-21, 35-36. Relevant here is the distinction between general duties or obligations and special ones. Special duties are those arising from special relationships or promises. Kant and Smith recognize, of course, that there are positive *special* duties.

3. The most influential contemporary example of the extreme libertarian view is found in Nozick (1971).

4. I have explored this conception of justice, or rather this type of theory of justice, at some length in Buchanan (1990). For a very enlightening discussion of a closely related distinction, between justice as impartiality and justice as mutual advantage, see Barry (1989), pp. 155-292.

5. Epicurus, *Kuriai Doxai* (*Key Doctrines*), Key Doctrine 32 and 33 (in Long and Sedley 1987, p. 127).

6. I have developed this argument in more detail in Buchanan (1993), pp. 233-50.

6 | Losses and Gains

Mary Douglas

Plural Democracy

"CHINK OR INK?" my London aunt would enquire brightly of each of us in turn. The question embarrassed her student nephews and nieces: the mild vulgarity was incongruous with the elegant tea service, and it was inappropriate for the daughter of a distinguished member of the Indian Civil Service to use the choice of China tea or Darjeeling to speak slightingly of Asian peoples. We were no doubt being oversensitive, for she was never the kind of person to say "Wogs begin at Calais," or to claim that she couldn't tell them apart, "They all look the same."

I feel something of the same kind of discomfort when I talk to liberal exponents of rational choice theory. At least my aunt was distinguishing between different cultures and places. But the experts on human rationality treat everyone as if there was no point in trying to tell them apart. To be sure, they distinguish themselves as experts on what is rational thinking, from the rest of the world. If they admitted to cultural imperialism I could appeal to their liberal conscience. After all, living in a plural democracy we cannot pretend there is only one rational way of behaving. As they see nothing wrong with their assumptions the challenge is to show why they are self-defeating and futile.

I have been making this complaint for a long time (Douglas 1985), but here I am asked to explain what it has to do with understanding charity. First, why do we want to understand charity? Presumably because people are sometimes selfish and sometimes generous, sometimes they give, sometimes they hold. An inquiry into what Robert Payton calls the different faces of charity is looking for explanations of human behavior. If you think that all humans behave according to the same laws, you are soon going to find massive exceptions to your theory. Do you treat them as anomalies and keep the assumptions of the theory? Or are you prepared to give a place to culture? One thing that humans do have in common is culture, but cultures vary and varied cultures filter experience and knowledge to the individual. If you really want to understand charity you will need a way of taking into account cultural effects on giving. But for some reason which I do not understand the experts on human rational behavior are very reluctant to weaken their monocultural assumptions.

Pulpit and Politics

Before I discuss the difficulties I should pay attention to the contributions of history to the understanding of charity. Historians do reflect on charity in different cultures. They do not assume a single cultural frame for all periods of history. However, the questions that historians can address about kinds of charity are limited by the nature of historical material. They can study the debates of a particular period, and from these can refine purely historical questions, such as how the Christian concept of *caritas* arose, how it was differentiated from Jewish or Greek ideas; or the differences between theory and practice at different times; or local theories of virtues and vices, whether lay or theological. The language of the historian glows with the heat of the political confrontations organized around the topic; is it right for the poor to go hungry? is charity inefficient? is it misguided? why should the deserving lose to the scroungers?

If we go beneath the language and beyond the appeals to nature, human and divine, the contemporary agenda for a discussion of charity is the same, reiterated through the ages. The same two positions are mustered in each generation, as freshly as if they had never been uttered before. One is the collectivist case for taking the poor to be inherently deserving because of their poverty, (either as victims of society, or as unfortunates commanding sympathy), or claiming the poor as brothers, to be loved as oneself, holy, close to God. In both variants of this view the poor require aid without question about how the alms will be used. The opposed view discriminates between worthy and unworthy recipients, expects accountability, values efficiency and wise allocation of resources. To employ terms that are nearly as highly charged, the first position can be described as communitarian, unjudging and inclusionary, the second as individualist, inculpatory and exclusionary; but anyway it is clear that both are exhortatory. Somehow a coherent theory of poverty will need a cooler, more neutral language.

But it is not merely a linguistic question. Supposing we took out each morally loaded word and scrubbed it, there is no alternative framework into which its cleaned-up equivalent can be inserted. The academic discourse on giving is still dragged in the wake of political and religious controversy. This is one of the reasons why the experiments of Tversky and Kahneman are important: they attempt to create a set of new theorems about loss and gain, starting from scratch and unbiased with moral prejudice.

Political science and economics also have some neutral terms, but when we examine how they are used outside of a strictly technical context, the moral tone creeps back. Take for example the term "efficiency": technically it relates ends to means without waste, but its contrast set, inefficiency, is wasteful, and who can justify that? The defense of inefficiency is doomed to be dismissed as traditionalist, obscurantist, confused, sentimental. We are back into the language of affray.

Or take the idea of the long term: surely an innocent expression, since it refers purely to the time dimension. Long term does not immediately seem to carry moral value, but as soon as the syntax of discussion develops, its contrast set, the short term, incurs opprobrium. To focus on the short term is myopic or blind, and often self-interested, or at least impatient; to focus on the long term is far-sighted, patient, and wise. The bias is a pity, since the contrast between long and short term could be made to frame most of what is involved in the contrast between the communitarian and individualistic views of charity. The long view means including a community that does not fear revolution from the hungry masses, is not rent by strife, and probably will show an egalitarian income distribution; the short term view is the normal view of private interests, in which it makes no sense to give funds to sturdy beggars who could work for their living, or to tolerate scroungers. More of that contrast below.

There is a reason why the neutrality of technical terms is so difficult to sustain. It is not the historians' fault. The source of the trouble is the weakness of theory in this field. The dominant intellectual framework for social studies is psychological, and, in default of an agreed standard theory of persons and emotions, that means there is no larger intellectual framework into which the theory of rational choice can be fitted (Douglas 1993). For what is left out of rational choice theory (and that is a lot) we have to scrabble around for disconnected bits and pieces of psychology. There is the notion that human beings are dominated by fear and love, an amendment of the original hedonic calculus, but without substantiation. And there is the collection of demonstrations that humans are basically irrational because biological considerations keep intruding into reason. But there is no accepted theory of culture.

The Right to Eat Salmon Mayonnaise

One place to start would be to convince philanthropists that questions about charity are culturally defined. If there are three or four or five different kinds of culture, there will be as many faces of charity, and as many explanations of how and why gifts are made. Anyone who assumes there can only be one correct reason is being naive about his own cultural bias. The last time I talked with the late Aaron Wildavsky he suggested that a good example of contradiction between theories of giving would be Freud's joke about the salmon mayonnaise, which he had discussed in an essay he was working on.[1] Freud gave the story as follows:

An impoverished individual borrowed 25 florins from a prosperous acquaintance with many asseverations of his necessitous circumstances. The very same day his benefactor met him again in a restaurant with a plate of salmon mayonnaise in front of him. The benefactor reproached him: "What? You borrow money from me and then order yourself salmon mayonnaise? Is *that* what you use my money for?" "I don't understand you," replied the object of the attack; "if I haven't any money I can't eat salmon mayonnaise, and then if I have some money I *mustn't* eat salmon mayonnaise. Well, then, when *am* I to eat salmon mayonnaise?"

In his explanation, Freud states

> . . . that it [the joke] has been very markedly in the form of a logical argument. But quite unjustifiably, for the reply is in fact illogical. The man defends himself for having spent the money lent to him on a delicacy and asks with an appearance of reason *when* he is to eat salmon. But that is not the correct answer. His benefactor is not reproaching him with treating himself to salmon precisely on the day on which he borrowed the money; he is reminding him that in his circumstances he has no right to think of such delicacies *at all*. The impoverished *bon vivant* disregards this only possible meaning of the reproach, and answers another question as though he had misunderstood the reproach. (Freud 1960, p. 60)

Commenting on this interpretation Aaron Wildavsky said that Freud's error was to have believed in one "only possible meaning of the reproach," whereas different meanings would have been defined within different cultures:

> In the hierarchical culture, full of status and role differences, borrowing money follows existing lines of mutual obligations which imply sumptuary rules for proper expenditure at any time. In the individualist culture based on contract, accurate accounting and the power of wealth, an important status difference distinguishes those who have money to lend and those who are needy. In these two cultures it is deemed legitimate to divide and stratify people, whether it be on the basis of status or power, so it follows that appropriate behavior may be attached to the reciprocal roles. The role of receiver is to be abstemious and deferential so as to show the giver that every possible care is being taken of the money so generously gifted. The role of the giver is to bespeak the norms of the society so as to bring each lower status individual up to a correct understanding. When the giver discovers a violation of these norms on the very day the money is given, it reveals the contempt with which traditional morality is being treated by the receiver.

Wildavsky went on to contrast these expectations with the perspective of an egalitarian culture in which unequal distribution is wrong in itself. The same story in such a case would start from the duty of the giver to share his money with others and it would be quite wrong of him to upbraid the recipient "for seeking gustatory equality":

> In an egalitarian culture the borrower, by replying that poor people have every much of a right to eat a delicacy as rich people, would be able to make his

benefactor feel guilty for wishing to deprive him of that right, especially on the very day that he borrowed the money.

In short, the act of giving is open to many interpretations, and it must be relevant to a study of philanthropy to have an idea of how they can be organized.

Asymmetry between Losses and Gains

I heartily applaud Aaron Wildavsky's tracking funny stories to their base in cultural conflict, and consider with him that the uses of money are prescribed in such different ways that it is unreasonable to look for a natural human response to owning or giving. However, I find myself drawn also to a universalist explanation: Freud's story seems to conform perfectly to the discovery of Kahneman and Tversky (1984) that people treat losses and gains asymmetrically. People are apparently made much more unhappy at the thought of a loss than they are made happy at the thought of a gain.

Apart from the Bible endorsement of the shepherd rejoicing more over one lost sheep found than the many which never strayed, many fascinating examples of this tendency have been reported. It has intuitive rightness. In the salmon mayonnaise story the person who has lost a sum of money (relatively small in relation to his wealth) feels bothered about what has happened to it, whereas the one who gained a large amount (in relation to his poverty) treats his gain flippantly. If equivalent gains and losses are considered to be events of the same kind, with just a difference of a plus or minus, they ought to provoke equivalent reactions, but be put to the empirical test. That this is not so is shown by hypothetical examples:
Question A.

> A small photocopying shop has an employee who has worked in the shop for six months and earns $9 per hour. Business continues to be satisfactory, but a factory in the area has closed and unemployment has increased. Other small shops have now hired reliable workers at $7 an hour to perform jobs similar to those done by the photocopy shop employee. The owner of the photocopying shop reduces the employee's wage to $7.
> (N.98) Acceptable 17%; Unfair 83%

Question B.

> A small photocopying shop has one employee . . . (as in Question A). . . . The current employee leaves, and the owner decides to pay a replacement $7 an hour.
> (N.125) Acceptable 73%; Unfair 27% (Kahneman et al., 1986)

The case is used to illustrate the principle that people "are more sensitive to out-of-pocket costs than to opportunity costs and more sensitive to losses than to foregone gains" (Kahneman et al., 1986, p. 731). This may be so, but what is unanalyzed and taken for granted is the responsibility of an employer to maintain his initial bargain with the employee. This which is known to be variable in different cultures weighs so heavily in the example that even if it is constant in these cases it cannot possibly be taken as an instance of a universal psychological principle.

The alleged discovery about asymmetry between losses and gains comes from applying the theory of rational cognition to all and any humans, regardless of cultural differences between Chink, Ink, or Wog. It is a put-down for human rationality, or at least it shows an unexpected anomaly which Daniel Kahneman has been kind enough to explain to me as related to biological origins.[2] Loss aversion is rooted in the deep asymmetry between pain and pleasure, in turn rooted in a necessary asymmetry between two biologically significant commands: "Desist" or "Proceed," and this in its turn is rooted in neurological signaling of pain and pleasure. Thus biology is harnessed to the support of the hedonic calculus.

The anthropologist has several worries about this. First, the rooting of the theory in biology is dubious because perception is underdetermined by biological factors. Recognition of a "loss" is a more complex process than recognizing that fire causes a pain. It is partly a question of expectations. An unnamed factor of suddenness in learning of the loss or gain might well affect the results. Further, the central thesis is self-validating insofar as it is supported by a method of inquiry which deliberately blurs cultural differences in recognizing loss and gain. Many of the examples given are financial losses, and the assumption that "humans" come to financial decisions uninfluenced by the culture they are living in is parallel to Freud's assumptions about universal right meanings for jokes.

The findings of the cognitive psychologists would appear less paradoxical, and I sincerely believe, more important for the study of charity, if cultural differences were to be incorporated into the comparisons of loss and gain. It would enrich the theory of rational cognition to be able to place it within a perspective of cultural theory.

Persons as Bundles of Entitlements

To start again at the beginning: if we want to understand charitable behavior, it will be a good idea to reconsider the idea of the person. There is often thought to be more scope for generosity in the long-term view than in the short. If the long-term view is accounted for by a personal (psychological) preference, what do we know about persons that can explain why some people prefer the "long term"? And what does that mean anyway?

A theory of the person that does not place it in the society of other persons is vacuous. The approach I favor would try to refurbish the idea of the person as an articulated set of responses to demands from other people. I recommend Daniel Dennett's definition of the person as an agent credited with theories about the world and goals to achieve in it, and essentially conceived to be operating in an environment of other persons similarly equipped. The person charts its way to its own goals by means of the theories, which of course include theories about how other persons are applying their theories to attain their own goals (Dennett, 1988; Douglas 1992).

Dennett's approach allows a first-level person to be a member of a higher-order person, a community or group with its own goals, and its own theories about how other groups behave. This I find a very acceptable and indeed necessary element in a theory of the person, since the higher level is where standardization of ideas and values takes place. His idea of a person always in an environment of other persons means always in a shared cultural environment. Something is still missing: he has left out the pressures that persons are able to put on one another and what they can do to make or disturb the unity of the goals and theories at the communal level. From anthropology the element is supplied by saying that persons organize their environment by blaming and claiming and upholding the obligations of reciprocity.

In the push and pull of daily life some claims will be rejected, and some will have general acceptance: for these acceptable claims we can borrow the word "entitlements" (Sen 1981). Our neutral vocabulary so far has persons, with private goals and theories which are always in the state of being negotiated, and adapted to culturally standardized goals and theories; the persons are carriers of conceded claims, entitlements, though these too are always in process of negotiation.

There will be more to say about the constituent elements of persons when we consider these entitlements further: they are claims with two-way implications. Entitlements are what an individual expects for his own case, and is prepared to defend for others. They are held in place by the eager scrutiny of individuals who are pressing hot claims against each other; if one rejects a claim he will not get away with his own request for the same claim to be conceded. This is simpler than the complex Aristotelian-Aquinas notion of reciprocal rights and duties: the right of a lord to fealty from his fiefs implicates him in a duty to protect them, and their oath of military service gives them a right to protection. The idea is to incorporate culture by defining persons as standard entitlement bearers. For example, a right of way: all expect it to be maintained, and it is maintained by their use; for example, a standard greeting, a seat in the bus, a golden handshake, a lottery distribution. A wedding present is part of an entitlement in this sense: it can be claimed from all relations of a certain order of propinquity or of friendship; if they reject the claim, they thereby redefine their relationship; the entitlements are varied and their terms are as negotiated. Though persons bear entitlements, this is only half the picture: the other half is the agreement of the other persons in that environment that the claims are valid.

Insofar as each culture is different because of a different history of negotiation between persons, there will be different standard entitlements. An actual person in a historic hierarchy bears entitlements to succeed to office in a nested structure of roles. The actual person in a historic market system bears entitlements to contract freely. The length of time for which contracts are binding will also be part of the pattern, with clauses of limitation. It may be legal to bind oneself for service for a limited number of years, but not for life slavery. A mortgage may be for any number of years, as agreed.

Term Structure

An advantage of focusing on entitlements in this way is that kinds of cultures can be compared according to the time span of normal responsibilities. This enables the idea of the long term to be discussed comparatively, without looking to anchor it in a special kind of far-sighted personality. The capacity to envisage the long term is not a private psychological endowment, but an aspect of the whole pattern of entitlements. There is no need to distinguish between persons' capability for looking ahead: the term of a person's view corresponds in this argument to the view which is provided by the social environment. So, in a time of stable entrenchment, it makes sense to save for the future, take and make loans, arrange mortgages for 50 or 100 years: the pattern of entitlements is long term. In a period of crisis, everyone knows that the entitlements for the long term are unlikely to be honored, and perhaps impossible; rational beings then shorten the term of their expectations (Douglas 1982).

The actual patterns of society and the actual personalities in it keep in step. It is easy to see how the term is shortened: no problem in saying that persons will skip out of their obligations when they do not see any chance of their own claims being honored. The much more interesting question is how the long-term perspective is ever made real. Collective time resources are as apt for treatment by the prisoner's dilemma game as any other collective good. As to the long term's dependence on trust, we can ask why the commons is not raided, why defectors do not continually reduce the trust that upholds it. We can wonder that the long term is ever actualized.

The anthropologist answers this by examining institutions for reminding neighbors of their interest in honoring claims (Douglas 1980). Certain processes encapsulate the future in the pattern of ongoing entitlement. A bequest, for instance, engages the future in one way, by expecting the beneficiaries to wait until the demise of the giver; it can engage the future more precisely by making a trust for the lifetime of a first beneficiary before the gift goes to another, and it can engage eternity with terms that endow an institution forever. Anyone with a relatively short-term interest in having the terms of the bequest honored just now, will vociferously protest against its permanence being attacked. Those who see themselves as the next generation of beneficiaries can easily be mustered in its defense. I am arguing that the long-term future is made safe by the strength of short-term demands. If that is plausible, there is a field for research in comparing the time structure of claims in different cultures at different times.

A hierarchical culture, for example, is a complex nested structure of entitlements defined by time spans. A king may reign for life, a parliament legislate for four years. Rules of succession which go from father to eldest son take in a span of one generation, but rules of succession which go from eldest son to the whole round of surviving brothers before the next generation is reached are much longer than natural generations in their periodicity. Anthropologists examining succession rules have suggested that a delaying principle of succession, or perhaps I should say, a wide range of successors involved in the rule, is a deliberate attempt to commit loyalties from a wider community and over a longer period (Gluckman 1954; Goody 1966).

Max Gluckman even went so far as to argue that though the Bemba wars of succession would seem in one respect to be destructive of solidarity, in another respect, the fact that there was a shared commitment to the royal dynasty and a shared belief that to hold one of the royal offices was desirable was a sign of or made possible a larger solidarity. This is relevant to the present topic since the villages which supplied military service in support of their own chief's claims (according to rules of succession of amazing complexity, delaying enjoyment of the rights over several natural generations) also allowed him to make levies on prosperous villages to feed those which had struck hard times (Richards 1939). It would be interesting if there turned out to be a correlation between time spectrum of entitlements and the range of solidarity. It is at least plausible that the ability to maintain the one depends on the strength of the other.

These are but scattered examples to suggest how the definition of the person could be amplified to take account of different possible time spectra written into their entitlements. The entitlement is a reciprocal relation between the person and the social environment of other persons. The bundle of entitlements that stands for a person's social being is variously set for timed claims and counterclaims. A person who is living in a hierarchical environment is a bundle of entitlements which is stratified and hierarchized for generations ahead. A person living in an egalitarian community is a bundle of short-term entitlements. And so on, the term structure of claims makes notches and slots and varied levels of committed resources in the bundle of entitlements.

On these lines we can reconcile the cultural approach and the rational choice approach to losses and gains. On the cultural approach, cultures vary in the commitments which they impose on the individual. The amount of what we could call free spending power varies, that is, spending that is not precommitted. For example, most of a man's income may be preempted for the house mortgage, the children's education, the ex-wife's upkeep, to say nothing of necessary hospitality. In *The World of Goods* I argued that these prestations (as Marcel Mauss called socially prescribed dues—Mauss 1990) are just as important for us in modern industrial society as for the archaic societies he instanced.

It is not that we live in a different society, but that we look at our society in a different way, as composed of individuals instead of holistically. It is the viewpoint that makes the difference. Any society, including our own, can be described as a total system of exchanges. In that book I also proposed the argument advanced here that different social systems impose their patterns of claims upon future time with different degrees of force and for different time spans, and that this aspect of a social environment is very revealing for most of the questions that in socioeconomics are approached as questions about individual behavior. It was also a main thesis of the book that the time spectra of internal distributions would account for variations in the tendency to save. The latter also has implications for the theory of charitable giving. I will now try to apply the idea that every bundle of entitlements has got a distinctive time structure to the discovery about losses causing more distress than gains cause joy.

Predictions

Here is a reason for why losses would be generally viewed with more concern, but not by everybody to the same extent. A loss means an unexpected deficit in a schedule of social obligations. The person who has suffered the loss holds a bundle of entitlements to maintain which he or she has given a lot of energy and persuaded a lot of other persons to support. The danger of not being able to meet a minor short-term commitment is understandably worrying. Defaulting means more than loss of face; a graver loss would be loss of creditworthiness, loss of standing, the fading away of those weak ties on which everyone depends and which are kept alive by little exchanges.

In *The World of Goods* I chose a paradigmatic case to illustrate the schedule of inescapable social obligations. The working man's code of public house good manners requires that accepting a drink entails standing a round of drinks when the time comes. This is not an expense which can be shirked, any more than paying rent or housekeeping money. The cost of not contributing to these prestations is not to be counted out in simple monetary terms. This is why I doubt whether the loss of a sum of money is an event equivalent to the gain of the same sum or more. The question does not make sense, or if it does the answer depends on how strongly differentiated and how fully committed is the schedule of expenses entailed in a set of entitlements.

Some individuals may be very uninvolved with the others in the same social environment. Durkheim talked about weak and strong social integration in terms of "moral density" (Durkheim 1951), and indeed social sparsity and density have the same effects on the toll of entitlements as physical sparsity and density. The symptoms of isolation would be in the number of transactional cycles in which persons are involved, how much influence they expect to exert and feel exerted upon themselves, how much they can say that their time is their own. It is possible to be in the midst of crowds and yet be alone. It may be a result of exclusion, or it may be a matter of choice. Such a person, I dare to predict, would not respond according to Tversky and Kahneman's predictions about loss and gain. There is no particular reason in the isolate's case for perceiving asymmetry between the two events. For such a person a loss does not disturb a prescribed allocation of funds, nor does a win necessarily offer to satisfy a need: the two events ought to be greeted by the isolate with the same amount of sorrow and joy.

On the other hand a person whose entitlements are heavily notched with timed repayments, one who is caught up in a round of social exchanges, such a one will consider that what they possess is already allocated to well-defined slots coming due now, in the near and the further future. There will be very little latitude in what they can do with their money. If something is lost, a hole will gape in the spending scheme, something lost will have to be replaced. For such a person losses and gains are asymmetrical. If a sudden windfall appears, it will have to be a big one to make a difference to well-articulated spending habits; rather than reorganize the allocation, easier to blow the winnings in a sudden spree. This is just what Friedman predicted for windfalls in normal savings and consumption behavior (Friedman 1957).

I am predicting that Friedman's theory of consumption and Tversky and Kahneman's theory of asymmetrical attitudes to loss and gain will apply more strongly to a hierarchized bundle of entitlements with a complex time component; it will still apply fairly strongly to a market-oriented individualist set of entitlements but only weakly to persons who are isolated or members of an egalitarian enclave or commune, because of their more weakly articulated set of entitlements.[3]

The unexpectedness of the loss or the windfall is important for the theorem. Even a small unexpected loss throws a complex system of intended allocations out of kilter, while an unexpected gain, especially a large one, poses tricky problems about how to allocate it. So the loss is to be grieved over, while the gain is a less serious matter. We can see why the one who gains in the transaction feels like going out and ordering a salmon mayonnaise and why the donor is annoyed about the money he has parted with, and of course the beneficiary is not the least put out at being discovered enjoying his feast. In fiction the giver discountenanced is a favorite comic character.

If Tversky and Kahneman are right about a general tendency to belittle gains and to magnify losses, one of the minor problems of philanthropy is solved. Professional philanthropists warn newcomers to their ranks not to expect their beneficiaries to show gratitude. If cultural theory is right, this will be true in some cases more than in others. Particularly will it hold good of the cultural isolate, the one whose entitlements are the least differentiated as to time, least complex as to other people's claims, or, another way of saying it, least integrated into any social environment. Their cultural type is known as "fatalist."

Aaron Wildavsky cites another joke of Freud's about charity's paradoxes:

> A *Schnorrer* [Jewish beggar] approached a wealthy baron with a request for a grant of some assistance for his journey to Ostend. The doctor, he said, had recommended him sea-bathing to restore his health. "Very well," said the rich man, "I'll give you something towards it. But must you go precisely to Ostend, which is the most expensive of all sea-bathing resorts?"—"Herr Baron," was the reproachful reply, "I consider nothing too expensive for my health." . . . This is no doubt a correct point of view, but not for a petitioner. The answer is given from the point of view of a rich man. The *Schnorrer* behaves as though it were his own money that he was to sacrifice for his health, as though the money and the health were the concern for the same person. (Freud, pp. 63–64)

Wildavsky goes on to comment that this is not what Freud calls it, a piece of faulty reasoning, but a conflict of cultures.

> In Yiddish, to begin with, a Schnorrer is not merely a beggar but a special kind of beggar who makes those who give feel it is their privilege to support him; indeed, it is his right to receive and their obligation to give. In short, a Schnorrer is an egalitarian beggar who makes givers aware that it is wrong to have disparities of resources among human beings who have similar needs. From an egalitarian cultural perspective, the Schnorrer's reasoning, far from being faulty, is punctiliously correct.

The remark of the Schnorrer that nothing is too good for his health is a lighthearted example of a normally asymmetric attitude to gains and losses. But once we learn that a Schnorrer is a special kind of beggar, we recognize him as a fatalist. He is not a sectarian determined to convert the world to his faith. He is an isolate, he is an uncoordinated bundle of entitlements, and his bland innocence about what is expected of him suits the typical fatalist.

These remarks may seem a frivolous contribution to the topic of charity. To me they are serious and important because two approaches to choice have hitherto seemed to be opposed. On the one hand a well-established tradition of rational behavior takes humans as a solidary block, and aggregates their answers without scruple. On the other hand there is a (not well-established) anthropological theory of how culture shapes choices, which though intuitively correct is extremely difficult to formulate. The asymmetry of responses to loss and gains has afforded scope for combining the two approaches, and perhaps a hope for reconciliation.

How will the schedule of obligations and social involvement help to understand charity? Four kinds of position are described, giving four kinds of entitlement-bearing persons, with four kinds of reasons for taking action. There will be four justifications for charity, four kinds of reasons for not giving, four kinds of expectation of proper behavior from the recipient. On the side of the judgment passed on the recipient's behavior, the culture that values efficiency and self-reliance will want to disqualify scroungers, the culture that values the unity and solidarity of the whole community will count desert as irrelevant.

Who says that this has no practical bearing? On the side of the beggar's judgment of the giver, cultural comparison predicts when episodic giving can be hoped for, and when it is plausible to ask for a regular donation. Episodic gifts are more to be predicted from isolates, persons who are freer to decide on a whim, and who do not carry a long and weighty schedule of social obligations. They carry few regular entitlements from others, their term structure is uncertain and short, so they are reluctant to commit themselves to an extended obligation to give year after year. Regular giving will come more readily from the person carrying the other kind of entitlements. In a complex but reliable series of exchanges with others, it will not be difficult for this person to be committed to giving an annual or monthly contribution, for the expectation is that the same conditions will prevail in the long term. It is nothing to do with class, or with education, language, race, or color, but everything to do with the pattern of claims vested in the cultural environment.

Notes

1. A. Wildavsky, from an August 1993 paper, "Freud on Jokes, a Postconscious Evaluation," unpublished, because Wildavsky died in September 1993.

2. In a personal communication.

3. These predictions are based on the identification of four cultural types, justified in cultural theory, and to be found in several databases. This is not the place to elaborate the theory beyond what has been said about the variety of bundles of entitlements. Unless the experiment is tried we cannot tell whether the suggested disaggregation of the population would yield the result. But for the argument, see again Douglas (1982).

7 | Motivation, Cognition, and Charitable Giving

Robert Frank

IN A Monty Python skit, John Cleese plays a banker who is asked to donate a pound to a local orphanage. His first reaction is that the solicitor must be proposing an investment opportunity, or possibly a tax dodge. Neither, the solicitor tells him, at which point Cleese is nonplussed.

> Cleese: No? Well, I'm awfully sorry I don't understand. Can you just explain exactly what you want.
> Solicitor: Well, I want you to give me a pound, and then I go away and give it to the orphans.
> Cleese: Yes?
> Solicitor: Well, that's it.
> Cleese: No, no, no, I don't follow this at all, I mean, I don't want to seem stupid but it looks to me as though I'm a pound down on the whole deal.
> Solicitor: Well, yes you are.
> Cleese: I am! Well, what is my incentive to give you the pound?
> Solicitor: Well, the incentive is—to make the orphans happy.
> Cleese: (genuinely puzzled) Happy? . . . You're quite sure you've got this right? . . . [1]

Cleese nicely epitomizes the *Homo economicus* stereotype who populates the self-interest models that increasingly dominate theoretical work in the social sciences. In these models, moral sentiments play no role. *Homo economicus* does not vote in presidential elections; he does not recycle; he does not leave tips when dining on the road; he pours unwanted pesticides down his basement drain; and, most certainly, he does not make anonymous donations to private charities. Yet despite the ascendancy of narrow self-interest models, most of us are amused by Cleese's portrayal of the selfish banker. And notwithstanding the predictions of these models, we give large sums to private charities. In 1992 alone, for example, Americans gave more than $250 billion, an average of more than $2,000 per family (Freeman 1993).[2]

The dominant behavioral models in the social sciences view people not only as self-interested, but also as rational. Although these models freely acknowledge that people often lack the information needed to make perfect decisions, the assumption is that people act rationally on the basis of whatever information they do have. Yet here, too, examples to the contrary abound.

Psychologists Daniel Kahneman and Amos Tversky, for instance, told one group of experimental subjects to imagine that, having earlier purchased tickets for $10, they arrive at the theater to discover they have lost them. They told members of a second group to picture themselves arriving just before the performance to buy their tickets when they find that they have each lost $10 from their wallets. People in both groups were then asked whether they would continue with their plans to attend the performance. If people are rational, the distribution of answers should be the same for both groups, since in each case the relevant change is that the decision maker is $10 poorer than before. And yet, in repeated trials, most people in the lost-ticket group said they would not attend the performance, while an overwhelming majority—88 percent—in the lost-bill group said they would.

In this chapter, I will argue that the dominant models of the social sciences provide a poor basis for thinking about the behavior of charitable organizations and the people who support them. I will begin by noting that, even in the most bitterly competitive environments, we should expect not just the narrowly selfish human motives emphasized in modern social science, but also motives of a more genuinely altruistic sort. I will suggest that although charities can hope to win support from both altruistic and selfish persons, the most effective strategies for appealing to these two types of donors will often be very different from one another. In the concluding part of the chapter, I will examine the implications of recent research in cognitive psychology for charitable giving.

Human Motivation in Competitive Environments

To study charitable giving, or indeed any other human behavior, we must begin with basic assumptions about human motivation. The dominant model in the contemporary social sciences is the self-interest model of rational choice, which assumes that people have essentially selfish goals and pursue them efficiently.

Cynical though it may appear, this model has yielded important insights. It tells us why people buy more fuel-efficient cars in the wake of rising gasoline prices; why people are more likely to recycle when garbage collection is billed by the container; why speeding is less common in states with high traffic fines; and so on.

Yet many other behaviors do not fit the me-first caricature. When traveling, we leave tips in restaurants we never expect to visit again. We often incur costs to dispose of unwanted pesticides properly rather than simply pour them down the drain. Soldiers dive atop hand grenades to save the lives of their comrades. Seen through the lens of modern self-interest theory, these behaviors might seem the human equivalent of planets traveling in square orbits.

The irony is that many noble human behaviors not only survive the ruthless pressures of the material world, but are nurtured by them as well.[3] If this claim seems self-contradictory, it is no more so than the fact that someone who deliberately tries to be "more spontaneous" is destined to fail. In the course of social and economic interaction, we confront many problems in which the conscious, direct pursuit of self-interest is self-defeating.

Imagine, for example, that you work for the owner of a profitable business, who is currently weighing an opportunity to open a branch in a distant city. She knows that if she hires an honest manager, the branch will return high profits, but that otherwise it will lose money. You want the job and are fully qualified for it. The owner would be willing to double your current salary if she could be sure you would manage honestly. She knows, however, that if you manage dishonestly, you will be able to make three times your current salary.

In standard economic models, this option to cheat spells doom for the branch operation. Reasoning from the self-interest model, the owner concludes that since you could earn more by managing dishonestly, you will do so. And since this means the branch will be a loser, she does not open it. The irony, of course, is that this choice leaves both of you worse off than if she were to open the branch and you were to manage it honestly.

In this scenario we have what economists call a "commitment problem." The problem could be solved if you could credibly commit yourself to manage honestly. In situations like these, the pursuit of material self-interest proves self-defeating.

Traditional economic models try to solve commitment problems by changing the material incentives people face. Thus, for example, the owner might try to hire an investigator to monitor the branch manager's performance. But in many cases, the relevant behavior simply cannot be monitored. In such cases, traditional models suggest that solutions do not exist.

Yet commitment problems can often be solved even when behavior cannot be monitored. Solutions require that we relax the assumption that people care only about material self-interest. Suppose, for example, that the owner had some means of discovering that you were a trustworthy person, and would manage his branch operation honestly even though you could earn much more if you cheated. She could then open the branch with confidence, even though she could not monitor you directly. Both of you would gain.

This solution relies on two premises: first, that there are people who behave honestly even when they could earn more by cheating; and second, that reliable means exist for identifying these people. The first premise is uncontroversial, but the second invites careful scrutiny. After all, managerial candidates have strong incentives to portray themselves as trustworthy, so personal declarations of honesty cannot carry much weight. Investigating a candidate's past record will be illuminating only in those cases where someone has actually been caught doing wrong. It will reveal little about the many cheaters who were shrewd enough to avoid detection. If these methods fail, how can trustworthy persons be identified?

The key is to recognize that honest behavior is motivated not by rational calculations but by emotions—by moral sentiments, to use Adam Smith's term. The employee who walks away from a golden opportunity to cheat is motivated by his sympathy for the owner's interests, and by his feelings of self-esteem, which depend strongly on right conduct. The problem for the would-be cheater is that the emotions that motivate honest behavior are difficult to fake. Once we get to know a person well, we are able to make reliable judgments about his character. The cheater's goal is to appear trustworthy, but given our ability to detect the presence of the emotions that motivate trustworthiness, the easiest way to *appear* trustworthy is actually to *be* trustworthy.

Perhaps the following thought experiment will help summon your intuition about whether we can make reliable character judgments about others. Imagine having just returned from a crowded sports arena to discover that you have lost an envelope with your name and address on it that contained $1,000 in cash. Can you think of anyone, not related to you by blood or marriage, who you feel certain would return your cash? Note that it is unlikely that past experience could have provided directly relevant objective evidence on which to base a prediction. Most people nonetheless report that there are people they feel certain would return their cash—that for these people, keeping the cash would just be out of the question. If you share this belief, then you accept the central premise of my argument—that it is possible to make reliable character judgments about at least some people. If these judgments are sufficiently accurate, they enable us to solve commitment problems.

Similar reasoning suggests that altruistic motives can survive and prosper even in harshly competitive environments. After all, the same moral sentiments that motivate trustworthy behavior—sympathy, a sense of fair play, and so on—cause people to derive satisfaction from helping others. If there are practical ways to identify people who have these sentiments, we will favor them as partners in ventures that require trust. Thus, although altruistic motives may cause people to incur costs they might otherwise have avoided, they may also yield important material benefits.

An Equilibrium Mix of Motives

It might seem that if moral sentiments help solve important commitment problems, then evolutionary forces would assure that everyone have a full measure of these sentiments. But a closer look at the interplay between selfish and altruistic motives suggests that this is unlikely to be the case. Imagine, for example, an environment populated by two types of people, selfish and altruistic. And suppose that people earn their livelihood by interacting in pairs, where the commitment problem they confront is the simple prisoner's dilemma shown in Table 1, which shows the possible payoffs for two representative individuals, X and Y.

If X and Y are both altruists, their interaction will yield a payoff of 2 units each. If they are both selfish, they will get only 1 unit each. It is thus better for both if both are altruists than if both are selfish. The difficulty, as in all prisoner's dilemmas, is that both X and Y would earn more by being selfish. Suppose X is altruistic. Then if Y is also altruistic, he earns 2, whereas he could have earned 3 by being selfish. Likewise, if X is selfish, Y earns more by being selfish (1 unit) than he would have earned by being altruistic (zero).

If altruistic and selfish persons were perfectly indistinguishable, interactions would occur on a random basis and the average payoffs would always be larger for the selfish types (owing to the dominance of the selfish strategy in all prisoner's dilemmas). In evolutionary models, the rule governing population dynamics is that each type reproduces in proportion to its material payoff relative to other types. This implies that if the two types were indistinguishable, the eventual result would be extinction for the altruists. In highly simplified form, this is the Darwinian story that inclines many social scientists to believe that self-interest is the only important human motive.

But now suppose that the selfish types were distinguishable at a glance from the altruists. Then interaction would no longer take place on a random basis. Rather, the altruists would pair off systematically with one another to reap the benefits of mutual cooperation. Selfish individuals would be left to interact with one another, and would receive the lower payoff associated with these pairings. The eventual result this time is that the selfish type would be driven to extinction.

Neither of these two polar cases seems descriptive of actual populations, which typically contain a mix of altruistic and selfish persons. Such a mixed population is precisely the result we get if we make one small modification to the original story. Again suppose that altruists are observably different from selfish persons, but that some effort is required to make the distinction. If the population initially consisted almost entirely of altruists, it would not pay to expend this effort because one would be overwhelmingly likely to achieve a high payoff merely by interacting at random with another person. In such an environment, the altruists would cease to be vigilant in their choice of trading partners. Selfish individuals would then find a ready pool of victims, and their resulting higher payoffs would cause their share of the total population to grow.

As the selfish types became more numerous, however, it would begin to pay altruists to exercise greater vigilance in their choice of partners. With sufficiently many selfish individuals in the population, altruists would be vigilant in the extreme, and we would again see pairings among like types only. That, in turn, would cause the prevalence of altruists to grow. At some point, a stable

X

		Altruistic	Selfish
	Altruistic	2 for each	0 for Y 3 for X
Y	Selfish	3 for Y 0 for X	1 for each

Table 1. Monetary Payoffs in a Joint Venture

balance would be struck in which the altruists were just vigilant enough to prevent further encroachment by the selfish types. The average payoff to the two types would be the same and their population shares would remain constant. There would be, in other words, a stable niche for each type.

Ecological models like the one sketched above can also be offered in support of a more nuanced portrait of individual human motivation. For example, rather than starting with a population in which people are exclusively one type or the other, we might begin with individuals with some mix of different motives. Such models would lead us to expect an equilibrium in which each individual experiences both selfish and altruistic motives to varying degrees.

But although the details of the story may differ according to the particular model chosen, ecological models as a group have an important feature in common: Each stresses that we should not expect a world populated exclusively by the *Homo economicus* caricature that populates conventional social science models. Such creatures may survive at the margins in environments where monitoring costs make it too expensive to ferret them out. But they are hardly a sensible basis upon which to ground a universal science of human behavior.

The ecological framework provides theoretical underpinning for a remarkably commonsensical portrait of human nature. It tells us that people are driven by a combination of selfish and altruistic motives, just as experience seems to suggest. The mix of motives is highly variable across individuals, yet polar cases are by no means common.

Similar views of human nature almost invariably informed commentary on human behavior in the eighteenth and nineteenth centuries. Contemporary social scientists, by contrast, increasingly ignore all but selfish motives. To their credit, however, modern scholars have developed much more carefully elaborated theories about how selfish motives translate into behavior in different domains. Our challenge is to discover how these theories play out under a broader conception of human motivation.

Motives for Giving

Once we acknowledge that people have purely altruistic motives, we can construct a simple, if uninteresting, theory of charitable giving. People donate because they *like* to donate, or at least feel it their duty to do so. There are several reasons people might take pleasure in giving. They might like the fact that their gifts will be put to specific uses of which they strongly approve. Those who donate to CARE's efforts on behalf of sub-Sahara famine victims fall into this category.

In other cases, altruistic giving need not signal approval of the specific disposition of the donated funds. Many donors, for example, derive satisfaction from providing extra resources to the impoverished, even though they may not approve of the specific uses to which those resources are put.

Note, however, that one can give to a cause one cares strongly about even in the absence of altruistic motives. The entire community may benefit from having a safe water supply, yet there may be only a single individual with sufficient resources to build a treatment facility. If that person has a sufficiently strong personal interest in safe water, it may pay her to build the facility on her own. And once developed, it may cost nothing extra to make safe water available to others.

But cases like this are surely rare. They should not be confused with much more common instances of donors who stand to benefit if the charitable organization's mission is carried out successfully. Suppose, for example, that generous relief for the poor would eliminate crime in the streets. Might not a person's gift to, say, the Salvation Army, then be rationalized by a narrowly selfish desire not to be victimized by street crime? Likewise, could not a gift to the Public Broadcasting System be viewed as a self-interested attempt to keep the MacNeil-Lehrer News Hour on the air? Except in unusual cases, the answer seems to be no. The problem is that the typical individual gift is far too small to affect the outcome in question. Any one person's risk of being a street-crime victim is virtually unaffected by even a generous gift to the Salvation Army. Similarly, the status of the MacNeil-Lehrer News Hour is, for all practical purposes, independent of any one person's gift. To explain such gifts, we must invoke some sort of altruistic motive (Andreoni 1986).

There are also cases in which donors benefit, even in narrowly material terms, by making gifts to charities whose work they care nothing about. For example, some donors may be subject to regulation in their business dealings, and being known as community benefactors may entitle them to more favorable treatment in the political arena. More generally, people may give because enhanced status is of value for its own sake, quite apart from any material benefits it may yield. Even in these cases, however, the altruistic concerns of the population at large will shape charitable giving. After all, a gift to a cause that few people favor will do little to enhance the donor's reputation.

A related selfish motive for giving is the desire to gain access to favored social networks. As with higher status, enhanced social contacts may be a source of pleasure in their own right. But as sociologists are quick to emphasize, they also have an important instrumental character. The allocation of jobs and other important resources, for example, are often decisively influenced by membership in social networks (Granovetter 1972, 1985; Podolny 1993).

That many gifts are consistent with self-interested motives is further underscored by the observation that the gifts of many donors come not at the expense of personal consumption but of leaving a smaller estate at their time of death. This is certainly true of the extremely wealthy, but is true of many others as well. In such cases, a gift involves no sacrifice in the donor's current or future living standards, yet may benefit the donor in any of the ways mentioned earlier.

To recapitulate briefly, my aim in this section has been to make clear that we may speak intelligibly of altruistic motives even within the bitterly competitive materialistic framework popular in the modern social sciences. This is not to deny, of course, the importance of selfish motives, which commingle with altruistic motives in most people. My claim is that any theory of charitable giving based exclusively on one type of motive or the other will inevitably fail to capture an essential aspect of reality.

Motivation is not the only respect in which conventional models of rational choice paint a misleading picture of human behavior. These models also assume that people are efficient in pursuit of their goals. But as the following brief review of recent findings in cognitive psychology will make clear, there are systematic exceptions even to this more limited claim.

Departures from Rational Choice

The Asymmetric Value Function

The rational choice model says that people should evaluate events, or collections of events, in terms of their overall effect on total wealth. Suppose you get an unexpected gift of $100 and then you return from vacation to find an $80 invoice from the city for the repair of a broken water line on your property. According to the rational choice model, you should regard the occurrence of these two events as a good thing, because their net effect is a $20 increase in your total wealth.

Daniel Kahneman and Amos Tversky argue, however, that people often seem to weigh each event separately, and attach considerably less importance to the gain than to the loss—so much less that many people actually refuse to accept pairs of events that would increase their overall wealth (Tversky and Kahneman, 1981). They propose that people evaluate alternatives not with the conventional utility function of rational choice theory, but instead with a value function defined over *changes* in wealth. One important property of this value function is that it is much steeper in losses than in gains. In Figure 1, for example, note how it assigns a much larger value, in absolute terms, to a loss of $80 than to a gain of $100. Note also that the value function is concave in gains and convex in losses. This means that the psychological impact of incremental gains or losses diminishes as the gains or losses become larger.

According to Kahneman and Tversky, it is very common for people to evaluate each item of a collection of events separately, then make decisions on the basis of the sum of the separate values. In this example, V(100) is much smaller, in absolute terms, than V(-80). Because the algebraic sum of the two is less than zero, anyone who employs this decision mechanism will refuse this pair of opportunities even though their net effect is to increase total wealth by $20.

There are really two important features of the Kahneman and Tversky value function. One is that people treat gains and losses asymmetrically, giving the latter much heavier weight in their decisions than the former. The second is that people evaluate events first, then add the separate values together. The first of these features does not necessarily imply irrational behavior. There is nothing inconsistent, after all, about feeling that a loss causes more pain than the happiness caused by a gain of the same magnitude. What *does* often appear irrational is the second step—treating each event separately, rather than considering their combined effect.

This is essentially a question about how to frame events. If someone pointed out to a person that the net effect of two events A and B was to increase her wealth by $20 she would probably quickly agree to allow the events to happen. Framed as an entity, they are obviously an improvement over the status quo. The problem is that, in actual decisions, it may seem more natural to frame the events separately. And as we will see, this tendency has implications for charitable giving.

Sunk Costs

Another basic tenet of rational choice theory is that sunk costs should be ignored in decisions. Contrary to this claim, sunk costs often appear to weigh quite heavily. Economist Richard Thaler offers the following example (Thaler 1980): Suppose you have just paid $40 for tickets to a basketball game to be played tonight in an arena 60 miles north of your home. Suddenly it starts snowing heavily and the roads north, while passable, are difficult. Do you still go to the game? Would your answer have been different if, instead of having bought the tickets, you had received them for free? Thaler finds that most people who bought the tickets would go, whereas most of those who were given them say

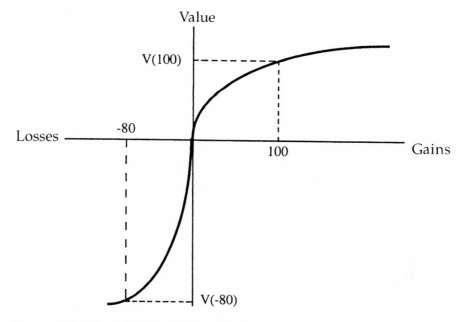

Figure 1. The Kahneman-Tversky Value Function

they would stay home. According to the rational choice model, of course, the decision should be the same in either case. If your expected pleasure of seeing the game exceeds the expected hassle of the drive, you should go; otherwise stay home. Neither element in this cost-benefit calculation should depend on how you obtained the tickets.

Out-of-Pocket Costs versus Opportunity Costs

Thaler suggests that our tendency not to ignore sunk costs may be given a simple interpretation in terms of the Kahneman and Tversky value function (Thaler 1980). Tickets to the 1988 Super Bowl sold for $100 through official channels, but in the open market went for prices as high as $2,000. Thousands of fans used their $100 tickets to attend the game, thus passing up the opportunity to sell them for $2,000. Very few of these fans, however, would have spent $2,000 to buy a ticket for the game. Thaler suggests that people code the $100 expense as a loss, but the $2,000 opportunity cost as a forgone gain.

Hedonic Framing

Kahneman and Tversky's value function suggests specific ways that sellers, gift givers, and others might frame their offerings to enhance their appeal.[4] Thaler mentions several specific strategies:
- **Segregate gains.** Because the value function is concave in gains, a higher

total value results when we decompose a large gain into two (or more) smaller ones. Thus, for example, Figure 2 shows that a gain of 100 creates more total value if decomposed into two separate gains of 60 and 40. The moral here, as Thaler puts it, is "Don't wrap all the Christmas presents in a single box."

• **Combine losses.** The convexity of the value function in the loss domain implies that two separate losses will appear less painful if they are combined into a single, larger loss. As shown in Figure 3, for example, separate losses of 20 and 30 have a combined value that is larger, in absolute terms, than the value of a loss of 50.

• **Segregate small gains from large losses.** A sample of subjects was asked which of these persons is more upset: A, whose car sustains $200 damage in the parking lot the same day he wins $25 in the office football pool; or B, whose car sustains $175 damage in the parking lot? 72 percent responded that B would be more upset, 22 percent picked A, and 6 percent said they would be equally upset. The rational choice model predicts they would be equally upset, because they suffer exactly the same reduction in their wealth. The Kahneman and Tversky value function, by contrast, predicts that B would be more upset, which accords with most people's responses. Thaler calls the segregation of a small gain from a big loss the "silver lining effect," and argues that it may help explain why so many merchants offer cash rebates on their products. ("Buy a new Dodge before October 1st and get $1,200 cash back!") Viewed in the context of the rational choice model, this practice seems to be dominated by the simple alternative of reducing the price of the product, which would lower the total amount of sales tax the buyer pays.

The Psychophysics of Perception

There is yet another pattern to the way we perceive and process information that differs from the predictions of the rational choice model. It derives from the so-called Weber-Fechner law of psychophysics. Weber and Fechner set out to discover how large the change in a stimulus had to be before we could perceive the difference in intensity. Most people, for example, are unable to distinguish a 100-watt light bulb from a 100.5-watt light bulb. But how large does the difference in brightness have to be before people can reliably identify it? Weber and Fechner found that the minimally perceptible difference is roughly proportional to the original intensity of the stimulus. Thus the more intense the stimulus is, the larger the difference has to be, in absolute terms, before we can tell the difference.

The Weber-Fechner law seems to be at work when people decide whether price differences are worth worrying about. Suppose, for example, you are about to buy a clock radio in a store for $25 when a friend informs you that the same radio is selling for only $20 in another store only 10 minutes away. Do you go to the other store? Would your answer have been different if you had been

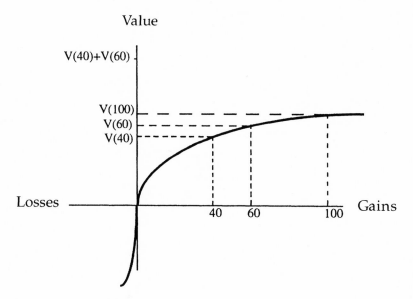

Figure 2. The Benefit of Segregating Gains

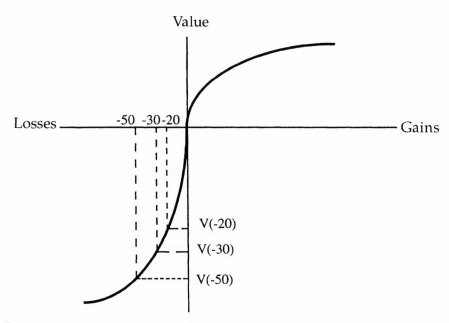

Figure 3. The Benefit of Combining Losses

about to buy a television for $500 and your friend told you the same set was available at the other store for only $495? Most people answer "yes" to the first question, "no" to the second.

In the rational choice model, it is inconsistent to answer differently for the two cases. A rational person will travel to the other store if and only if the benefits of doing so exceed the costs. The benefit is $5 in both cases. The cost is also the same for each trip, whether it is to buy a radio or a television. If it makes sense to go in one case, it also makes sense in the other.

Earlier proponents of the rational choice model were under no illusions that people were flawless decision makers. But early research on decision making under incomplete information seemed to suggest that any departures of behavior from fully informed rational choices were essentially random. By contrast, more recent research in this area suggests that the rules of thumb people use, although adaptive in many contexts, often give rise to systematic departures from rational choice. What is more, many errors occur predictably in contexts where decision makers have all the relevant information at hand.

Some Implications for Fund-Raisers

In this section, I will consider how the preceding discussion of motivation and cognition might be put to use by the managers of charitable organizations.

The Strategic Problem of Appealing to Multiple Motives

Earlier we saw that charitable organizations can hope to appeal even to potential donors who are motivated primarily by narrow self-interest. And there has never been any mystery about how charitable organizations might appeal to donors with altruistic motives. Once we recognize the plurality of motives for giving, however, any given charitable organization's task becomes more complex. Indeed, it may seem natural to question whether a single charity can hope to appeal simultaneously to both altruistic and selfish motives.

Yet consider the difficulty of a charity that attempted to appeal only to donors with selfish motives. As noted, charitable organizations have much to offer such persons, both in terms of business and regulatory contacts and heightened status and respect in the community. The fundamental problem is that the community is more likely to admire donors whose gifts are motivated by altruism than by self-interest. Of course, outsiders have little way of knowing what any individual donor's motives might be. But if a charity openly appealed to selfish motives, and managed in the process to attract primarily selfish donors, it would eventually be colored by a community perception to that effect. Such a charity would thus be ill positioned to confer status upon its donors, and hence less able to attract the kinds of donors with whom selfish donors might wish to associate.

These considerations suggest that if a charity is to appeal to selfish motives, it must do so indirectly.

There is a parallel difficulty, however, that confronts any charity that ignores the self-interested motives of potential donors. Most donors, even those with strongly altruistic concerns, have narrowly self-interested goals as well. Consider a charity that determinedly resists any opportunity to facilitate its donors' pursuit of selfish objectives. It collects their donations for an unquestionably worthy cause, but resists any step that might advantage them in the community. It does not publicly recognize major gifts, it does not hold social events, and so on. Charitable giving is an intensely competitive industry. Support for many worthy causes is organized by charitable groups that afford donors public recognition for large gifts, chances to mingle socially, and so on. Facing competitive pressures from charities organized along these broader lines, it would be difficult for a charity to survive if it refused to acknowledge, and attempted to serve, its donors' self-interested motives.

Note the parallels between the forces that govern the evolution of different types of motives in human populations and those that govern the evolution of different types of charitable organizations. In both cases it appears that populations consisting only of pure types are unlikely to be evolutionarily stable. In human populations consisting only of trustworthy persons, the level of vigilance will be low, which in turn will enable cheaters to make inroads. Likewise, in an environment in which all charitable organizations ignored the self-interested motives of their donors, there would be opportunities for organizations that took these motives into account.

At the other end of the scale, human populations in which cheaters predominate give rise to a climate of vigilance that fosters the growth of cooperative motives. The analog in the organizational context is that an environment consisting of charitable organizations that catered only to the selfish motives of donors would foster the growth of new organizations that broadened their appeal to include altruistic motives.

In sum, it appears that ecological forces will give rise to human population in which most people pursue a mix of selfish and altruistic motives, and a population of charitable organizations in which most groups attempt to appeal simultaneously to both types of motives. This characterization of charitable organizations and their donors has numerous specific implications for how these organizations might appeal most effectively for support.

The Central Role of the Cause Itself

Perhaps the most important message is that despite the importance of self-interested motives for most donors, a charitable organization's appeal for support must focus primarily on the worthiness of its cause. A campaign that begins with a fundamentally worthy cause at its core then has many opportunities to enhance its appeal by providing donors with opportunities to advance a variety of self-interested goals. But one that lacks a worthy cause is, for the reasons discussed earlier, almost certain to fail.

The Role of Affect

Many gifts are motivated not by rational deliberations about self-interest but by moral sentiments like sympathy and guilt. The most effective appeal in these cases will thus focus on triggering the relevant emotions. That this principle is well understood by many charitable organizations is evident from specific strategies for personalizing both the cause and the direct connection between organization and donor. Let us briefly consider these in turn.

STATISTICAL VERSUS IDENTIFIED LIVES

Thomas Schelling cites the example of a community that is willing to spend several million dollars to rescue a child trapped in an abandoned mine shaft, yet is unwilling to spend half a million dollars on an emergency coronary care ambulance that will save an average of five lives per year (Schelling 1984). The explanation is not that the community values the lives of trapped children much more in the abstract than it does the lives of potential heart attack victims. On the contrary, the community might very well be willing to spend even less per expected life saved on measures to prevent accidents in mines than on measures to save heart attack victims. Rather, the critical difference is that the child trapped in the mine is a known individual while the potential beneficiaries of the money are merely statistics. We see the child's grieving parents, we imagine ourselves in their position, we contemplate our sense of remorse if we fail to intervene. An identified life is vivid, it engages our emotions fully. Of course, we know in the abstract that future coronary victims will also be real people with grieving relatives. But the power of these imagined victims to engage our sympathies is much more limited. And hence the difference in our willingness to expend resources in the two situations.

Many charitable organizations appear to have grasped the importance of tying their cause to the plight of specific identified individuals. The March of Dimes, for example, has its poster child, and the Jerry Lewis telethons bring the beneficiaries into our living rooms. CARE knows that a photograph of a starving child will summon many more donations than an abstract appeal to end world hunger.

PERSONAL SOLICITATION

In a recent paper, Richard Freeman has found that, holding the worthiness of the cause constant, people are much more likely to make charitable donations when they are asked than when they are not (Freeman 1993). People may understandably feel that there are many more causes that deserve support than they can possibly support themselves. One could of course apportion one's limited support on the basis of an abstract assessment of the relative merits of the various causes. But it is hardly surprising that a given cause is more likely to make a donor's short list if it appeals to him directly. Most people are strongly motivated to win the approval of other people—friends in particular, and, to a lesser degree, even strangers. Failure to donate to an organization that doesn't ask courts no risk of face-to-face disapproval. When a friend requests a donation for a worthy cause, by contrast, both the abstract desire to support the cause and the more concrete motivation to please the friend work in tandem. Most charities are aware of this, of course, and rely on volunteer networks to solicit friends.

Opportunities for Anonymity

Although many, perhaps even most, donors find public recognition gratifying, there are at least some with a strong preference to remain out of the limelight. This group will include some whose motive is to avoid being solicited by charities they have no wish to support. But it will also include some whose pleasure in giving is enhanced by the fact that it was in no way motivated by the hope to win others' approval. Still others may wish to give anonymously in the secret hope that their identities will somehow leak out, thereby placing them in the admirable, if paradoxical, position of being known as generous anonymous givers. Attempts to accommodate such donors are fraught with practical difficulties, although we may suspect that in equilibrium there will inevitably be organizations that are willing discreetly to leak the identities of anonymous donors.

That there exist donors who prefer anonymity does not mean that organizations should call public attention to the fact that they offer opportunities for anonymous giving. Public announcements to that effect may create the impression that donations that receive public recognition are somehow less praiseworthy. Even if this is true, it is no reason to discourage donors who seek public approval. And in any event, those who really want to donate anonymously hardly need to be made aware of that possibility through public pronouncements. A charity need only recognize that some such donors exist, and to make every effort to maintain confidentiality if that is the donor's desire.

Matching Grants

Many charitable organizations have discovered the efficacy of matching grants—contingent donations under which a benefactor pledges to match others' gifts up to some specified amount. From the perspectives both of the initiator of a matching grant offer and of those who respond to it, this practice creates additional leverage. And if the ceiling of the benefactor's grant is not reached, or if the benefactor would not have given as much on other terms, the format does indeed increase total giving. Given that matching grants have positive effects and are virtually costless to administer, the puzzle is that they are not used even more widely. Even someone contemplating a $100 gift to her local radio station, for example, could achieve more impact by making her gift a matching grant. Yet most small donations are not in the form of matching grants.

Marketing Status

People acquire status in a variety of ways, almost all of which involve being compared favorably with other persons. Status acquisition thus has a zero-sum character. Actions or behaviors that enhance one actor's status involve reductions in status for others. When we frame the issue in these stark terms, it seems natural to wonder whether charitable organizations ought to act as agents in their donors' quest for status.

A moment's reflection about alternatives, however, suggests that this is an attractive role indeed. After all, the quest for status would continue unabated even if charities stood completely aloof from it; and many of the alternative means of pursuing social status are distinctly less attractive than charitable giving. For example, many people display their wealth by conspicuous consumption. From a social perspective, such behavior is a wasteful alternative to the display of wealth by charitable giving (Frank 1985; Glazer and Konrad 1992).

If a charitable organization wants to facilitate potential donors' quest for status, what can it do? One valuable service is to create opportunities for their leading donors to mingle with one another, as in fact many charitable and other nonprofit institutions routinely do. Universities, for example, often appoint, and convene regular meetings of, advisory councils that include their leading benefactors. The "charity ball" is another time-honored institution in this tradition. Still another device is to recognize donors by attaching their names to facilities, positions, or projects, as when a university creates an endowed professorship in a donor's name.

All of these activities confront the organization with the strategic calculation of how to distribute recognition and opportunities for association in the way that maximizes total value. To take an illustrative case, consider a university's decision about how many endowed professorships to create. The law of demand states that the lower the price of a good or service, the more units of it the public will wish to buy. Put slightly differently, it says that the more units of a good or service people already have, the less they will be willing to pay for an additional unit. This proposition will hold doubly for a "good" like public recognition, for as an institution attempts to distribute ever more recognition to its donors, its power to confer effective recognition on any of them diminishes sharply.

Suppose the curve labeled D in Figure 4 is the demand schedule for endowed professorships on the part of a university's donor community. If the uni-

Price ($/endowed chair)

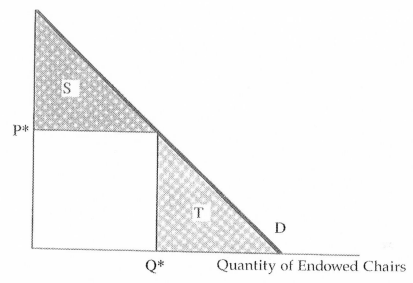

Figure 4. The Donor Demand Curve for Endowed Chairs

versity's goal were to maximize its total revenues from the sale of rights to endow chairs, and if it were forced to charge the same price to all donors of endowed chairs, its best bet would be to sell Q* endowed chairs at a price of P*
each, for total proceeds equal to P*Q*.[5] Donors who support endowed chairs
would receive an aggregate consumer surplus equal to the shaded triangle
labeled S in Figure 4.

This arrangement is inefficient in several respects. Note first in Figure 4 that
there are many donors who would be willing to donate less than P* to endow a
chair; and since there is no physical cost when a standard faculty position is
transformed into an endowed position, there is an implied loss in consumer surplus equal to the area of the shaded triangle labeled T in Figure 4.

Note also, however, that at the other end of the spectrum there are many
donors who would have been willing to pay much more than P* for the privilege
of endowing a chair in their name. At least some of these donors would actually
have preferred that the group of people whose names are attached to chaired
professorships be smaller, and hence more elite.

From the perspective of professors as well, the pricing policy described in
Figure 4 is inefficient. Among the group of professors not holding endowed
chairs, for instance, there are many who feel themselves worthy, and indeed
many who genuinely are worthy, of holding such positions. And among the
most distinguished of those currently holding endowed chairs, there will be
some who wish the number of chairs was considerably smaller than Q*.

By tinkering slightly with its endowed chair policy, the university can mitigate many of these inefficiencies. Suppose, for example, that in addition to the standard endowed chair it currently offers, it added a premium category with a title something like "distinguished university professorship." Chairs in both categories would bear the names of their respective donors, as now, but the distinguished professorship would sell for a premium price P_1^* that is greater than P^*, while the ordinary endowed professorship would sell for a price P_2^* that is less than P^*, as shown in Figure 5. With suitably chosen levels of P_1^* and P_2^*, it would be easy to assure that the total revenue raised from donors of endowed chairs, $P_1^*Q_1^* + P_2^*Q_2^*$, would exceed the total raised previously. What is more, the combined consumer surplus for the two categories of donors (S_1+S_2) would exceed aggregate consumer surplus under the single-category policy. And finally, the unexploited consumer surplus in the two-category case (shaded area T' in Figure 5) is smaller than the unexploited consumer surplus in the one-category case.

The number of categories of course need not be limited to two, and in general the more finely the market can be partitioned, the smaller the unexploited consumer surplus will be. Nor need the process be limited to the endowment of chairs. At the higher end, it can include endowed buildings, and even colleges. At the lower end it can include relatively modest scholarship or research endowments. Some institutions even allow donors to purchase named seats in auditoriums.

Issues similar to those that arise in connection with the marketing of endowed professorships, programs, and facilities are encountered in a host of other contexts. Universities elect boards of trustees, whose positions they reserve for their most influential and generous supporters. Often they also maintain much larger advisory councils, and here membership is more inclusive. Many other charities maintain several tiers of advisory boards, and also sponsor larger gatherings of supporters, such as annual social events. In all of these cases, the interests of donors and beneficiaries alike can be advanced by careful attention to the partitioning of the relevant markets.

Framing Manipulations

The recent work in cognitive psychology summarized earlier suggests a variety of possible ways in which a charity might frame its appeal for greatest effectiveness:

IN-KIND CONTRIBUTIONS

Richard Thaler describes the incongruous example of the man who would not mow his neighbor's lawn for $20, yet mows his own lawn even though his neighbor's son would be willing to do it for only $8 (Thaler 1980). The explanation, Thaler argues, is that people mentally code out-of-pocket expenses (here,

Price ($/endowed chair)

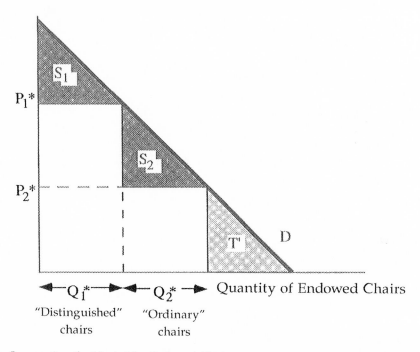

Figure 5. Segmenting the Market for Endowed Chairs

the $8) as losses, but code opportunity costs (here, the $20 not earned by mowing the neighbor's lawn) as forgone gains. The asymmetry between gains and losses discussed earlier lies behind the man's seemingly inconsistent decision.

The knowledge that forgone gains are psychologically less painful than out-of-pocket expenses suggests that a charitable organization may often be able to increase its support by appealing for donations in kind rather than in cash. Many charities, for example, sponsor benefit concerts in which services are donated not only by the featured musicians, but also by a constellation of other, much less visible support personnel.

The same principle may help explain why the parents of children attending expensive private schools often spend harried Friday evenings preparing items for the school's semiannual bake sale. Since most of these parents are highly paid professionals whose time is both scarce and valuable, it might seem more sensible for them simply to make additional cash contributions to their children's schools. The irony is that if out-of-pocket costs are accorded greater weight than opportunity costs, the bake sale may nonetheless be the more effective vehicle.[6]

"FREE" GIFTS TO DONORS

Many charitable organizations, among them public radio and television stations, offer contributors free gifts in return for their cash donations. This practice may seem puzzling at first glance, but on closer scrutiny it appears to make sense for at least several reasons. First, there is the silver-lining effect, which says that the overall disutility of a loss will be significantly reduced if it can be framed as a package that includes a small gain. Here the cash contribution is the loss and the token gift the small gain.

Gifts to donors might also be attractive because the gifts themselves can often be obtained as gifts from their manufacturers, whose generosity is enhanced by the perception that forgone gains are coded as less painful than out-of-pocket costs. Even without that perception, promotional gifts can generally be obtained at wholesale prices, whereas their value to donors is likely to be coded at the much higher retail prices. Another attractive feature of gifts is that they often bear the charity's logo, thereby calling favorable attention to donors.

SELLING DISCOUNT COUPONS

In the private sector, retail merchants often band together to sell books of discount coupons, which entitle bearers to reduced prices on various goods and services. This device is attractive in part because it enables sellers to target discount prices on those buyers for whom lower prices are most likely to affect purchase decisions. The reasoning here is that buyers for whom price matters little are unlikely to go to the trouble of buying, storing for future use, and then redeeming discount coupons. Another attractive feature is that the coupon books, like many other promotional devices, are a useful way to introduce new buyers to products. Offering a deep discount is good business if the buyer turns out to like the product and becomes a regular customer. Finally, the discount coupon booklets may be attractive because they encourage buyers to go to a particular retail district, where their trip to buy from one merchant may result in additional purchases from other merchants.

An interesting feature of discount coupon booklets is that, having bought one, people apparently feel duty bound to use it, at least for a while. Standard economic theory suggests that, once bought, the purchase price of a coupon booklet is a sunk cost, and hence the likelihood of using particular coupons in it ought to depend only on how the discounted prices compare with how much value a consumer assigns to the various products. As with many other sunk costs, however, there is evidence that buyers do not ignore the sunk cost of these booklets. Often they buy products that as non-coupon-book purchasers they would not have bought even at similarly deep discounts.

Ironically, a different pattern holds when discount coupon booklets are sold not by merchants but by charitable organizations. Here, people seem to ignore the sunk cost of their booklets, just as traditional economic theory predicts (Nye 1993). People seem to encode the price booklets as a charitable donation, not as a sunk cost they need to justify by subsequent purchase behavior. As a result, it may be possible that when the proceeds from the sale of discount booklets accrue to charitable organizations, merchants may be able to offer even deeper discounts than before, and this in turn should raise the price that consumers are willing to pay for the booklets.

EARMARKING

The free-rider hypothesis of traditional rational choice models is predicated on the notion that any single donor's gift constitutes such a small proportion of a charity's overall budget that it cannot appreciably alter the extent to which the charity achieves its mission. If the charity will succeed or fail independently of your own contribution to it, the argument goes, then why make the personal sacrifice?

The Weber-Fechner law discussed earlier suggests a psychological mechanism whereby charitable organizations might reduce the attractiveness of free riding. What an organization wants to prevent, specifically, is having the individual view her donation as a proportion of its overall budget. To this end, it can offer donors the opportunity to earmark their contributions for specific activities on a much smaller scale. Several decades ago, for example, I was a volunteer fund-raiser in a political campaign and was surprised to discover that the fee for 30-second radio commercials on local stations was only $10. We then framed our call for contributions as a request to fund individual radio spots ("Your gift of $100 will put 10 more George-Brown-for-Senate commercials on the air"), and donations increased substantially.

There is indirect evidence that giving donors a choice between funding any of several different specific activities may also enhance contributions. Gilovich, for example, found that sales of state lottery tickets increase dramatically when consumers are given the opportunity to pick their own winning number, rather than having it assigned by a random number generator (Gilovich 1991).

Concluding Remarks

In recent decades, the self-interest model of rational choice has become increasingly influential in the social and behavioral sciences. I have argued that this model provides an impoverished framework for thinking about the behavior of both charitable organizations and their donors.

The standard model is flawed not only in its characterization of human motives, but also in its portrayal of the efficacy with which people pursue these motives. Drawing on signaling and game theory in an evolutionary framework, I have described a broader portfolio of human motives, one that includes concerns not only about the well-being of others but also about status in various social hierarchies. I have also described recent work in cognitive psychology that suggests that people often pursue their goals inefficiently, and that the errors they make are often systematic rather than random. Finally, I have tried to show how the insights of this recent work help us achieve a clearer understanding of what charitable organizations and their supporters are up to.[7]

Notes

1. *The Complete Monty Python's Flying Circus: All the Words, Vol. 2.* New York: Pantheon, 1989, pp. 93–94.

2. Freeman, 1993. These estimates include imputations of the value of time spent in volunteer activities.

3. I develop this claim at length in Frank (1988).

4. The material in this section draws extensively on the arguments and evidence presented in Thaler (1985).

5. Of course, the university's calculation must also include another dimension, namely, the effect of variations in the total number of named chairs on the satisfaction received by the holders of those chairs. More on this point below.

6. Of course, bake sales and other in-kind contributions also promote social interaction, which may itself be of value to the donor.

7. I thank Daniel Kahneman for helpful discussions.

8 | Philanthropy in the African American Experience

Adrienne Lash Jones

WHILE THE PIVOTAL role of philanthropy and individual philanthropists is most often included in studies of African American history, as part of an examination of forces which helped to shape black social and institutional life, rarely is philanthropy itself the focus of study. Similarly, the emerging literature on the history of philanthropy rarely focuses on topics in African American history as part of the complex social history of America. Unfortunately, this discrepancy has resulted in misinterpretations about the history of African American experience, and the importance of the relationship of African Americans to the history of philanthropy in this nation. Emphasis on the importance of white philanthropic activity on behalf of blacks (which has indeed been considerable) has tended to underemphasize the philanthropic initiatives of blacks in their own behalf. Thus, the participation of black Americans in the philanthropic life of the larger society remains to be explored.

In order to reassess the history of black participation as both donors and recipients, however, it is critical to challenge modern conceptualizations and definitions of philanthropy, which separate acts of benevolence into basically two arbitrary categories. The first category, "charity or voluntarism," involves terms traditionally used to describe personal acts of compassionate gift giving, including gifts of time and talent. Until recently the term was mostly used to describe the work of women of means. "Philanthropy," on the other hand, describes large gifts of money or items of great monetary value by individuals, organizations, or institutions. As a result, the term "philanthropy" is most often identified with wealth, and wealthy people, while charity or voluntarism is more often identified with institutions or organizations which provide aid to and for the needy.

Neither of these definitions is concerned with the motives of the donors, or with the fact the recipients may be specified by the donor. The assumption seems to be that race and/or ethnicity of donor and recipient are not taken into consideration when decisions are made as to the nature and proportion of the acts or gifts. Yet, when the benevolent actions of African Americans are discussed, the term "self-help" is applied. Presumably, because their contributions are likely to be combinations of individual and organizational voluntarism, and/or monetary or material gifts of relatively small value whose beneficiaries are more clearly identified with the donors, this special category functions as a way to indicate a presumption that there is no benefit to the larger society. In other words, gifts of time, talent, and fortune of black Americans are less often acknowledged or considered for inclusion in our descriptions of charity and philanthropy because they are usually given by blacks for the specific purpose of raising the quality of life for members of their own community. Moreover, the historic low position which African Americans occupy in the nation's economy has sustained the presumption that their place in the history of philanthropy is inconsequential.

In this chapter I will argue that both the history of philanthropy and African American history can benefit by turning to a definition of philanthropy which not only recognizes the links between charity and philanthropy, but which also does not make a distinction between large and small gifts, or between those gifts which are especially targeted to particular interests, and those whose beneficiaries are more subtly defined by the donor. Thus, we will use the term "philanthropy" to describe "*any act* which expresses loving mankind; goodwill to fellow men [humanity]." These acts may be especially manifested "in *donations of money, property, or work* to needy persons or to socially useful purposes."[1] Further, we will use the term "benevolence" to qualify our definitions to emphasize the motivation for such acts, or in other words the disposition to do good, or to perform acts of kindness. By using these definitions, it is suggested that no distinction need be made between monetary gifts and gifts of labor, and that all gifts which are intended to serve socially useful purposes may be included without regard to the portion of society for which such donations are intended.

In addition, it is my contention that the term "self-help," which describes "a wide range of activities designed to promote the interests of an individual or a particular group," (E. Carson 1989, p. 93) in actuality describes the motive for most philanthropic initiatives. Although the term has most commonly been used to describe the collective efforts of minority racial or ethnic-oriented groups prior to their acceptance into the nation's mainstream, "self-help" is in no way particular to the experiences of these groups. Traditionally, gift giving, both large and small, benefits select populations whether by class, race, religion, or ethnicity, simply as a function of the nature of the gift. For example, though churches and religious organizations are very favored recipients of gifts from their particular constituencies, and are most likely solicited to enhance their work among a similar population, this form of philanthropy is rarely described as "self-help." Yet, because their gifts are dedicated to providing institutional and individualized support to encourage self-sufficiency and upward mobility for their own people, when describing similar efforts among blacks, the term "self-help" has effectively diminished the purpose and the benefits of their gifts of time, talent, and money.

By expanding or reconceptualizing definitions of philanthropy, and by refusing to continue to use terms which separate the various forms of gift giving, we provide a way to reanchor these acts of benevolence to the historic experiences of the majority of Americans. With this broader definition, the experiences of African Americans, as well as for other particular groups, are more easily identifiable as part of the larger tradition of philanthropy.[2] This reexamination is by no means an effort to diminish the enormous benefits of traditional forms of philanthropy. Rather, by using nontraditional examples as a means to rethink the concept, it is meant to suggest that by the use of new paradigms and definitions, we may better describe the experiences of a larger part of the population.

African Origins and Transformation of Traditional Gift Giving

Although the harsh realities of the slave system overwhelmed the lives and experiences of African American people during the antebellum period, the system could not eradicate all cultural memories of African people. These memories, which included traditions of sharing and giving, were important features of communal, familial life patterns on the African continent. They also served as critical links to the ways that many African people responded to their new environment and their new circumstances. However, these are also themes and traditions which demonstrate some of the difficulties inherent in trying to compare very dissimilar cultures. For example, although over time African people in the United States and the Americas embraced Judeo-Christianity, it is important to consider that they came with belief systems and values which were well grounded in a more ancient religious philosophy. Among these was a way of life which valued and understood the importance of achieving and maintaining the balance between individual or personal identity with one's responsibility as a member of society (Mbiti 1991). This ideal required cooperation and mutual support in all segments of life. Thus, an important feature of the socio-religious system of the African before slavery and colonization was to measure status according to one's ability to disperse wealth, rather than by accumulation of wealth. According to this tradition, there was no perceivably distinct category of sharing or giving which can be used to compare with Western notions of philanthropy.[3] Rather, giving aid and sharing resources was part of the fabric of everyday life.

Although the transition to slavery in the Americas completely disrupted the lives and traditions of the Africans, at the same time by its very nature, the institution of slavery did not permit their complete assimilation into the culture of the masters. Rather, the conditions under which most slaves lived required that they adapt and expand upon traditional forms of mutual support as a means to survive. Slave narratives and studies of slavery are the source of countless illustrations of the ways that the tradition of sharing, and the tradition of individuals taking responsibility for members of their group or community were among the most beneficial of these strategies. Though individual acts of benevolence could not include vast financial donations, there are many accounts of slaves sharing meager food supplies, clothing, and whatever other resources they could obtain. Also, there were the clandestine midnight reading and writing lessons which placed teachers and pupils at risk of severe punishment or death, informal child adoptions by kin and non-kin, and the sharing of information, which could be invaluable aids to facilitate escape for members of the slave community. Within the constraints of the slave system, these were acts of benevolence which cannot be measured in dollar amounts, but because of the risk to the donor, could be counted among the most precious, that is the gift of life.[4]

Yet, despite obvious limitations, such acts of benevolence and altruism in fact accomplished positive goals for the survival and maintenance of values for their communities in much the same measure as the more visible and acknowledged altruism of their more affluent and famed counterparts in the majority society. In their own way, each segment of society was motivated by the will to improve the circumstances of their community, and each produced personal satisfaction on the part of the "donors," even though there is no easy basis for comparison. For the wealthy, philanthropy functioned as a vehicle for upward social mobility. The benevolent activities which took place within the slave community were meant to improve the lives of individuals who were caught up in a system of physical, emotional, and cultural oppression. Thus, this form of benevolence has been overlooked and dismissed as merely a form of personal survival. However, a reassessment of the motivation and "cost" to the individuals who participated in the routine subversion directed the effects of the slave system, may suggest that African-descended people managed not only to survive, but they were able to sustain many important values and practices from their traditional cultures. Moreover, recent studies increasingly suggest that this somewhat hidden community life of the slaves was influenced and molded to a much greater extent than had been acknowledged, by a fusion of traditional cultures and values which are directly traceable to their African origins. Thus, it is imperative that we continue to study traditions of benevolence in order more accurately to recreate the spirit in which many unselfish acts were performed.

The difficulties in trying to trace the transition of values under the slave system, from traditional religious principles to their incorporation of the values and traditions of Christian charity, are great. They are somewhat less formidable in the study of free blacks during the same period. For the latter, the blending of traditional and Christian values becomes apparent as early as the eighteenth century. With the formation of black church denominations and secular societies, traditions of communal responsibility as well as the larger sense of societal responsibility are found among their records.

For example, even though money was scarce, in most African American congregations members were constantly called upon to collect clothing, to provide shelter, and to share food and other necessities with runaway slaves and poverty-stricken neighbors. Careful scrutiny of church records reveals that these activities were not undertaken as special appeals or efforts, but rather they were considered to be part of the routine business of the church. Also, women's aid societies, Dorcas societies, and benevolent societies, particularly in Northern black communities, were constantly involved in fund-raising activities, and their sole purpose seems to have been to provide charity relief for the poor. However, these activities have been overlooked by researchers, because the efforts of these groups were ongoing and they did not always describe themselves as charitable organizations. For this reason, researchers must look beyond written documents to examine certain cultural practices, some of which are common even today. For example, multiple collections were and are commonplace during services in many black churches. Collections for special purposes have always been part of the routine within the worship service. Consequently, monies are difficult to track, as neither donor nor recipient is required to account to an intermediary, other than their immediate constituency. Moreover, since these donations came from the poorest segment of the population, it is important to recognize, acknowledge, and interpret them as acts of philanthropy.[5]

Voluntary services to churches and organizations within their own communities were also sometimes extended to benefit the larger community, particularly during times of crisis. One often cited example is the response of blacks to a crisis in the city of Philadelphia in 1793. When a cholera epidemic swept the city, church founders Absolam Jones and Richard Allen personally went out among the sick to offer public assistance work along with many of their church members. Their motivation to respond to the crisis was recorded in a pamphlet in which the two leaders attempted to answer what they determined to be racially based, false accusations of misconduct on the part of black church members. "It was our duty to do all the good we could to our suffering fellow mortals," they wrote, "[because] it is . . . a generally received opinion in this city, that our colour was not so liable to the sickness as the whites" (Jones and Allen 1962, pp. 32–36). Unfortunately, color proved not to make the difference as to who survived and who died from the disease, and some of the black Samaritans lost their lives in the effort to help their fellow human beings.

Along with the religious groups, early secular societies also organized to meet basic needs in their communities. For example, an advertisement which appeared in the Philadelphia *Gazette* on March 1, 1831, detailed the purpose of the establishment of numerous benevolent and mutual aid societies. This rare document also lists the expenditures of the organizations. Here the authors stated that most organizations were formed to pool resources for mutual protection, much like their African ancestors who had similar benefit societies.

However, they also suggested a philosophy of philanthropic outreach within the black community as their Preamble makes clear:

> Whereas, we believe it to be the duty of every person to contribute as far as is in their power towards alleviating the miseries, and supplying the wants, of those of our fellow beings who, through the many misfortunes and calamities to which human nature is subject, may become fit objects for our charity. And whereas, from the many privations to which we as people of colour are subject, and our limited opportunity of obtaining the necessities of life, many of us have been included in the number dependent on those provisions made by law, for the maintenance of the poor; therefore, as we constitute a part of the public burden, we have deemed it our duty to use such means as was in our reach to lessen its weight.[6]

The authors also explained that "by contributing a trifling sum to these funds while in prosperity, we not only secure to ourselves a pension in sickness and adversity, but also contribute to the relief of our distressed brethren" (Aptheker 1964, p. 110).

Earlier, minutes of the Boston African Society, established in 1796, indicate the genesis of the kind of initiative which has been most persistent among African Americans; namely, the pooling of funds to aid families who were left without their primary provider. Organizations such as these have most often been categorized as precursors to mutual aid or insurance societies. However, their documents indicate a secondary purpose which is consistent in organizational documents during that period: the responsibility to care for the youth among them. This is evident in the "Laws of the African Society," which set out as their purpose,

> When any Member, or Members of the Society is sick, and not able to supply themselves with necessaries, suitable to their situations; the committee shall then tender to them and their family whatever the Society have or may think fit for them. . . . Should any Member die, and leave a lawful widow and children, the Society shall consider themselves bound to relieve her necessities . . . and that the Society do the best in their power to place the children so that they may in time be capable of getting an honest living.[7]

Although this example indicates that benefits were specifically designated to be used for members who contributed to the general fund through the regular payment of dues, the emphasis is on community responsibility, and does not appear to be exclusive to members. For these early African Americans, there was no question that they considered it to be their responsibility to provide access to a pool of funds for *any* needy person in the community.

These examples are not unique. A study of the Prince Hall Masons, the nation's oldest black fraternal order, founded in 1776, emphasizes its tradition of charity among members and in the general community. According to William Muraskin, in *Middle Class Blacks in a White Society*, the organization has long boasted that "charity is inseparable from Masonry and requires that the brethren never turn a deaf ear toward others" (Muraskin 1975, p. 65).[8] Likewise, studies of early free black women's societies indicate that although their primary purpose was to function as quasi-insurance societies, a secondary function of the organizations was to provide aid to women outside of their immediate circle in the way of emergency funds, personal attention, and material goods (Jones 1984).

During the antebellum period, perhaps the most poignant acts of charity were those efforts which free blacks made to raise money to purchase freedom for those who had been left behind in slavery. In some cases they were relatives or friends, but not in every case. In spite of limited earning opportunities and poor wages, accounts of this brand of charity and fund sharing are found in numerous official documents and personal accounts from the antebellum period. These particular efforts help make the most compelling arguments of all for reconsidering the categories into which we have artificially compartmentalized philanthropy and self-help. Charitable actions and benevolent gifts among African Americans were inextricably tied to antislavery activity. The underground railroad, mutual aid societies, antislavery publications, and all other forms of community involvement were dependent upon personal and organizational voluntarism, and upon donations from blacks as well as from their white sympathizers. It would be hard to refute the notion that the motive to uplift humankind from the horrors of the slave system was as compelling as the will to survive.

During that same dark period in America's history, there is no question that African Americans were the recipients of a great amount of philanthropy from white church groups that furnished books, clothing, and other necessary items to aid the needy. These groups also financed much of the abolitionist activity in the Northern states. However, it is also true that white philanthropy has in many ways overwhelmed the literature. As a result, the idea has persisted that African Americans are only recipients of philanthropy, and never providers. Yet upon reexamination of the evidence, it is clear that from the perspective of African Americans, their philanthropy can best be understood as necessarily based on a history of both practical and philosophical concerns, which while at times different from those of European Americans were nonetheless selfless and altruistic. At a time when help from whites was limited to contributions from a small group of abolitionists, church and organization records provide countless indications that blacks were active volunteers and donors, even though their contributions were mostly invisible.

The Postbellum Era

For black Americans during the first twenty-five years after Emancipation, philanthropy became critical for survival and progress. At this time, the major philanthropy within the community came from the same sources as during the earlier era; namely, the churches and an increasing number of secret/benevolent societies. Simply put, organizations which existed on a small or localized scale in the antebellum era, were pressed to expand southward, and some, as in the case of the religious denominations, became national institutions. Fraternal societies, churches, and women's organizations continued to do what they had always done, that is, collect and pool funds and material resources for a variety of causes, carry members of their communities through periods of illness and difficult times, and provide for burials.[9]

In his ground-breaking study of Philadelphia's black population, W. E. B. DuBois noted the importance of secret societies among blacks as second only to the church for organized philanthropic activity. According to his accounts, these societies were originally popular among blacks because their practices of ritual and secrecy were reminiscent of traditional African mysticism (DuBois 1970). However, the societies quickly evolved to incorporate a range of functions, including, in many cases, very effective and efficient work as insurance and benevolence associations.

Though their primary function was to provide help for members who paid in as a form of insurance, evidence of philanthropic activity outside of the membership of these organizations is found in numerous examples. One such example is the Independent Order of Saint Luke, organized in 1867 as a women's sickness and death mutual benefit association. The organization grew to become a powerful business empire among blacks in Richmond, Virginia, and at one time included ownership of a department store, a bank, and a weekly newspaper.[10] According to Elsa Barkley Brown, the organization and its leader Magi Lena Walker were not only interested in becoming business and financial leaders. They placed equal importance on the social and spiritual growth of the community, and the profits from the businesses often supported a number of other organizations and efforts, including an industrial school for girls and a national training school. In explaining the mixture of interests which were represented in the group, and the motivations of women who were the backbone of the Order, Barkley Brown highlights their sense of the importance of continuity in their benevolent activity, building on traditions of caring for the needy from an earlier era. The women emphasized the need to provide support for training and enrichment for youth, and offer a good example of the merger of the value of collective consciousness and racial identity and the concept of race as family. In her analysis of the purpose of the organization Barkley Brown concludes,

> Saint Luke women built on tradition. A well organized set of institutions, maintained community in Richmond: mutual benefit societies, interwoven with extended families and churches, built a network of supportive relations. The families, churches, and societies were all based on similar ideas of collective consciousness and collective responsibility. Thus, they served to extend

and reaffirm notions of family throughout the community. Not only in their houses but also in their meeting halls and places of worship, they were brothers and sisters caring for each other. (Brown 1988, p. 182)

Just as the cultural context for the tradition of sharing was maintained and reinforced by the conditions of the slave system, legal and de facto segregation outside it served to nurture the sense of racial identity and community, and to transform the idea of mutual aid and self-sufficiency for the race. This included demonstrating their sense of responsibility through philanthropic acts. Following the example of other religious and ethnic minorities, black Americans struggled to build communities by creating institutions and coalitions among themselves, and by forging coalitions with wealthy white sympathizers.

For some this meant accommodating to a system of race exclusivity, and at times this also meant pandering to racial stereotypes. The stereotype of the dependent African American after slavery ended was in part the result of severe poverty and critical needs. Because African Americans could appeal to the sensibilities of potential individual benefactors, institutional representatives resurrected and reinstituted the demeanor of the humble beggar. Black fund-raisers realized that this was an effective way to facilitate fund-raising activities. Perhaps the best-known user of this kind of appeal to donors was Booker T. Washington, the most successful fund-raiser of the era. By articulating a race ideology which essentially conceded that African Americans were better off by not attempting to compete with superior whites for political and economic opportunity, Washington was rewarded with the largest share of philanthropic support for his school, the Tuskegee Institute. Moreover, because his ideas became so enormously popular, white philanthropists came to rely on his opinion and approval for nearly all of their support for black educational institutions. Washington's success as a fund-raiser made him a role model for others who desperately needed the support of white donors. Thus, not only his manner, but also his accommodationist ideas, became key to getting positive results from donors.

This form of dependency was the result of two important factors. First, because no provisions were made by the government to compensate the former slaves, blacks became the largest and most needy group in America. Second, and equally compelling, was the fact that black Americans represented a vast reserve labor force at a time when labor unions were challenging their industrial employees. The fact that labor unions usually excluded blacks, and they were eager to work, made them perfectly suitable potential strikebreakers. Donors recognized that even though the funds which they directed to black institutions usually were only a fraction of the amount given for similar causes for whites, they were critical to this impoverished population. Moreover, the institutions which were designated as recipients of their philanthropy were most often those which stressed ethics and skills which would be most useful if blacks were needed in the workforce. In spite of sometimes questionable motives, however, were it not for these same benefactors necessities such as education, health care, and social services would have been almost nonexistent. Perhaps not by coincidence, the industrialists and philanthropists whose charitable donations built countless schools, hospitals, and social service agencies for blacks also augmented implementation of the newly emerging race segregation laws which effectively assured black Americans a place at the bottom of the economic ladder.

A tragic secondary result of this form of benevolence in the post-Reconstruction era was its confirmation of a popular and persistent perception of the relationship of African American citizens to organized philanthropy. Prior to that time, pious justifications for maintaining the nation's slave system included rationalizing that because Africans and their descendants were dependent, childlike creatures, they were best-off when cared for by white masters and mistresses. Although this characterization of the slaves was in fact distinctly contradictory to reality, these images were part of an evolving rationale for maintaining race separation.

The Era of Organization

In the period between the late nineteenth century, and the end of World War I, while wealthy white Americans established and supported numerous institutions of education, culture, and social service, black Americans also were involved in a virtual frenzy of philanthropic activity in response to the tremendous needs within their community. With more than four million blacks released from slavery with little or no education, and few social structures to support them, black and white church denominations and secular organizations scrambled to open schools, orphanages, homes for the aged, and hospitals. These institutions were founded not only because of the tremendous needs of blacks, but also in response to their systematic exclusion from institutions which were already established to serve a white clientele. At a time when public resources for needy Americans were minimal at best, the passage of legislation to separate the races in the South, and a growing sense that this was an acceptable and preferable way to manage race relations in both North and South, meant that white institutions were not inclined to accommodate blacks, and blacks were hard-pressed to find ways to help their own.

In many ways, exclusion from majority institutions became the impetus for unity among black citizens. All-black organizations and institutions, which became the model for so-called "race uplift," satisfied yearnings for self-improvement as well as providing access to education and social services for an increasingly isolated population. By successfully managing minimal funds and meager resources, virtually thousands of black Americans were taught to read and write, manage small farms, and launch a variety of projects which moved them closer to self-sufficiency.

At the same time, the era was fraught with contradictions in regard to relations between the races. Consequently, idealistic aspirations held by black Americans to achieve self-sufficiency were compromised by severe economic realities. Moreover, as jim crow laws grew ever more restrictive, donors were likely to force recipients to conform to increasingly stringent requirements which at times, rather than fostering independence, made them less well equipped to move up the economic ladder.

For example, in order to allay concerns that classical education for blacks would make them dissatisfied with menial employment, Northern donors were likely to fund what they referred to as "practical" education such as domestic sciences and industrial arts. Many of the all-black schools which started out with aspirations to create an elite leadership group, were forced to subtly alter classical curriculums, to emphasize more lower-grade vocational courses.[11] Also, inferior segregated facilities such as libraries, hospitals, YM and YWCAs were rationalized by white benefactors to be better alternatives for blacks than mainstream institutions, because there they would not have to compete with superior whites for education and services. Further, the separate institutions were thought to be the best sites for personal improvement. In other words, the promise of the American dream was to be pursued by both races by gaining experience within segregated institutions (Mjagkij 1992).

Excellent illustrations of the complexities of this period are found in the records of black women's clubs, where records of the organizations indicate that in order to cope with the economic and social realities in their community, members worked to achieve race uplift on two fronts. On the one hand they worked to build local and national independent all-black organizations like those clubs which were under the umbrella of the National Association of Colored Women. At the same time black women also pressed for integration as members of segregated units of predominantly white movements and organizations like the Young Women's Christian Association and women's suffrage and temperance organizations. In these examples, self-sufficiency meant utilizing all opportunities, in spite of the economic and social limits which defined the boundaries of a racially segregated society.

To illustrate their work in all-black organizations, the National Association of Colored Women, the most prominent organization of black women at the turn of the century, provides an excellent case study. Their motto, "lifting as we climb," succinctly expresses their optimistic belief that the race would and could overcome the obstacles of segregation and degradation, and that they, as women, would be active participants in the process. The motto of racial uplift also spoke to their condition as black women, burdened with racially charged sexual and sexist stereotypes. The organization served as a national umbrella for a federation of state and local women's clubs whose activities ranged from sponsoring and leading so-called Mother's Clubs to teach hygiene and parenting skills, to building full-fledged social service institutions such as day care centers, orphanages, settlement houses, and safe homes for working women.

As part of their commitment to the national organization's goals, local affiliated clubs usually worked independently in their communities, raising funds by a variety of sponsored events such as cake and handicraft sales, auctions, contests of all kinds, bazaars, and teas to subsidize indigent families, and to furnish supplies for classes which were taught by club women volunteers. In other cases, with larger projects, such as organizing social service institutions and schools, the women had to look outside of the black community to find sufficient funds. This meant soliciting the support of white businesses and individual donors. Nevertheless, the consistent common motivation for all of these efforts was a desire to improve the quality of life for all black people. Club members were dedicated to supporting women and their families in all aspects of their lives, and in their own way within the limits of race relations during this era of jim crow, were phenomenal in their ability to accomplish so much with so few resources.

One important kind of independent philanthropy which was typical for these organizations was the in-kind contributions of their more affluent members, who incidentally were usually the leaders. As an example, in Buffalo, New York, club woman Mary B. Talbert opened her home for classes to teach young women the manners and morals of their middle-class mentors. Such topics as proper dress, personal hygiene, diction, and contemporary politics were stressed, as the women mixed training in practical skills with their enthusiasm for race consciousness. Talbert also allowed the young women to conduct social functions in her home, as a way to make sure that they would be in a safe and supportive environment and away from the possible embarrassment of being turned away from a white facility (L. Williams 1992). For Talbert and other women of her class, philanthropy meant finding a means to build pride and self-esteem among the young and to model the social skills which they considered to be imperative for upward social and economic mobility.

While this kind of activity would not at first glance seem to qualify as philanthropy, when placed in the context of the racial climate of the times their priorities seem appropriate. The era is often described by historians as the "Nadir," or worst of times for blacks in this country. Given the severe economic restrictions for blacks which resulted from limited access to higher education, lack of job opportunities, social instability, and the violence to which many were subjected because of race, what these women were offering to their communities was a formula for maintaining dignity and self-confidence, however meager the funds which they were able to raise, and however distorted their motivations and methods may seem today.

Local organizations affiliated with the NACW also prided themselves on their ability to raise funds toward nationally identified causes. While some of these efforts directly benefited their home communities, quite a few were directed to larger-scale national projects. For example, the New Jersey Federation of Colored Women reported that they "put Negro books in the library in Summit"; gave out "many baskets to the poor and needy in [their] community and in Mississippi, Georgia, and Florida"; and "rented rooms for very small sums" to young women with low-paying jobs. At the same time, they also proudly donated monies to the organization's national project which was to purchase and restore the home of Frederick Douglass in Washington, D.C (E. Davis 1933, p. 360).

On a larger scale, an illustration of the way locally based organized philanthropy, fully funded by the efforts of black club women, is Atlanta's Neighborhood Union. As in most cities where women's clubs were organized, the Union's founders and leadership core comprised mostly middle-class, educated women, many of whom were wives of faculty members at local black colleges or wives of prominent black Atlantans (Rouse 1989, p. 89). The women organized after they learned of an incident in the city in which a black woman died, apparently as a result of a lack of medical care because her neighbors failed to recognize the seriousness of her illness and did not intervene in time to be helpful. When the women learned of the tragedy, Lugenia Burns Hope, wife of the president of Atlanta Baptist College (later Moorehouse College), called a meeting for neighborhood women to "become better acquainted with one another and to improve the neighborhood in every way possible."[12]

After completing a survey of the neighborhood, the group quickly identified the need for a more systematic approach to improving communication within the community, and for working with young people and their mothers. Between 1908 and 1919 the organization grew to be a citywide entity among black women, with community work in nineteen neighborhood zones. The group also opened a centrally located Neighborhood House, a health center, a day care facility, and a variety of projects for the improvement of conditions among Atlanta's black community.

During the earliest meetings, the group determined that their members would not be "beggars." Rather, they would make and pay their own way. This determination was consistent with their sensitivity to negative stereotypes of blacks and especially black women.[13] To accomplish the work, each member was assessed a set fee which she could either raise herself or pay outright. The goal was to foster cooperation within the community, and to encourage racial independence in financial matters.

The first outreach program for girls by the Union followed a typical pattern. Usually, as in Buffalo and Atlanta, middle-class black women leaders began by opening their homes for community projects. Mrs. Hope, an extraordinary organizer and social reformer, opened her home for embroidery lessons for young girls in her community. Lessons were taught by volunteers who used this opportunity not only to become acquainted with the girls, but to gather information about what other classes the young women would like, and most importantly, about health problems in their families. Subsequently, the group organized classes in cooking and nutrition and sewing. They also brought in a nurse professional for "demonstrations on care for the home and bathing the sick" (Neverdon-Morton 1989, p. 147).

When classes outgrew their homes, members began a campaign to find other quarters which could accommodate a full schedule of activities. After several false starts toward renting their own space, and by adding classes which met at various sites, including "colored" public school buildings, churches, and college facilities, the Union finally purchased a building in 1912 and still better quarters in 1914.

Fund-raising followed strict guidelines, which kept the Union's finances completely within the control of the black community. In order to supplement the minimal fee assessment, Union members organized suppers and charged admission, sold books, sponsored activities such as benefit banquets, bridge tournaments, track meets, bake sales, carnivals, and baseball games, and printed formal solicitation cards for donations. They also organized a men's auxiliary "whose duty it [is] to assist the Union in stamping out anything that tends to injure the morals of the community."[14] The auxiliary also aided in the solicitation and disbursement of funds.

The funds which were raised were placed in the Colored Savings Bank, where assets could have a direct impact on the economic health of the community. Black businesses were always featured in their solicitation program booklets as donors as well as advertisers. For health projects, black physicians and nurses were enlisted to donate services, and teachers from black colleges were recruited to offer classes on a variety of subjects. While classes were given for no charge to community residents, for those who lived outside of the original targeted community, the Union charged ten cents a lesson. Later, fees were assessed according to ability to pay, and for the specific services which were rendered. Members also made pledges to raise or donate funds to cover the payments on their mortgaged property.

On rare occasions, the women solicited political help from white women, and a few white organizations supported the group with financial donations. For example, after investigating the poor conditions of most of the city's colored schools, members decided that they needed to solicit the support of "other factions of the community." In order to confirm their findings, and to gain the political clout needed to improve the situation, they visited "every influential white woman in Atlanta" (Neverdon-Morton 1989, p. 153). However, the group self-consciously remained as independent as it could in order to minimize the possibility that they might be forced to compromise their goals to accommodate the wishes of white donors.

The work of the Neighborhood Union in Atlanta helps to demonstrate the difficulty inherent in trying to categorize philanthropy among blacks. By the use of active voluntarism and creative fund-raising, and in a few cases with the help of private philanthropy, the women modeled the true meaning of benevolence within their community. Because the work was done by women and men of the race, and their efforts were directed to help others in the race, it has been marginalized and categorized as "racial self-help," rather than as philanthropy. However, we do not apply this label to similar efforts, when wealthy business and industrial leaders designate funds for single denominational or segregated facilities to uplift their particular clientele. The only difference in these efforts seems to be the race of the donors and recipients. The tireless benevolent work of black women, with cooperation from the men of their community, would certainly seem to merit consideration as philanthropy, even though their efforts were purposely directed toward the purpose of improving the quality of life for African Americans.

In an alternative to the work of Atlanta's black club women, where funds were raised from wealthy whites to provide much-needed services for blacks, we still find the black community contributing volunteer services and a lesser portion of the monetary commitment. This very prevalent model helps to highlight the contradictions between categories such as "self-help" and "philanthropy," and again indicates the difficulty in trying to find ways to make such distinctions.

To illustrate the case, it is useful to consider the founding of a social service institution for black women in Cleveland, Ohio. In 1911, when a small group of black domestic workers organized an effort to provide safe housing for black women migrants, they were essentially responding to conditions which they felt were critical, out of their own personal experience. In doing so they also provided a way for whites to solve a problem regarding race which was increasingly confronting fast-growing Northern cities. The black women in this instance were not members of the middle class, but were women who had come north to work. When they arrived in the city, they discovered that the Young Women's Christian Association, which housed newly migrating white women, would not accommodate them. Even worse, there was simply no systematic way to find safe housing for rent. However, all this changed when the small group, who called themselves the Working Girls Home Association, elected Jane Hunter as their leader. The group of mostly Southerners started out with traditional local fund-raising efforts within the black community, such as dinners, rallies, and special events, and as in the previous model, each member pledged to set aside a nickel of her earnings each week, toward rental of a house for newly migrating women like herself. However, Jane Hunter had bigger ideas.

When she first came to the city, like many before her, Hunter sought assistance and housing from the YWCA, but was turned down because of her race. This initial rejection did not deter her from going back to ask for help for her organization. The idea of a separate facility was very appealing to the leadership of the YWCA, because it would relieve them from pressures from the black community to integrate their programs and their newly built residence. Thus, with very little prodding, Hunter gained support from the organization, as well as from a number of white church women in the city.

However, the financial support for the project came at a price. Hunter and her group were forced to relinquish control of their organization and the institution which would grow out of their original plan. The tone was set early on. A potential major donor demanded that members of the original group disband and reorganize to make room for what he considered to be a more "competent" group of white women. He further stipulated that the white women must compose the majority of board members and assume the management of finances for the home. The white women who accepted the offer to serve were mostly officers of the YWCA, including its president, who then also became head of the new organization, the Phillis Wheatley Association. Another concession was made when white board members demanded that in exchange for their voluntary "expertise" they should be allowed to choose the blacks who would serve along with them. This meant that black community leaders could not select their representatives as leaders of their own race institution. Perhaps the most serious concession was a promise that along with providing living quarters for the women, the new institution would also be responsible for providing training for domestic work, so that the residents would be eligible for referral as servants for their white supporters.

Although these concessions were bitterly opposed by the majority of blacks in the city, because of their opposition to segregated services and facilities, there seemed to be no alternative. Although blacks had successfully resisted attempts to start up a segregated YMCA, and several attempts to open an all-black settlement house, in the era when blacks were moving north in large numbers, there was no time to continue the fight. The need was immediate, and there were too few funds available among the relatively small black population to open and sustain the much-needed facility. Eventually, it was this reality which gained support among a number of black women and men. While many would continue to argue that white institutions had an obligation to open their doors to blacks, at the same time in this prewar period, there was no argument that social services for these migrants were virtually nonexistent. The home opened in 1913, in a twenty-three-room house, with a predominantly white board of trustees, a white president, and a year's payment on the rent.

After the first flack, blacks in Cleveland came around to supporting the home because it filled a critical need. Large donations from wealthy whites were supplemented with funds raised from the black community. Although they could not control the institution, black women volunteers played an important role in the day-to-day operation of the home, and black organizations were formed to support the many skills training and social uplift programs which were introduced. Even though many disliked the home's domestic work referral service activity, it was conceded that it was a practical solution to employment needs for the women in the home, since this was the only work available to most black women at the time.

In 1918, just at the end of World War I, the Phillis Wheatley Home moved into a forty-five-room apartment building, which they renovated. At that time, suggestions that the home might become a branch of the YWCA were fiercely resisted by the city's largest donors, who threatened to withdraw support. Because blacks in the city had long resisted segregation, whites feared that if they were allowed to become affiliated with the YWCA, they may not be content to stay within the limits of programs and the facilities of the Phillis Wheatley, but would demand to be included in other YWCA activities. Therefore, when the issue of merger was raised as a serious consideration, wealthy benefactors threatened to cut all support for the Phillis Wheatley.

In 1922, the association announced a capital fund-raising drive for $550,000 to build a new, larger facility. This campaign, racially the most integrated effort in the city, was headed by two very wealthy and prominent white women, in cooperation with the white president of the board. According to Hunter, black women and men established a nucleus of $15,000 to start off the drive. Soon, a major gift of $25,000 came from one of the white board members, and by 1924, pledges of $90,000 had come from other major (white) donors. With these gifts, the fund grew to $130,000. Hunter was thrilled to note that many of the gifts came from ordinary working black people like the cook at the Phillis Wheatley, who gave $100, and another worker who gave $250 of her life savings.

Armed with the local pledges, the women were able to obtain a matching pledge of $100,000 from John D. Rockefeller, Jr. They broke ground for an eleven-story building in 1927, the largest independent facility for black women in the nation. When the issue of merger with the YWCA was raised once again, white donors put the matter to rest by making it very clear that they would support the Phillis Wheatley Association *only* if it remained a separate institution with an interracial board. There was to be no alternative. The campaign was split into a colored section and a section for white donors. Fund-raising committees met separately, with whites meeting at the city's most exclusive men's club during the day and blacks meeting in the evenings at any facilities which would accommodate them. At times, Jane Hunter was forced to enter the white meetings from the service elevator. However, by then black leaders were more comfortable with having a "race uplift" institution, even if it was basically a project to keep the races separate. The building was dedicated in April 1928, with Dr. Robert R. Moton, President of Tuskegee Institute, delivering the main address (Jones 1990).

Jane Hunter was a true disciple of Booker T. Washington. This brand of philanthropy, white support for so-called race institutions, was accepted as the practical way to cope with some of the realities of race segregation, and was tolerated as a means to establish larger and more financially solid institutions than funds from within the black community could support. Moreover, some black people felt that even though the institutions were controlled by white philanthropists, blacks themselves, who were the majority of the volunteers and staff, could influence positive results by their daily interactions with clients. Thus, blacks rationalized that the sacrifice of control of institutions was well worth the good that could be done for their community. Black women and men also were very dedicated fund-raisers and donors. In spite of the obvious limits to their ability to play a principal financial role, in proportion to income their pledges and their participation were outstanding indications that these institutions were seen to be essential philanthropic work.

The Second Half of the Century

While such efforts as those illustrated above were understood by blacks to be part of the strategy toward eventual equality of access to economic and social opportunities, in many ways they also profoundly effected the perception that black Americans could be placated and satisfied with little effort and minimal funds from the majority society. This notion persisted in the literature of church denominations, philanthropic foundations, government agencies, and charitable institutions during the entire first half of the twentieth century, and was not changed until after the civil rights movement, when protests by blacks for more "power" over their own destinies and within American institutional life signaled a change of mood. Undoubtedly, the stereotypes which grew from the circumstances of an earlier era, help to explain how and why race relations in the United States remained basically static through the first half of the century. Although there were incremental steps toward race integration, with significant court victories and the post–World War II abolishment of strict segregation in the armed forces, jim crow laws continued to prevail in the Southern states until the mid-1960s, and race discrimination was blatantly practiced in the North and West.

In spite of an increase in the numbers of black businesses and trained professional personnel as an immediate result of opportunities which followed World War II, the lag between the incomes of white Americans and their black counterparts remained sufficiently significant to suggest that race patterns were the determining factor in shaping opportunities for economic and social mobility for most Americans. Moreover, access to white collar jobs, which resulted from mid-1960s civil rights legislation, failed to bring parity to the economic positions of the majority of blacks and whites with similar education and work experience (see Sinton 1990).

At the same time it must be noted that each decade of the post–World War II era brought about significant changes in black Americans' lives, which are reflected in their philanthropic activity. White responses to appeals from blacks changed as well, though more slowly than might have been expected. In the period between 1950 and 1990, only a detailed decade-by-decade retrospective could adequately assess patterns of philanthropy as they reflect radical changes in race relations. Still, a few points stand out as key to understanding yet another generation of transitions in the experience of philanthropy as it affects and is affected by African American people.

For example, in the immediate post–World War II era, when Americans finally came to terms with the real effects of an economic and social segregation system which threatened to impede the nation's progress as a world power, it also became clear that the jim crow system must be dismantled. Black soldiers returned from a war in Europe against a racism and fascism, to a system of racism and oppression which they could no longer tolerate. In spite of the slow and deliberate efforts of organizations such as the National Association for the Advancement of Colored People, changes in segregationist practices in the South did not occur fast enough to prevent the escalation of activities which indicated massive dissatisfaction and more vigorous resistance on the part of blacks. Thus, the period between 1945 and 1960 witnessed the largest migration of black families in the nation's history, from rural areas in the South to what they hoped would be more hospitable industrial areas in the North.

Unfortunately, the migrants found that the move north and west did not relieve the racial isolation of their former segregated communities. Although the move sometimes gave them access to better-paying jobs, housing practices were such that blacks were again relegated to pockets within large urban areas in which they recreated, for a time, the same kinds of support networks as had always sustained them. New churches opened on street after street, and the middle class, who were also trapped in the segregated neighborhoods because of racial constraints, focused the major portion of their energies as well as their funds on actions to open up the broad range of social services which had excluded blacks from their clientele. Often with particular newly energized campaigns, Northern blacks moved to force established agencies to integrate their staffs as well as their facilities. At the same time, they also fought for fair housing laws which would allow them to integrate formerly all-white neighborhoods. Older, more established organizations within the community strained to meet the complex needs of the growing black population, and as a result, blacks were often likely to be encouraged to look to government for assistance. Obviously, this disruption in the structure and stability of familiar patterns of intracommunity support also presented a challenge to more familiar patterns of philanthropic activity. The shift in population, from South to North and West, also meant that white philanthropy, formerly directed to supplement Southern black institutions, was also challenged to increase its efforts, and to change its expectations about the kinds of compromises that had been traditional.

In the wake of the civil rights movement many institutions, North and South, which had long served the African American community, and which had long been the focus of its gifts of labor and financial support, such as the colored branches of YWCAs and YMCAs, were dismantled with the expectation that black supporters and members would become part of formerly all-white institutions. It was also anticipated that the enthusiastic voluntarism which had been so key to the success of many of the black institutions, along with the dollars which were traditionally raised from within the black community, would naturally follow. However, this did not occur for several reasons, not the least of which was the fact that the focus of black philanthropy shifted for a time, to respond to the more immediate needs of a movement to dismantle the jim crow system.

During the 1950s and 1960s, as black Americans fought for equal rights and opportunities, and while the black church served as the center of activity, philanthropy and "the movement" were difficult to separate. Certainly, pressures from outside the community, such as the banning of traditional organizations like the NAACP in some Southern states, meant that new organizations had to be established and funded, mostly out of the same churches as those which were most active in the civil rights struggle. At that time, donations which were collected at mass rallies, boycotts, and other movement activities, formed the nucleus of support for related expenses. In spite of misrepresentations by earlier scholars, which suggested that the movement was mostly funded by Northern white liberals, more recent scholarship provides evidence that much of the "outside" money sent South, came from Northern black individuals and organizations (A. Morris 1984, p. 57; Haines 1992; Garrow 1987). Through national organizations like the NAACP and black church denominations, fund-raisers for "the cause" became a critical link between disillusioned Southern blacks, who found that they had not escaped the racism that precipitated their move north, and their home communities, where friends and relatives had remained.

Besides monetary support, African Americans were also the primary providers of food, shelter, and emotional support for civil rights workers. For example, during the Mississippi voter registration drive, young workers were housed, fed, and supported by poor rural black residents who risked their jobs, their livelihoods, and their lives to give what they could. These acts of charity again illustrate that for poor people, philanthropy may take the form of personal sacrifice, rather than money, with the hope that their efforts will change systems of oppression, much the same as their ancestors had done during the antebellum period. Most important, "the movement" provided a common impetus for giving, whether this meant volunteering services, donating funds, or risking life. The prospect of change appealed to blacks at all social and economic levels.

Although the period of most active protest, between the late 1950s and mid-1970s, showed remarkable similarities to the abolitionist period a century earlier, the results were not nearly as tangible. Blacks who thought that they could "integrate" formerly all-white institutions and social and political structures did not anticipate that whites had a corresponding expectation that what were considered inferior all-black institutions would be dismantled. For blacks, however, these institutions represented history and stood as historic symbols of their struggle to sustain African-centered values and culture. For a time there was some doubt that they could or would be sustained. This also meant that many black Americans faced divided allegiances. On the one hand, having been denied access to all-white institutions and organizations, they were determined to exercise newly won opportunities to make them integrated. However, there was no will to give up their own. For a brief time, the result for black institutions was decline or closure, because they could not compete with their white counterparts for the funds and resources which had traditionally been available from mainstream philanthropic sources, and blacks had not yet mobilized to raise sufficient funds to save their institutions. This was especially true when in their rush to remedy past segregationist practices, formerly all-white institutions were able to promise potential large donors that the end of segregated facilities and practices would eliminate the need for dual agencies and institutions.[15]

Promises that the "great society" would solve the most urgent problems for the poor led African Americans to shift their focus from efforts to aid needy individuals to more sophisticated attempts to find remedies to inequities in governance and power. Paternalism and racism, although accepted in earlier times when white donors were allowed to dominate decision making at black institutions, were now considered intolerable. However, in many cases the thrust by black Americans to assume control of their own institutions was premature. Civil rights victories could not significantly change the economic equation overnight, and in spite of the emotional appeal for "self-determination," the community could not quickly absorb all of the financial responsibilities associated with operating the institutions. Moreover, except for the churches, few other institutions were completely funded without financial support from the white community, either from local government or from individuals. For this reason, communities that had historically rallied together to raise their share of monies for race institutions were divided by calls to burn buildings or take them over. Younger people were impatient with the slow pace of change. Older blacks were torn between their desire for control of their institutions and their fear and understanding of the financial implications of such demands. This dilemma was particularly evident in the case of a few of the historically black colleges, when students rallied against predominantly white boards of trustees, and in some cases destroyed buildings which symbolized what they claimed were pay-offs from their oppressors.[16] These contradictions, along with more individualized efforts to "move on up" to partake of the American middle-class dream, may account for yet another shift in black philanthropic activity among blacks.

In spite of expectations by whites that black churches and institutions would no longer be attractive, once opportunities were opened to integrate, blacks did not rush to fill white pews or institutions. Moreover, in many cases what had previously been known as natural constituencies for agencies like the YMCA and YWCA, simply dispersed. On the other hand, as traditionally all-white institutions began to respond to charges of racism and segregationism, and made an all-out effort to recruit blacks to join their ranks, it is my speculation that for the mainly middle-class and upwardly mobile blacks who responded, their major efforts shifted for a time to the more immediate needs of their families: a traditional source of informal support and another important venue for sharing of resources.

The tradition of raising money from community and family members to help one of their own to take advantage of opportunities as they are presented is one which is age old within the black community. Stories of communities and families pooling funds are so well known that they are often overlooked for their importance as sources of philanthropy.[17] Once again, the tradition became crucial, as new opportunities opened to younger blacks. In spite of a virtual avalanche of new programs to fund scholarships, social services, and training programs, families and church members strained to provide the supplemental monies which were necessary. Though this kind of philanthropy is not unique to African Americans, it is significant because of its implications within the tradition of the extended family and the black church as community. However, it is also the hardest to quantify. While sociologists have long acknowledged these kin relationships and the ways that they differ in terms of the responsibility which members of the family are expected to assume, the phenomenon is not taken into account when we try to assess benevolent contributions within the community or the philanthropy of African Americans. However, the evidence of the importance of these contributions is suggested by the figures indicating the rapid increase of black college graduates, and the expansion of the black middle class during the post–civil rights era. Personal narratives and autobiographies of the era very clearly acknowledge the contributions of cousins, aunts, and even fictive kin, which supplemented new opportunities such as scholarships, home mortgages, and training programs to facilitate the upward mobility of many individuals.[18]

Yet old images and stereotypes persist, particularly when black dependency provides a useful and convenient way to represent the undeserving poor. Without acknowledging the persistence of racism in education and the workplace, politicians and the media have been able to encapsulate some of the most complex problems in American society by perpetuating images which subtly reinforce the nation's historic disdain for poverty. Moreover, the high visibility of welfare and programs to aid the poor have focused on the disproportionate numbers of black Americans who are dependent on public assistance. In some ways, their poverty has become a scapegoat for the failure of our economy to include opportunities for all American citizens.

At the same time, deliberate misinterpretations of the results of affirmative action goals and the new visibility of the black middle class suggests to much of the public that poor blacks are particularly undeserving. This perception is also compounded by the high profiles of the minuscule class of black athletes, entertainers, and professionals, whose enormous incomes are regularly publicized and whose philanthropy is mostly ignored. There are suggestions that the resolution to problems within the race should be the responsibility of those who have succeeded. But since funds to support education, adequate housing, and health services are declining for all Americans, it is increasingly clear that private philanthropy cannot adequately address historic patterns of racial exclusion from opportunity, nor can it solve the massive problems which are now faced by society. African Americans are not the exception. In fact they are more likely to be directly involved in finding and funding solutions than their white counterparts.

A survey published in 1987 showed than no less than 60 percent of blacks with incomes under $20,000 made charitable contributions and 38 percent reported that they had performed some volunteer service in the community. Among blacks with incomes over $40,000, 88 percent made monetary contributions and 67 percent reported participating in some form of volunteer service. Further, the data indicate that black churches are the major recipients of dollars and volunteer time, and black organizations continue to receive the major part of their energies and resources (Carson 1990). These organizations often combine social and civic activities, and most take some responsibility for providing a variety of services to the poor through fund-raising, private donations, and direct volunteer activities. Moreover, the survey found that altogether, even though their financial contributions do not represent the largest amounts when compared to other groups, African Americans donate a higher proportion of their income than others. Most often, these donations are targeted for direct services, without benefit of intermediary external institutions, and thus they are harder to track. Because of their historic role as providers of multiple services within the community, black churches are the chief conduit for black philanthropy. The strong second recipient of funds and services are institutions which directly benefit youth. These facts refute the notion that the black community has grown to expect that the government can or should provide all solutions to its problems.

Conclusion

The history of Africans in America is very much a history of giving as well as receiving. Their relationship to philanthropy must be considered an important part of the total picture. At the same time, the history of American philanthropy must include African American traditions if it is to be considered accurate and comprehensive. This will require new definitions and new models for analysis, with qualitative measures weighing in along with quantitative indices. In many cases, because of historical circumstances, philanthropy among black people was necessarily responsive to overwhelming political, economic, and social realities. It thus resists comparison with philanthropy in the majority community. Moreover, cultural traditions have also helped to shape the ways that philanthropic acts are carried out. These include formal and informal giving practices within churches and community organizations, as well as within the extended family.

I would suggest that a more thorough analysis of such institutions as black churches, sororities, and fraternal organizations, social clubs, and grass-roots community associations would reveal that philanthropy, in a more inclusive definition, is a way of life among black Americans and has been so historically. Further, because giving and receiving are part of the pattern of life among blacks who are less well-off, these practices will have to be the deliberate focus of study if we are to fully understand the true meaning of benevolence and philanthropy within cultural groups.

By reexamining practices of philanthropy to include a variety of acts of charity, and by reassessing what is implied by the use of the ambiguous category of "self-help," historians and analysts can discover the importance of these rich and diverse patterns of sacrifice and giving. Further, similar networks of family and community service, fund-raising, and personal and direct donations within the community, while part of the pattern of giving among blacks, may be useful models for exploring patterns of giving among other racial and ethnic populations.

The history of segregation, separation, and isolation out of the main economic stream, has undoubtedly played a role in shaping the ways in which African Americans responded to social and economic needs in their community. This means for the most part that they have focused somewhat meager resources to *respond* to crises, rather than giving priority for their time, monies, and attention to activities which can be directed toward resolution of problems for their communities in the future. However, this is an issue which is widely recognized at this time. Historically black colleges and universities and historically black organizations, like many of their white counterparts, are currently actively involved in developing ways to encourage donor constituents to plan their giving in order to shore up endowments and operational funds. In addition, community foundations, which in the past tended to ignore the minority donor, are now actively soliciting smaller, more donor-targeted funds from the African American community. These efforts will undoubtedly mean that the gross underestimation of their philanthropy will be corrected by some measures, but they will not redress the problem of reassessing the history of their many contributions.

I have attempted to suggest new ways to conceptualize and define philanthropy and have used examples for reexamining materials which have been largely overlooked as sources for understanding philanthropy. I would also like to emphasize the need for more in-depth and specialized study of black institutions and individuals. For example, the public benevolence of Bill Cosby and his wife Camille should be seen as continuing a tradition of giving. So should the missionary work in Africa by black church denominations, which dates back to the nineteenth century, or the project of Links, Inc., a national women's organization, to supply funds to build water wells in Africa, or Alpha Phi Alpha Fraternity building homes for the aged. These are all part of African American history and the history of American philanthropy.

However, the major story of black philanthropy is not now, nor has it ever been simply "self-help," nor is it about doing good with excess wealth for the most part. Rather, it has been about giving "a hand up" to the less fortunate, including those among them. It has also always been directed to finding a way to promote self-reliance, and in some cases, it has provided a means for survival. In the final analysis an old saying in the black cultural vernacular best describes black philanthropy. It is mostly a history of "making a way out of no way."

Notes

1. *Webster's New Collegiate Dictionary.* A similar definition which defines philanthropy as "the philosophy and practice of giving to nonprofit organizations through financial and other contributions; all voluntary giving, voluntary service and voluntary association and initiative" is cited from *The Lexicon for Community Foundations,* in *Donors of Color: A Promising New Frontier for Community Foundation,* a report published by the Council on Foundations Association of Black Foundation Executives, Washington, DC, 1993, p. 24. In this report, a survey conducted by the Winters Group, Inc., the argument is also made that the term, as currently commonly used, fails to include non-structured philanthropy, which is the principal philanthropic activity of minority groups.

2. E. Carson (1989) makes the case for the inclusion of voluntarism as part of the definition of philanthropic activity. However, he uses "self-help" to refer to activities which are designed to promote the interests of an individual or a specific group.

3. Accounts of the practice of "gift-giving" are found in most descriptions of western African life. For example, in Chinua Achebe's *Things Fall Apart*, along with his achievements as a warrior, the protagonist is obliged to disperse foods and favors in his effort to gain status in his community.

4. One account of the existence of benevolent societies within the slave community is found in a petition to President Andrew Johnson from a group of black men in Richmond, Virginia, barely two months after the fall of Richmond. The petition recounts the good deeds of slaves such as taking care of the aged, burial for the slaves, and reading and writing lessons in spite of "the law of slavery [which] severely punished those who taught us" (Rachleff 1984, pp. 13-14).

5. For discussion of worship services and practices in the black church see Lincoln and Mamiya (1990).

6. "Negro Societies in Philadelphia, 1831," in Aptheker (1964), p. 112.

7. "Laws of the African Society, instituted at Boston . . . 1796," in Aptheker (1964), pp. 38-39.

8. In addition to founding black Freemasonry, Prince Hall was among founding members of the Africa Society in Boston.

9. Studies of black communities in practically every city where blacks lived in enough numbers indicate the existence of such societies. See for example, Rachleff (1984), p. 11; Horton and Horton (1979), ch. 3.

10. See *Some Efforts of American Negroes for their own Social Betterment*, Atlanta University Publications No. 3, 1898; also, Brown (1988).

11. For full discussion of this phenomenon, see J. Franklin (1991), ch. 16; Berry and Blassingame (1982), ch. 8; and Bullock (1970).

12. Neighborhood Union Minutes, 8 July 1908, Minutes Book, p. 1, Neighborhood Union Box 5, Archives Department, Atlanta University Center Woodruff Library, Atlanta, Georgia. Quoted in Neverdon-Morton (1989), p. 145.

13. Negative stereotyping of black women provided the original impetus for the formation of the National Association of Colored Women. For a full discussion of the founding of the organization see Lerner (1972), ch. 8; also Giddings 1984, ch. 5-6.

14. Neighborhood Union Minutes, 11 Nov. 1908, Minutes Book, p. 40, Neighborhood Union Box 5, Atlanta University Woodruff Center Library, Atlanta, Ga. Quoted in Neverdon-Morton (1989), p. 149.

15. An excellent example of the rush to integrate, and the ultimate loss of neighborhood-based institutions for blacks is found in the case of YWCAs and YMCAs throughout the country. In many cases, outside of the churches these associations were the centers of social activities for youth, and represented the focus of a good amount of voluntarism and fund-raising activities on the part of blacks of all classes. Therefore, for example, when the YWCA decided to close all segregated facilities, the result was a decline in black memberships, and in many black communities, the loss of an important social service agency. For more detail see Jones (1990b).

16. As in the student takeover at Fisk University, Nashville, TN, and the turmoil and board takeover at Karamu House in Cleveland, Ohio. In both cases, white domination of the boards of trustees were the focus of protest. This kind of protest occurred in large and small institutions across the nation.

17. See, for example, Washington (1965); also selected autobiographies in Gates, ed. (1991).

18. An excellent illustration of the role of the extended family is found in Ione (1991) and Gayles (1993). Also see sociological studies of black family life, such as Billingsley (1968) and McAdoo (1981), which discuss the kin network function at length.

9 | "Human Communion" or a Free Lunch

School Dinners in Victorian and Edwardian London

Ellen Ross

CHARITABLE ACTIVITY IN nineteenth- and early twentieth-century England occupied a central place in the cultures both of its upper-class purveyors and of the needy people who were its objects. The commercial and industrial middle classes of the late eighteenth and nineteenth centuries claimed and maintained their place in Britain's political sun in large measure through their voluntary charitable organizations, which also provided generations of middle-class men and women with pleasure, interest, and occupation. As for the poor, household survival was often postulated on charitable donations, offerings which, in one form or another, surely made up an element in the household budgets of a majority of Britain's poor and near-poor households. The social status and personal fulfillment achieved by charity giving, of course, had only a tangential relationship to the recipients' view of charity as one among many inadequate survival resources which, if pieced together carefully, could add up to security or even modest comfort.

For my contribution as a historian to this collective investigation of charity, I will, using material from my own research in London history between 1870 and World War I, sketch out some of the meanings and functions of charity to donor and recipient. These meanings changed as state policies developed and as the objects of the charity began to interject their own opinions into the charitable enterprise. I will, first, briefly look at charitable work in the culture of its upper-middle-class practitioners and in that of its working-class recipients. Then I will turn, by way of a case study, to the operation of a characteristic charitable activity of the late nineteenth and early twentieth centuries, the provision of lunches and breakfasts to schoolchildren.

My purpose is to urge a view of charity as all parties in the project, including the working-class wives and mothers who were its main objectors, found it. Making them actors in this drama of giving and receiving gifts provides a fresh way of evaluating the charities of the Victorian and Edwardian eras. By watching charities in their daily work with their clients we can begin to judge their significance both in helping the poor materially, and in shaping the experiences and views of the philanthropists themselves. My research stressing the concrete way in which poor housewives incorporated resources provided by charities into their household budgets was originally intended to challenge both the naive view of nineteenth-century philanthropists as generous and disinterested, and the more skeptical position pervasive in historical scholarship until quite recently which viewed philanthropy primarily as a nexus in which the rich controlled and scrutinized the poor. I hope this research will also advance our thinking about the structure and mission of philanthropy and social welfare programs today.

A powerful charitable impulse was one product of the wave of evangelical Christianity that swept over Britain in the late eighteenth century, generating the first "Age of Benevolence" (in the words of novelist and moralist Hannah More). Studies of the shaping of middle-class culture in the early nineteenth century are unanimous on the significance of charitable associations in the shaping of the claim of the new professionals and industrialists to a share in political power; as Davidoff and Hall comment in their study of Colchester and Birmingham between 1780 and the middle of the nineteenth century, "[These] societies provided opportunities for the public demonstration of middle-class weight and responsibility. . . . The experience of such associations increased the confidence of middle-class men and contributed to their claims for political power, as heads of households. . . . "[1]

Women, though excluded from the powerful voluntary associations, were nonetheless very active in charitable causes from the early nineteenth century. They were engaged in less formally organized kinds of charity such as "visiting" the poor, and were active also as donors and as members of female auxiliaries of the major associations. Female charity bazaars raising money for churches, hospitals, and other causes of all kinds were a ubiquitous element of British social life. Mothers' activism enticed children into charitable work and their own auxiliaries. Child philanthropists favored missionary and Bible societies offering Christianity to the heathen in the colonies, and Sunday school pupils of all social classes contributed thousands of pounds to organizations like the British and Foreign Bible Society, the Church Missionary Society, and the Methodist Missionary Society from early in the century (Prochaska 1980, ch. 2–3).

By the 1870s or 1880s British charity had entered a new phase. Many organizations were attempting to operate on a more systematic, even scientific footing, arguing that charity (now more often dignified by the name philanthropy) must advance the long-term interests of the receivers as well as the moral and civic welfare of the donors. A "consciousness of sin," to use Beatrice Potter's (later Webb) phrase, stimulated in the 1880s by revelations of East End poverty and by the political demands of workers not only generated large increases in charitable donations but also new cohorts of young people to administer charity, run slum churches, and work with the poor. Young male Oxbridge graduates began to invade the slums in the 1870s and especially 1880s, often intent on "transforming rough lads into model adult citizens" (Koven 1992, p. 375) through settlement house residence, and work with boys in clubs and sports.[2] By the 1880s the world of philanthropy was one in which women and men mixed reasonably freely and women were active as leaders and as rank and file during this era. Indeed, charity was one of the leading professions for females by this time. According to an 1893 estimate, twenty thousand women worked as full-time paid officials in charitable organizations nationally, a number that excluded nurses and women in religious orders.[3]

Charity was big business in late Victorian and Edwardian Britain. In the 1870s eleemosynary contributions were greater by far than the whole tax-supported national expenditure on poor relief. In 1885, donations to charities in London alone (some of this money was spent in other towns, though) were worth more than the entire national budgets of several nation-states, Portugal, Sweden, and Denmark among them. Though there were changes over time in the ways philanthropists spent their money, neither David Lloyd George's extension of the income tax nor the general expansion of state services in the early twentieth century diminished the British enthusiasm for philanthropy. London was the hub of British charity. By the turn of the century there were nearly a thousand private charitable agencies based there. In addition, several of the London boroughs were among the leaders in Britain in providing private or public services—medical care for mothers and babies, clinics, and school meals among them (Owen 1964, p. 469; Prochaska 1980, p. 21; Harrison 1966, p. 354).

London charities in the late nineteenth and early twentieth centuries made available to various categories of poor people a wide assortment of goods and services. Charity permeated the operations of church and state: police court "poor boxes" supplied the needy at the magistrate's discretion; vestry or borough sanitary officers offered free disinfectants and white-wash; church- or settlement-sponsored mothers' meetings ran clothing, boot, blanket, or coal "clubs," through which members saved for these necessities a penny at a time for goods purchased wholesale. Several (free) district nursing services operated in inner-London neighborhoods, not counting the midwives and nurses employed by the large maternity charities attached to major hospitals. For children there were Sunday school teas and "treats," similar Band-of-Hope events, evening and after-school clubs and classes, and, by the later decades of the nineteenth century, summer holidays, only partly covered by fees paid by parents and which by 1899 supplied nearly thirty-four thousand London schoolchildren with two weeks at farm or seaside, a number that increased to forty thousand in 1908.[4] Breakfasts and noontime dinners for children were offered in larger and larger numbers and were eventually served to a large minority of the public (Board) school population of the metropolis.

As the great London teaching hospitals expanded, they provided ever more free hospital and clinic visits and absorbed an increasing portion of the money donated to charity; medical charities received about half of the nation's charitable donations in the years before the First World War.[5] In 1889 about a fifth of the Greater London population used a hospital in- or outpatient service at one of the region's ninety-one hospitals; in 1901 a quarter of the population used the ninety-two hospitals now in the region, and more than three hundred thousand more took advantage of smaller charitable dispensaries.[6]

Much of this charitable work brought the donors right into the slums. This traffic, while it never amounted to a stampede, was certainly considerable. It consisted, first of all, of the kinds of workers who had been a fixed part of the charity world for decades: clergymen, church lay workers, London City missionaries (operating since the 1830s), Ellen Ranyard's Bible women who sold installment-plan Bibles (since the 1850s; she also founded a district nursing program in 1868) and representatives of various agencies supplying coal, blankets, food, even trusses to the "ruptured poor."[7] The 1870s and 1880s added newer figures, a large proportion of them women: school teachers; school managers (social/charity workers associated with poor schools); district nurses; more specialized charities supplying children's boots, eyeglasses, and country holidays, or offering job training for the disabled; and Charity Organization Society (COS, founded 1869) caseworkers. The numbers of visitors grew with the 1884 opening of Toynbee Hall in Whitechapel and, in 1887, the Women's University Settlement in Southwark, followed by other settlement houses. By the twentieth century, new professions, many of them open to females, brought still more women from London townhouses or from country estates to work in poor districts as sanitary inspectors, health visitors, providers of rate-subsidized school dinners, or as school nurses.

The variety and profusion of charitable activity in London alone by the turn of the twentieth century is well exemplified in historian of religion Jeffrey Cox's catalog of those sponsored by churches or chapels in the borough of Lambeth alone. The list included

> *at least* 56 mothers' meetings, 36 temperance societies for children, 36 literary or debating societies for young men, 27 Bible classes, 27 girls' or young women's clubs, 25 cricket, tennis, or other sports clubs, 25 savings banks or penny banks, 24 Christian Endeavour societies, 21 boot, coal, blanket, or clothing clubs, 19 adult temperance societies, 17 branches of the Boys' Brigade or Church Lads' Brigade, 13 vocational or adult classes, 13 men's clubs, 10 gymnasiums (usually devoted to recreational classes of some sort), and 10 maternity societies. There were 16 nurses and two part-time doctors as well as a part-time dentist in addition to those sponsored by the provident dispensaries which were closely linked to the churches. Furthermore there were two "servants' registries," two lodgings registries, two "industrial societies" which employed women at needlework, one burial guild, one convalescent home, one

hostel for the dying, one invalid kitchen, cripples' classes, a children's play-time, a day nursery, a "prostitutes' institute," several libraries, and dozens of Sunday Schools in addition to the extensive work of extra-parochial and transdenominational organizations.

About half of the Nonconformist chapels and all of the Anglican parishes in the borough also provided relief to the poor in cash or in kind (Cox 1982, pp. 58–59; see also McLeod 1974).

Women Charity Givers

Female activism obviously had burgeoned under the umbrella of philan-thropy. To young upper-class women just finishing school, Hoxton or Bermond-sey could be as satisfying as the Rockies or the Congo River. After her father's death and still in her teens, vivacious Henrietta Rowland (later Barnett) went to London to serve an apprenticeship with housing reformer Octavia Hill. Katharine Symonds, daughter of the classical scholar, yearned to work in the 1890s at Toynbee Hall in Whitechapel "but mother was afraid that I should pick up some infectious disease." The compromise was a clerical job at a COS office in Whitechapel Road. By the 1900s the school charity bureaucracy and borough health visiting programs were supplanting the COS and the settlements as places where a young lady could find interesting work. Indeed as soon as she left school in 1908, Mary Brinton (later Mary Stocks) a girl who had visited the St. Pancras workhouse many times with her aunt, and spent her school holidays helping her mother with her COS rounds among the West London poor in Lad-broke Grove and Kensal Green, took a position as (volunteer) secretary of the managers attached to the Saffron Hill Elementary School in Holborn (Koven 1994; Furse 1940, p. 156; Stocks 1970, pp. 47, 51, 58).

New freedoms for middle-class women had opened up opportunities for world travel and exploration, and, while some set out for Africa or the Middle East, others were satisfied to journey only as far as the London slums. Clara Grant, whose lifelong ambition had been to be a missionary in Central Africa, gave it up in the late 1890s in order to live, teach, and establish a settlement house among the East London poor. Gertrude Ward, sister-in-law of novelist Mary Ward, worked for years as the illustrious author's secretary and also vol-unteered with the Women's University Settlement in Southwark. At age thirty, in 1891, she began her longed-for training as a missionary nurse; five years later she sailed for Zanzibar (Grant 1930, p. 72; Birkett 1989, pp. 8–9, 11; E. Jones 1973, pp. 97–98).

Thanks to London's very good regional railway network, work with the poor could be quite easily combined with the routines of middle- or upper-class life. Devastated by her husband's death in 1890, Charlotte Despard threw her-self into the ladylike charity of supplying fresh flowers from her country house to the poor of Nine Elms, a desolate island of riverside poverty in Lambeth. Her clients' warmth, sympathy, and ability to acknowledge grief, she found, "best helped me bear my desolation," and eventually Despard moved to Nine Elms, founded a settlement in her new home, and established a new life as a neighborhood social activist. Other philanthropists continued to commute from country to town. For thirty years, beginning as a young girl in 1875, Constance Battersea, born a Rothschild, journeyed in from her various country houses to do home visits in Whitechapel and Mile End for the Jewish Ladies' Benevolent Loan Society. For most of 1885, Beatrice Potter (later, Beatrice Webb) living in her family's town residence, York House, in Kensington, made her way regularly by rail to the Katherine Buildings just east of Tower Bridge. Ellen Chase, a Bostonian who came to London in the 1880s to work with Octavia Hill, took a steamer up the Thames several times a week to Vicarage Lane in Deptford where she collected rents on forty-eight houses whose landlord, "a man in the City," had given Hill charge of the management. Mary Ward, the novelist, began to commute in 1892 from her country home in Buckinghamshire to St. Pancras station in Central London, only a short walk from the Marchmont Street branch of University Hall, the first of the London settlements with which she worked.[8]

Slum life forms the background for numerous literary romantic encounters,[9] and these plus the many real-life marriages that took place in this community of social investigators and charity workers (Henrietta Rowland and Samuel Barnett, Beatrice Potter and Sidney Webb, Helen Dendy and Bernard Bosanquet, among many less well known) are suggestive of the significance of philanthropic activism in the social and emotional lives of this generation.

Whatever their work, the well-off slum dwellers radiated pleasure and interest. The poet Amy Levy, and Eleanor Marx, East End labor activist and daughter of Karl Marx, both suicides as quite young women (and both of them Jewish), ultimately paid a high price in personal suffering for their commitment to independence and to work among and for the poor. But both had struggled on in poverty themselves.[10] For the daughters of the country houses surrounding the metropolis, poverty was a chosen destination rather than a fate, and it provided life and movement normally denied to women of their class. Beatrice Webb was impressed in the 1880s by the serenity of her fellow rent collector Emma Cons, at Surrey Buildings south of the river, at the "calm enthusiasm in her face, giving her all to others." Settlement youth worker May Craske wrote warmly in 1908 of her nine years in an ugly inner East London district: "Happy years to us . . . years in which every moment has been a living one, each day full. . . . " Flora Lucy Freeman was open about the moral benefits of this work: "You will learn much about yourself, perhaps more than you teach them. Above all, the sight of 'the pathetic patience of the poor' will do much to shame away the vague discontent which shadows so many girls of the upper classes." But she also more guardedly intimated that there were other advantages for slum workers: the sense of mastery in shaping the rough stone of slum childhood into "the beautiful statue which the sculptor designed it to be," and, more mundanely, opportunities to do such unladylike things as "indulging in cricket or rounders" in full public view in Kensington Gardens (B. Webb 1979, p. 267; Craske 1908, pp. 184–89; F. Freeman 1901, pp. 139–40, 65–66, 70).

The Poor and Charity

The poor were by no means exclusively *receivers* of charity. Working men collected money informally when coworkers were ill or needed money in emergencies, and there were more formal trades union or workmen's benefit clubs. The great private hospitals in and outside London collected thousands of pounds in tiny donations from working people. Working-class women taught Sunday school and did parish visiting in their own neighborhoods.[11] The poor also, as a normal element of their existences, gave help, goods, and money to their neighbors and relatives, so much so that, as observers began to register the extent of this "unstinted and abounding charity of the poor to the poor" they had to recognize its significance in the survival of the one-third of households in London classed as poor (Jephson 1910, p. 21; Dendy 1893, pp. 612–13; Prochaska 1980, p. viii). This neighborhood self-help, however, which I have written about elsewhere (Ross 1983), falls outside of this chapter's scope, which is "official" charity administered across class lines.

Philanthropy was certainly not a good substitute for wages as the basis of working-class family survival. Also, neighbors' help, the pawnshop, and the landlord's indulgence were, in general, more important sources of temporary income than formal charity. But at certain moments in a household's cycle, the formal charities were crucial, and wives, who were in charge of crafting household survival from the wages of husbands, children, and their own paid work, worked actively to procure and maintain philanthropic offerings—the best sign we have of their value to them.

Charity is nearly invisible in the household budget studies by social scientists that proliferated from the 1880s. But domestic budgets surely underrate the value of charity to families. Some services, like children's school dinners, were often accepted as a right connected with school attendance and not noted as income. Others, like fuel or food from individual benefactors contacted by teachers, parish visitors, or settlement workers, may have been covered up to preserve family honor from the investigators. Certainly such sources were hidden as well as possible by applications for poor law or Charity Organization Society aid. Investigators usually asked only about money earnings, but charities generally doled out goods in kind. Finally, many people would never have considered such things as placing "extra" children in poor law custody during hard times, or using hospital outpatient services as charity, though for our purposes they certainly are.

Examples of household thrift from another source, children's autobiographies, suggest the range of charitable help which housewives used. A Tottenham woman remembers the pints of soup and milk and the bread tickets her mother was granted by a local Congregational church, as well as the regular loan of "maternity bags" of linens for new mothers and new Christmas outfits made by the church's needlework guild. Children's boots, an expensive item, were received with gratitude by parents, if not always by children, from parish sources or via the Londonwide Peek Fund for schoolchildren. One housewife sent her daughter weekly to pick up free disinfectant, probably from the local medical officer of health. Another bought cheap, sturdy dresses made by a local order of nuns for her daughters, which—unlike many charity garments—the daughter remembered with pleasure.[12]

The working-class family cycle with its points of poverty and of plenty drew some more than other households into contact with charities. When people were in trouble with such routine problems as old age, illness, unemployment, or drunken spouses they were likely to call on charities for aid. Widows, the elderly, and the handicapped were not only attractive as recipients of charity but also needed aid for longer periods than other households. Half of the children in poor law custody in England and Wales, for example, were those of widows. A study of children getting school dinners in 1915 similarly found that the fathers of 45 percent were either dead or invalids. Old people, especially old women, used charities to carry themselves along, keeping the workhouse at bay with a combination of expedients that included parish aid, visits by district nurses, care by neighbors and landladies, and earnings as laundresses and childminders. The old-age pensions which, from 1909, provided five shillings a week for single people over age seventy, or half again as much for couples, merely injected one more source of income into these delicate systems without transforming them.[13]

All of the seven Lambeth households hit by long periods of unemployment whose budgets were recorded in Maud Pember Reeves's *Round About a Pound a Week*, a 1913 study of life at the poverty line, had recourse to modest contributions by public and private agencies. One man had spent a month in a poor law infirmary; a deserted wife got parish relief during an illness that prevented her from working; the school-aged children of four of the households had school dinners daily during their difficult weeks. All of the infants were receiving free milk as a part of the Fabian Women's Group project in which they were participating (Pember Reeves 1979, ch. 14).

Another South London couple with three small children, the man an unemployed plumber, the wife too ill to work, exhibited a somewhat different pattern. Economics Club members who published their household budget in the

1890s noted their heavy use of charity during their very difficult months, which contrasts with the Lambeth households' sparser reliance on charity or the poor law. This husband had spent a month at St. Thomas's Hospital, during which time the wife, after much cruel delay, received home (parish) relief. The woman's doctor had contacted a "charitable lady," who supplied them once with coal, and they used a free dispensary when they were ill. The sister of another doctor with whom they came into contact had also been helping them, as had the wife's former employer. The Lambeth husbands and wives were well established in their district, with kin, neighbors, and landladies close by and available to help, whereas this South London couple "receives no visits and conceals its privations." This isolation, often a token of respectability, prevented participation in neighborhood aid networks and made them more dependent on the charity of the wealthy (Collet and Robertson 1896, pp. 19–20).

A woman who was chronically short of money because her husband was a heavy drinker combined traditional neighborhood survival strategies of the poor with aid from formal charities. The COS was one of the many expedients to which Violet Dawes, of Hornsey Street in North London, had recourse when she applied to that agency in 1908 to "place" her three children so that she could leave her violent husband and take a position as a live-in servant. At that point she owed several weeks' rent, had a "great many pawn tickets," and had debts to a draper as well. Mrs. Dawes had applied to and been rejected by the poor law guardians but had help from the Salvation Army. Her husband's parents also "have helped till they are sick and tired." (The COS denied her request because she was reported to have slept away from home several times.)[14]

Meant by the givers to bridge the chasm between the classes, charity was invariably distorted as it traveled from one side to the other: recipients lied, cheated, and used donations in ways charity givers did not intend. The enormous influence of Lévi-Strauss's stress on the "laws" of reciprocity has obscured the fact that with all gift giving, there is always the possibility of nonreciprocation, rejection, and ingratitude. To dispel their chronic suspicion of "charity mongering" many charities carried out endless extra casework: middle-class female time, the foundation on which the COS method of "thorough investigation" of cases was built, was plentiful in the nineteenth century. Charity in Victorian and Edwardian Britain was based on two dilemmas which made cheating on the part of the users and distrust on the givers' side inevitable. First, the rich seldom gave the poor what they most wanted: cash to use as they pleased—to pay the rent, redeem the bedding from pawn, buy the "pieces" from the butcher, or even send for a pint of stout from the pub. Second, charities frequently gave to individuals, but most working-class individuals had powerful family obligations, and resources flowed in the direction of those obligations. Thus gifts from rich to poor were, as a matter of course, "deformed" (to use Stedman Jones's useful misreading of Marcel Mauss).[15]

Recipients of charity seldom used it in the ways they were intended to; the offerings were not necessarily used by the people to whom they had been given, nor in the form in which they were offered. Relief given to children in the shape of clothes or boots, indeed even school prizes like books or cricket bats, often went to the pawnshop for food money, for working-class schoolchildren did not have private possessions. Schoolteachers who brought secondhand clothes to distribute to their pupils noticed how few they ever saw the children wearing; the middle-class clothing donated was obviously too valuable to wear (and was often too dressy and fussy for comfort) and was placed in pawn or sold to secondhand shops. Tickets for children's meals distributed at the schools were regularly sold by the children or their parents for the penny or half-penny they could bring in. And children given charity meals also pocketed bread and butter or bread and meat to be "relished by the parents" later on.[16] Grace Foakes and her sister, in early twentieth-century Wapping, regularly sat through hours of Sunday church services so they could attend the teas that followed and stock up on scones and rolls for their family's Monday meal. Elderly people might, after 1909, check into the workhouse or infirmary while drawing and saving their old-age pensions (technically illegal so as to donate them to a needier married son or daughter) (Foakes 1972, p. 128; Bailward 1912, p. 552; S. S. J. F. 1911, p. 72).

Charity mongers were both stock literary figures[17] and the bête noire of the philanthropic world because their cool instrumental approach to the gifts denegrated the donors. "Working" charities for a livelihood nonetheless required time, dramatic flair, information, and luck. Individuals who supported themselves this way were rare, whole households rarer still, though charity mongers received considerable sensationalized attention in the press. In fact, they were small-scale operators indeed. City missionaries thought they spotted one in one of the little streets running out of Drury Lane, half demolished in a late-nineteenth-century slum clearance project. The husband, an old soldier and semi-invalid, made only a small contribution to the household. One assumes that the writer's reference to the mother's "hard work" is facetious, yet her hustling (to use a term from another time and place) was indeed energetic.

> The mother works hard for her children and attends every [church-sponsored] mothers' meeting she can, as well as every mission hall if possible. This brings her soup three or four times a week and sometimes a loaf of bread, and so the poor woman keeps her little room, and the children with bread. At Christmas she may contrive to get two or three Christmas dinners from different places. (Booth 1969, p. 54)

The Hardings of the Old Nicol in the 1880s and 1890s were also genuine charity mongers, according to their son Arthur's detailed account. The father, having lost or disqualified himself from a number of livelihoods, spent his last "working" years collecting surplus food from restaurants. The mother did not so much cheat local charities as display herself and her children to best advantage, a technique described with intelligence and sympathy by the son when in his late eighties:

> My mother was a forager. God bless her, she foraged all her life, that's how she brought us up. She got a few bob off the people in the [Shaftesbury Society's Ragged School] Mission. She would tell the hard-luck story as to get herself in. Well it was a true story. The whole thing was having your poverty well known to the people who had the giving of charity. They noticed that mother was a dead cripple, and that father was a loafer, and that she had children to bring up. . . . If you wasn't poor you had to look poor. . . . But you had to be clean and that was easy—soap and water didn't cost a lot of money.

Mrs. Harding sent her children to daily bread and milk breakfasts at the mission in exchange for which the children had to go to the mission's Sunday school. She also—and this was her only real racket—went to church rummage sales, whose existence she was informed of by a male friend, stole rather large quantities of used clothing, and sold it to wardrobe dealers in nearby Petticoat Lane (Samuel 1981, pp. 24–25).

Cheating one way or another was obviously a way of life for the poor, as services by local and national government mingled with charitable donations and other resources in the homes and on the dinner tables of the poor. By using several sources of aid—the recipients implicitly stated their ingratitude toward all—none was generous enough to sustain them. Furthermore the user, not the donor, was in charge of the household whose livelihood she had pieced together from many sources. She had obviously rejected a proper client relationship with the donors. The elementary survival needs of the poor were bound to undermine the apparent moral simplicity of the charitable relationship.

Children's School Meals

Schoolchildren's breakfasts and noon dinners are a deceptively mundane form of London charity. No one who has read Charles Morley's vivid account of hundreds of hungry children in the Borough sitting down to rapidly devoured hot meals supplied by the *Referee* (a London daily newspaper) Free Dinners Fund will dismiss the school feeding projects as bland exercises of upper-class benevolence (Morley 1897). Because they involved the highly charged issue of feeding hungry children—a mother's job, after all—school meals were the object of hopes, fears, accusations, and fantasies for both the givers and the receivers, all the more so because the uncertainties about the meanings of reciprocity when services were offered across classes were still greater when their objects were children often too young to be expected to exhibit gratitude. For the study of charity as a social issue, the London meals provide a striking case study in the gift relationship, its meaning for both parties, and its concrete results for children's nutrition, mothers' budgets, and even party politics. From the vantage point of charity practice and policy, school meals serve as a good case study of the way in which donors' ambivalence about their project and suspicion of recipients distorted their gift even before it reached its object.

Throughout the period 1870–1918 the providers of the meals were volunteers (the kitchen workers and a few administrators were paid after 1907), whose impulses were on the whole generous, even loving, toward the poor, especially toward their children. Their soaring hopes for the feeding had sacramental overtones; volunteers spoke of the "spiritual beauty" of the feeding and of the meals as moments of "human communion."[18] But these ideals came into thudding contact with the ideological outlines of Victorian and Edwardian charity with its suspicions of charity mongering and fears of "demoralizing" the poor. The caregivers' colorful fantasies also clashed with the gray hues of the mothers' (and occasionally fathers') highly practical approach to the meals; the parents simply wanted decent food for their offspring at some saving to themselves. To them, the meals represented no sacramental linking of the classes involving reverence and gratitude but a household resource.

Feeding hungry children has, of course, a long history among charities. But it was compulsory education, introduced in 1871 in London, daily exposing hundreds of thousands of children, many ragged, barefoot, and hungry, to public view, that generated the charitable offering of children's meals on a massive scale years before the 1906 Education (Provision of Meals) Act regularized and publicly funded these proceedings.

The meals themselves were supplied by volunteer organizations such as the *Referee* Fund (founded in the 1870s by journalist George Sims and his newspaper), the London Schools Dinner Association, the Jewish Penny Dinner Society, and the London Vegetarian Association. These organizations worked with subcommittees of school managers, whose structure changed in 1907 and were renamed school care committees (Gordon 1974). In the winter of 1904–1905, at least thirty different associations were supplying funds or goods for these volunteers to use, as were countless private individuals contacted by the school managers. The feeding was carried out on a large scale, though the schools differed greatly in the number and quality of meals offered. During one week of cold weather and high unemployment in February 1895, more than a tenth of the children on the London School Board rolls were being fed (52,000 out of 490,000 children) an average of two and one-third meals each week per child.[19] Over the course of a given ordinary year, such as 1903, about a sixth of London's board (public) school population was served meals for some period. In the year ending March 31, 1909, the London schools supplied over four and a half million meals; in the entire remainder of the country only about seven million meals were served.[20]

Feeding children attracted donors across the political spectrum. Schoolchildren's meals had long been a priority of the British Left, supported by trades councils in many large cities, by the Social Democratic Federation, the Trades Union Congress, the London Trades Council, and the Labour Representation Committee. The bill authorizing public funds for meals to "necessitous school children" was introduced by a newly elected Labour M.P. in the 1905 session of the new Liberal-dominated Parliament, and, though plastered with amendments, it became law at the end of 1906 (Thane 1984; Simon 1974, pp. 134–37, 278–79, 282–83). But the Left shared its commitment to feeding schoolchildren with such organizations as the Ragged School Union, The Women's Total Abstinence Union, and hundreds of churches and missions. Matilda Hyndman, a leading light in the Social Democratic Federation's meals program, was doing exactly what her peers among Tory and Liberal women were doing.

Although all adults involved agreed on the rightness of feeding the children, political chasms divided their views on the significance of the meals. For the Left, school meals were a foot in the door of state-funded universal social services available as entitlements. Many nonleftists, on the other hand, while responding warmly to the obvious hunger of the children, worried about the implications of feeding them: were they not taking on a responsibility that properly belonged to parents? The issues were sharpest for the hundreds of Charity Organization Society members who participated in meals programs. As an organization, the COS always opposed free feeding and maintained that position well past the point when the meals had begun to receive funding through local taxes. It was this ambivalence about the legitimacy of the feeding programs that generated so many of the obstacles the committees placed between the dinners and the children, obstacles we label, collectively, their stigma.

Funding problems combined with moral ambivalence contributed to the rather poor quality and small portions of the meals themselves, which compared favorably only with the bread-and-butter meals which were often the only food the children got during the day. An experienced soup kitchen volunteer grimly testified in 1886 that the charity food served to the children was normally not generously supplied: "You cannot, as a rule, supply as much as they could eat, but [only] as much as doctors state to be necessary." In 1885, a meat pudding and vegetable meal, which cost the children a penny, contained only about one and a half ounces of meat (which supplied only 360 calories). Christchurch School Shadwell, in the 1880s, served five hundred children lentil soup, which cost only a pound in all to prepare![21] The number of dinners rejected by thin, hungry children—a worry and an embarrassment for the mealsgivers—suggests more than the notoriously finicky appetites of the young;

the food was often inedible. The smell of the dinners cooking could be nause-ating. A London schoolmistress who had pioneered school dinners in the 1870s, spoke glowingly in 1895 of the fortitude of the teachers at a school where soup was prepared daily, exuding a smell so pleasant that "it is wonderful how the teachers endure it."[22] Children in the south London district of Walworth voted with their feet against a penny dinner program at board school there which offered them an unfamiliar food. "They called the macaroni lumps of fat, and said it made them sick, and they really were sick," the headmaster reported graphically in 1885. On macaroni days many of them took their pennies to the local coffee house where they could get a more appealing portion of pudding for the price. The meals workers themselves were often distressed by the bad quality of the food or by its unappetizing or unedifying presentation. One care committee member who visited a Shoreditch dining center that he was respon-sible for in June 1911 found the potatoes there "very bad." A committee in Islington tried successfully in 1909 to break its meal contract with the Alexandra Trust, but two years later the children were still getting the same dreary carbo-hydrate-heavy menu:

Monday and Thursday: rice pudding, two slices of bread and butter
Tuesday and Friday: stewed mince beef, vegetables and bread
Wednesday: hot bread and milk, fruit, jam roll[23]

For the children's mothers, of course, feeding them was not a voluntary ac-tivity but a desperate necessity. Settlement worker Anna Martin spoke for doz-ens of other observers of the poor in 1910 when she referred to the "skill and ingenuity with which [mothers] contrive to keep their families, on about half the weekly sum per head found necessary in the poor law schools for each child's food and clothing."[24] Just as they negotiated most of the contacts with the school bureaucracy in general, it was the mothers who dealt with the meals committees, paying the large price in effort and humiliation that getting charity usually exacted. By the early twentieth century, in many districts, mothers had to apply for meals in person or in writing and then to reapply at frequent inter-vals, as more, and more elaborate, casework was demanded by the school meals bureaucracy in the London County Council. In other districts, teachers or doc-tors selected "underfed" children, whose homes were then visited and in-spected by subcommittee members. Keeping the meals coming for one or more children could thus require considerable maternal vigilance, as demonstrated by the case of Mrs. U., a Lambeth woman who was part of the Fabian Women's Group's study of infant life in the district in the 1910s. When her husband lost his job in the summer of 1910, she attempted to get school dinners for her three school-aged children, but despite her persistence she did not entirely succeed. Two were granted meals "after weeks of application," but a third, at another school and thus under the jurisdiction of another committee, was rejected because, due to the mother's conscientious housekeeping, the household did not appear poor enough (Pember Reeves 1979, p. 206).

But when literally every penny counted, the meals were obviously worth the trouble, many women calculated. Mrs. U. found them a considerable help as she tried to maintain her family on the small savings she had managed to make while her husband was in work, together with what he could bring in through odd jobs. In August 1910, she was spending under twopence a day per person on food for her family of five children and two adults, a sum that was typical of other poor housewives at the time. As a woman in Rotherhithe commented, "If you spend a bit less on food there's a bit more for coals and boots; and if your big girl falls out of work you can feed her on what you save on the little ones" (Pember Reeves 1979, p. 204; Martin 1911, pp. 13–17, 31). Those programs that were not free but charged a penny, given the minuteness of the housewives' calculations, had far fewer takers. One observer thought that even if only a halfpenny were charged for a school breakfast, mothers would not use them because they could feed their children more cheaply on "good bread and bad tea." Mrs. B, another mother from Rotherhithe, explained that penny school dinners were far too expensive for her to use: "It's no good to us if they provide the children with dinners at the school for 1 d. each. Four of mine are attending . . . school and I can do better for them at home. I make a stew of three-pennyworth of pot-herbs [carrots, celery, onion, etc.]. If I've got it I throw in a handful of rice. This makes a good dinner for all of us, including myself" (Price 1893; Martin 1911, p. 14).

Meals providers often offered the dinners in unpalatable forms, both gastronomically and socially. The Charity Organization Society's commitment to thorough investigation of home circumstances—interviews, home visits, papers to fill out—even when only small donations like boots or meals were at stake, and which was especially well entrenched in several East London districts, was only one of many barriers between the child and the meals, barriers "calculated to deter all self-respecting parents from making an application [for meals] on behalf of their children," as an Independent Labour Party pamphlet put it in 1909. Even with the more formal and publicly financed operation of the school dinner machinery in the 1900s, at least some of the basic elements of stigma were enforced by most of the committees: careful investigation of the receivers; unattractive food or surroundings for the meals; public identification of the children in their classrooms; attempts to extract repayment from parents when their circumstances improved (McMillan and Sanderson 1909, p. 1). In a suburban South London school in the 1900s the meals program "was conducted in so condescending a way that the snobbery of the other children was invoked, and the recipients of the charity were made to feel their lowliness," as Ethel Mannin, a schoolgirl from a socialist household, remembered with distaste. A Shadwell woman refused to ask for school dinners on behalf of her children after her request for milk for a sick husband had been humiliatingly rejected by another charity at a nearby church. Obviously recalling that experience, the woman, as well as her daughter, thought the school meals were also "degrading."[25]

The minutes of the care committees show sporadic attempts to get parents to justify their use of the meals, to harass them for payment, and to cut the children off from the meals (which could be appealed from 1909 on). But the minutes also demonstrate the limits of the committees' capacity to compel gratitude or even cooperation. The Popham Road committee in Islington, which fed attractive meals to an average of over two hundred children each month during the winter, sent out many summonses each year to parents to come to their meetings to justify their continuing the meals. In 1910 only half actually appeared at first call. At a school in Shoreditch, the proportions were even lower. When in the winter of 1909–1910, a Mrs. O'Brien failed to come to two hearings to which the committee summoned her; they then demanded that she repay the cost of the meals. A divisional officer sent to investigate, however, found that Mrs. O'Brien was an office cleaner whose evening work kept her from attending the hearings and recommended that the committee give up its plan to extract compensation from her. Obviously feeling that she had made her point, Mrs. O'Brien then ignored a third summons as well.[26]

Another East London committee, which deliberately set out to stigmatize its users, was met with popular surprise, hostility, and rejection. The committee deliberately offered children breakfasts of "an unvaried diet of porridge [deeply loathed by London working people] and milk." As one member, the Reverend Henry Iselin, stated without embarrassment, "This food was distributed at such an hour [between 8:15 and 8:45 when school did not begin until 9:15] and was of such a character as to constitute in itself a definite test of need. . . . This policy has restricted the number considerably." Many potential users would have nothing to do with the meals. "I can give them better at home than what you gives them," one woman hissed. "It ain't worth while to tell lies about a bit of porridge," said another.[27]

The experience of Henry Iselin's East London committee in those years suggests that even in the heart of COS country, by the twentieth century the poor were beginning to view school feeding as a kind of entitlement. When the LCC began to levy a small property tax to defray the feeding costs in 1909, Iselin found the parents of the children he fed even less likely than before to feel either gratitude or loss of prestige. One father, whose children had been assisted sporadically for a few years, simply sent a note to the committee secretary saying, "I am out of work so will you do the needful?" Committee members elsewhere in London reported the same attitudes among the recipients. On Campbell Street, Islington, "the vilest road in London," the local committee in 1909 had a great deal of trouble with the rough population who inhabited the furnished rooms on the street: "Sometimes the parents are most abusive, and seem to take it for granted that they are entitled to Free Meals." In another district, "The poor generally regard the whole affair as a kind of food lottery without an entrance subscription." The only way the committee could convince people that meals were not available for the asking was to promote "the prevalent idea that every child sent is keeping another out." (Although this was not technically true, it spoke to the way people actually did collectively ration scarce resources and was an effective alternative to stigmatization as a way of keeping numbers down.) A committee member in 1912 reported a conversation with an artisan, who, though employed, applied for school meals because his workmates' children were getting them. When his request was rejected, the man indignantly responded: "You people don't do the work properly, what you're paid for."[28]

Though their correspondence registers distress at being taken for granted and confidence in means testing their offerings, the logic of the food charities' situation—they did want to feed poor children and were judged to some degree on their effectiveness in doing so—demanded that they adapt their offerings to pressures from the recipients. The committees' practices were in fact the product of a delicate and usually unspoken series of arrangements between givers and receivers. The charities became resigned to the fact that, despite their anomalous civic status, it was the mothers, not the fathers, who were the "heads" of households when children were the issue, and would be the ones to conduct the family's public business. The committees also offered the meals at the times when London's poor were usually the hungriest: in the winter and early spring months when work was short or nonexistent in many male trades, and on Tuesdays through Fridays, when the wages brought home on Saturday began to dwindle. As far as the food itself was concerned, vegetarians, oatmeal devotees, and other food faddists who had gravitated to the world of school meals were, mostly, eventually overruled by those more observant of the tastes of the children (though oatmeal exponents were the most tenacious). Determined to summon parents fortnightly to justify their continued aid, some committees accepted that many would never come, grumbled, but continued to feed the children. Thus the programs' functioning was a kind of compromise between the donors and the recipients.[29]

After the Education (Provision of Meals) Act went into effect in 1907, the number of London consumers began to climb. According to Sir Charles Elliott, who had served before 1907 as head of the Joint Committee on Underfed Children ("more soup than joint," quipped school headmistress Clara Grant), the average number of children fed per month rose dramatically. The 1909 annual average was double the figure for 1906. Elliot's explanation for the sudden increase was that the money granted by the act, which provided better food and paid kitchen staff and administrations, inspired the local committees, still volunteers, to undertake more meals, for which there was no shortage of hungry children, a development Elliot himself found "insidious" (Grant 1930, p. 71; Elliott 1909, p. 805). Though the 1906 Act explicitly stated that taking school meals did not carry any of the legal consequences of pauperization, donors and most legislators continued to find it impossible to offer the food as the routine service that primary education itself had become and as the parents themselves were increasingly tending to see the meals.

On the eve of World War I, Sir George Newman, the chief medical officer for the (national) Board of Education, eager to get Parliament to support a bill authorizing more local tax money for school feeding, offered an argument hitherto unheard among those supporting school dinners, and one of the few likely to succeed in Parliament: "Experience shows that food riots are inspired largely by the hunger of children; and if that problem can be met, a large operating factor in the causation of riots is removed." The bill became law with unusual speed, and a record number of children were fed during the school year 1914–1915, a year of enormous unemployment and social dislocation. The next year, however, the number of meals declined drastically, in London by about three-fourths.[30] Though war work and wives' allowances improved living standards for a large minority of London households, the children's meals would have been very helpful for wartime working wives. But their social price was too high, as it indeed continued to be until World War II. With the edge of desperation temporarily blunted, the London mothers withdrew their children, or saw them ejected wholesale, from the dining centers.

Separated from us in time and place and by its outmoded language, the British practice of charity a hundred years ago with its successes and failures leaves us with some more permanent insights perhaps by virtue of its very distance from our own world. The British charity givers' lack of control over the ultimate use to which recipients put their donations certainly offers one permanent cautionary tale for philanthropists today, as does the futile and ungenerous accumulation of punitive methods designed to control the destination of their gifts. And, as the administration of stigma along with London school dinners demonstrates, ambivalence about the justice of the cause or the worthiness of the recipients distorts the offer of charity as much as material obstacles in the form of funds and personnel.

Notes

Portions of this paper have been adapted from other work by the author: Ross (1990) and Ross (1993), ch. 1.

1. Himmelfarb (1991), p. 2; Davidoff and Hall (1987), p. 416; Koditschek (1990), ch. 10–11; R. Morris (1983) and R. Morris (1990).

2. There is a large literature on the settlement movement, but a recent discussion which focuses on the male side of this movement is Koven (1992).

3. Prochaska (1990), p. 385. On women settlement workers see Vicinus (1985), ch. 6.

4. Children's Country Holiday Fund, *Report for 1899*; "The Children's Country Holiday Fund," *Toynbee Record*, December 1908, p. 45.

5. Owen (1964), 479; and on charitable support for hospitals in general, pp. 483–89.

6. Montefiore (1903), p. 18. Another 12,137 people (a far smaller number) used state funded institutions, either poor law infirmaries or Metropolitan Asylums Board hospitals according to 1884 figures (Thorne 1888, p. 262).

7. See Prochaska (1980) and Prochaska (1990), p. 371. The provision of trusses, he points out, is not just a quaint and odd taste of the philanthropists but a response to a great need in a society where so many people did heavy manual labor and hernias were very common.

8. Linklater (1980), p. 59 and passim; Battersea (1922), ch. 20; B. Webb (1979), pp. 274, 285; Chase (1929), pp. 23–24; E. Jones (1973), pp. 102–103.

9. For romances of this kind, see, for example, Besant (1889); also the sketches in Honnor Morten, *Tales of the Children's Ward*; and Free's (1907) story of the socialite and the slum clergyman. Also see the romantic encounter against a slum background in Gissing (1976), pp. 219–20.

10. On Eleanor Marx, see Kapp (1972); on Amy Levy, see the discussion in Nord (1990).

11. For a good general discussion of working-class charity, see Prochaska (1990), pp. 362–70; also Peterson (1989), p. 140; and Chinn (1988).

12. Tottenham History Workshop, *How Things Were: Growing up in Tottenham, 1890–1920* (n.p., n.d.), p. 21; Hine (1980), p. 40; Foakes (1972), p. 22.

13. S. Webb (1907), p. 18; *School Child* 6 (January 1916), p. 1; Bailward (1912), p. 548.

14. Case records of the COS (now Family Welfare Association), Area 4, St. Pancras North, in the GLRO, no. 22478. I am grateful to the Family Welfare Association for giving me permission to examine these records and have used a pseudonym as promised. The woman, eventually accepted as a client, remained an active case through 1946.

15. The corrective, acknowledging the uncertainties of gift giving, is found in Bourdieu (1990), pp. 98–99; also G. Jones (1976).

16. Elizabeth Rignall, "All So Long Ago," typescript, ch. 10, Brunel University Library; School Board for London, *Report of the Special Sub-Committee of the General purposes Committee on Underfed Children 1898–99*, Appendix I: Evidence of Witnesses, testimony of Mr. J. Morant, February 27, 1899, p. 17, in Greater London Record Office; Bulkley (1914), p. 16; Free (1907), p. 142.

17. As in Edwin Pugh's sketch, "The Charity Mongers," a conversation between two old women complaining about the poor quality of the multiple offerings available through the churches at Christmas (Pugh 1914).

18. Elliott (1909), p. 869; McMillan and Sanderson (1909), p. 2. Another rhapsodic account is Price (1893), p. 43.

19. London County Council, *Report of the Joint Committee on Underfed Children for 1904–05* (London: King, 1905), pp. 15–21; School Board for London, *Report of the Special Sub-Committee, 1898–99*, p. iii. Also see the discussion in Hurt (1979), p. 121.

20. The meals tended to be discontinued in March or April and resumed about November, because London unemployment rates were higher during the winter. See Bulkley (1914), p. 143; Rubinstein, p. 82; Board of Education, "Report on the Working of the Education (Provision of Meals) Act 1906 up to 31 March 1909," Great Britain, House of Commons, *Parliamentary Papers (PP)* 1910, vol. 23, p. 24.

21. *Charity and Food: Report of the Special Committee of the Charity Organisation Society*

upon Soup Kitchens, Children's Breakfasts and Dinners, and Cheap Food Supply (London: Spottisswoode & Co., 1887), pp. 55, 11; Hurt (1979), pp. 118–25.

22. "Report on the Working of the Education (Provision of Meals) Act," PP 1910, vol. 23, pp. 17–20; Hurt (1979), pp. 119.

23. *Charity and Food*, p. 33; Minutes of Children's Care Committees: Curtain Road School, June 20, 1911; Popham Road School, October 1909, May 1911. All in the Greater London Record Office.

24. "The Women's Socials at Beatrice House," *Bermondsey Settlement, Eighteenth Annual Report*, 1910, p. 14.

25. Manin (1930), p. 34; Family Life and Work Experience Archive, collected by Paul Thompson and Thea Vigne, housed at the University of Essex, transcript no. 331, p. 42. See also no. 368, p. 58.

26. Care Committee minutes, Popham Road School, Curtain Road School.

27. Iselin, "Story of a Children's Care Committee," p. 43.

28. Iselin, "Story of a Children's Care Committee," pp. 59–60; The Secretary of an Islington Care Committee, "Difficulties in a Very Poor District," *School Child* 2 (February 1912); Tallents (1909), p. 97; "Saturday Afternoon in Fulham," *School Child* 2 (April 1912), p. 13.

29. These conclusions are based on a study of the minutes of several of the London committees, most of which begin in 1909: Curtain Road School, EC2; Popham Road School, N1; Wood Close School, E2; Bay Street School, Central Hackney; St. Matthews N. School, NW. All in Greater London Record Office.

30. Thane (1984), pp. 75–76; Hurt, "Feeding the Hungry Schoolchild," p. 182; *Women's Dreadnought*, September 29, 1917, summarizing Newman's annual reports; Beveridge (1928), p. 327.

10 | Compromising to Achieve

Choices in International Charity

Alex Rondos

POPULATION GROWTH, environmental degradation, political inequity, and the replacement of social order with a world of multiple civil conflicts have combined to produce the simple statistical fact that more people are more vulnerable to the threat of death or deprivation than ever before. This has been accompanied by an explosive growth of international charitable initiatives. Whatever the current debates about "foreign aid," governments give substantially, either directly to foreign countries or to the United Nations system. Private charitable initiative has expanded to such an extent that it has become a political constituency of its own in donor societies, affecting the course of conflicts and altering social issues overseas. This growth has meant a major increase in the number of charitable organizations and of administrators and workers who are charged with the responsibility for the proper definition of crises, selection of programs, management of projects, and accountability for funds. Motivated by goodwill, of religious or secular inspiration, they daily confront realities which prompt a series of ethical questions that they cannot avoid if they are to continue their missions.

Whether the issue is the military protection of delivery of food and medicine to a besieged town in Bosnia, organizing a group of women to develop their own savings scheme in some distant African village, or providing cash to support a leprosarium in a country where lepers are otherwise stigmatized, there is a set of five related issues which shape the course of any charitable decision and action.

(i) To what extent is any charitable action an intrusion in the working of a society, cloaked in the language of impartiality?

(ii) Is the purpose of the charity to provide immediate relief, or is it a longer-term pursuit of justice, requiring support for or perhaps manipulation of indigenous entities so that they are "empowered" to overcome the injustices of the environment in which they live?

(iii) Is the activity shaped by reasonably objective analysis of the needs of prospective recipients, or is it more strongly influenced by a perception of what the donor would like to see happen as a result of his gifts?

(iv) To what extent are charitable activities shaped by the fear of not being accountable?

(v) Finally, how, in a world where needs exceed the availability of assistance, is the triage between beneficiary of charity and those rejected to be conducted?

For the charitable worker these are not theoretical issues. They require making hard decisions quickly about what to do next. The questions are made more difficult for the philanthropic bureaucrat because they arise at a time when much of the context within which charity is being conducted is being redefined.

Central governments that once assumed a monopoly of responsibility for the well-being of their citizens are beating a collective retreat from their social obligations. This began well before the collapse of the communist systems of the Soviet Union and Eastern Europe, when creditors of many Third World countries forced those governments to cut back on social programs (subsidized food, medicine, housing, and transport) to meet their financial commitments. Given that state charity greased the wheels of political legitimacy in most countries with unrepresentative political systems, the decline in social services has contributed to a social and political vacuum that is now being filled spontaneously by community initiatives, on a scale that has yet to be fully appreciated.

In organizing themselves, the poor of the Third World countries, and increasingly also those of Eastern Europe, have had recourse to institutions with which they have the most traditional affinity. Organized religion has emerged as an essential purveyor of social services. Mosques in the Middle East now provide relief, day care, primary health care, and even economic assistance to help people set up business. The same trend is emerging among the newly liberated churches of the former communist bloc, and religious institutions are being called upon to play a greater role in the alleviation of Africa's crisis. In all these locations the poor have also begun to construct their own new forms of group action. Secular interest groups, such as women's cooperatives, associations that represent environmental concerns, and organizations of parents with handicapped children are mushrooming in a world where these services were once carried out by, or at the very least claimed as the domain of, central government.

Thus, in the redefinition of the social contract where the state and its role are significantly reduced, the entire indigenous structure and dynamics of charity also change. It is to this constellation of initiatives and interests that an equally diversified and expanding group of international charities are responding.

From the perspective of the donor there are three main categories of charitable bureaucracy. Governments make public finance available for a wide variety of emergency and long-term assistance. The U.S. Government annually makes some $15 billion available for foreign aid, though over half of this is devoted to a small group of countries deemed strategically important. The majority of this money, often for poverty alleviation, is given directly to governments in the form of direct finance or technical assistance. The so-called grassroots sector of a society rarely receives U.S. government funds directly: the administrative cost of such an effort is prohibitive.

The United Nations constitutes the next major bloc of donors and is divided into several technical agencies of varying wealth and mandate. UNICEF, the World Food program, and the UN High Commissioner for Refugees are among the best known. Depending on the intensity of a crisis, they may collaborate to great benefit or they can compete bureaucratically with fatal consequences. They too make the majority of their funding available to local governments, and as United Nations agencies they are, to a large extent, the least independent of actors. Being a creature of its member states the United Nations is deeply beholden to its constituency. Only lately has one detected a willingness by the United Nations to take a less constrained definition of national sovereignty, and this has resulted in controversial initiatives such as those in Somalia or Rwanda.

There is, finally, the growing family of voluntary organizations. Names like Oxfam, CARE, and Catholic Relief Services have, for many years been synonymous with "relief" work. Each represented a constituency: some are faith based, others have a secular concern for social justice; more recently still others have come to represent specific concerns such as the environment or women's interests. Beyond this formal network of agencies there are a multitude of small parish or community acts of charity that represent a massive but unquantified transfer of resources to the overseas poor and their representatives.

It is against this global background of fragmenting structures of political authority and proliferating charitable initiatives that the questions raised at the beginning of this paper acquire a certain urgency. They need to be illustrated more fully.

(i) The first question concerns the intrusiveness of charity. Even if the donor claims to be impartial, who benefits most from charity, and to what extent can or should the donors impose their preferences? Can charity pretend to be impartial? In the shorthand of the editorialist this may come under the heading of the "politics of foreign aid." As some of the subsequent remarks will suggest, there is no way in which the politicization of charity can be avoided. Indeed, if charity is at its "purest" in pursuing social justice, then it is by definition political. To the practitioner, as opposed to the political advocate, the question is not whether the politics are good but whether they are clever. Do the ethical compromises permit the work of charity to be carried out?

At one level the debate has revolved around the "colonial" nature of charity—the imposition of goodwill without adequate understanding of the expressed or elicited desires of those for whom the charity was intended. The significant aspect of this debate was that it originated from the protests of the so-called beneficiaries. In the aid being given to them they saw not an instrument of liberation from poverty or for social justice, but a means of perpetuating their degradation and failure to challenge the prevailing power structure. Out of this debate emerged the theology of liberation and the work of such men as Paulo Freire.

The discussion and the practice of international charity have been significantly expanded by the challenge made in the last decade to the once unassailable protection of sovereignty behind which many an oppressive government has hidden. The militarization of philanthropy which first occurred in northern Iraq in 1991 and subsequently in Somalia and Bosnia, dramatically illustrate the operational tension between the desire to reach people in desperate need and the political consequences of that action. For the first time, the international community has intervened militarily in a sovereign state to protect or guarantee access to people deemed physically at risk because of civil conflict. The subordination of sovereignty of a recognized state to the needs of the suffering is arguably a milestone in legal and practical precedent in the history of international charitable action. Hitherto charitable organizations had to accommodate themselves to the political whim and constraint imposed by one side or another in a conflict.

Iraq, Somalia, Bosnia today, and Ethiopia a decade ago also sharpen the focus on the abiding paradox that cloaks any act of charity in a conflict. The charity which keeps people alive has also perpetuated the carnage. Sarajevo has been relieved from hunger by a very successful relief effort: There are no recorded deaths by malnutrition in Sarajevo. Yet Sarajevo has not been relieved, as one might associate the word with a siege: Its agony continues.

Likewise in Ethiopia in the 1980s, hundreds of thousands of tons of food reached Ethiopia in response to a famine created by civil war, not drought. Food was brought in to areas controlled either by the government or by rebel nationalist factions that represented Eritrea or Tigray. Organizations operating in Ethiopian government territory were accused of abetting a vicious war conducted by the government against rebels with a real cause. Agencies which helped on the rebel side were accused by the government of assisting "bandits." But despite the invective, it is beyond doubt that a famine of even more catastrophic proportions was averted by these relief efforts.

The real issues, though, rarely rise to the forefront of public debate. To give just one example: Large numbers of trucks are required to move enough food across treacherous terrain if one wants to feed over two million geographically scattered people a day. The Ethiopian government announced that there were insufficient trucks and the international donor community cravenly acquiesced by supplying a fleet of over 600, all of which remained in Ethiopia. Meanwhile, the Ethiopian army was conscripting larger numbers of men and moving them throughout the territory with their own military trucks, use of which they denied to the humanitarian programs.

Emanating from this central ethical conflict in humanitarian work is the moral price paid for silence in the face of conspicuous abuses of human rights.

When the Ethiopian government decided in 1985 to "resettle"—a euphemistic precursor of ethnic cleansing—up to half a million Tigrayans from the central highlands to the southwest, in malaria-infested territory on the border of Sudan, only one of the many relief agencies spoke out and eventually had to leave the country.

Silence in the name of operational survival grew even more perverse in Ethiopia when the government refused to admit that a cholera epidemic had broken out. It claimed instead that this was a case of "violent diarrhea." So millions of warning leaflets remained locked in warehouses, while thousands of people were dying from what were classic symptoms of cholera, a disease that need not be fatal if treated in time. The government preferred the path of fatal obfuscation because the official admission of a cholera epidemic would have halted the international sales of Ethiopian coffee, the primary source of hard currency with which the government was able to purchase fuel and other supplies for its war effort.

A decade after the Ethiopian crisis, a newer ethical twist is posed by the growing use of sanctions against renegade governments such as in Iraq or Serbia. If the purpose of sanctions is to coerce a regime into some form of compliance with international policies, it is assumed that forces within the country will react politically to make the change. Charitable organizations, and especially religious groups, argue that those who suffer most under sanctions are the ones who are beneath politics. They are the shut-in elderly, infants, the institutionalized who cannot affect the political system. The evidence tends to suggest that sanctions create a new class of profiteers who are coopted by the local regime against whom the sanctions were initially imposed. With equal cause, others argue that any assistance sent to these countries will permit the regime to divert its diminishing food and medical resources to those who might otherwise take political action.

The debate over the political impact of charity has been most contentious in Somalia. Beyond the immediate hand-wringing over the transformation of a military expedition intended to protect the delivery of humanitarian assistance into an embarrassingly unsuccessful punitive expedition against one Somali faction leader, there lies a much larger issue. There is a fundamental difference between delivering aid to civilian victims of a conflict and making or keeping peace. The relief worker, not unlike the military planner, has to have one simple objective in mind: to ensure the most effective and timely delivery of assistance to a target population. The obstacles are invariably political as opposed to logistical and involve a degree of negotiation and even collaboration with the parties to the conflict to ensure access. International peacekeepers have to ensure that opposing forces are kept apart. The more fashionable term—"peacemaking"—implies that an external force is willing to engage in combat in order to assert not just peace but some attendant political solution. What really happens in a foreign military intervention is the replacement of local capacity, however politically compromised, by external forces whose durability or even purpose is less than clear.

The relief worker is concerned with identifying those indigenous entities who can not only carry food (because they have the access, at least, to their communities) but also because they are representative of communities which must eventually be party to some form of reconciliation. Thus, in the midst of war and suffering one might begin to fashion the beginnings of a climate of reconciliation rather than continued alienation. The best relief operations are in fact those that identify indigenous organizations, or individuals, that command a degree of local respect, to carry out the work of delivering food. They know the terrain, they know the principal actors, and invariably they are the people who will play the critical role in the future reconciliation of a society.

(ii) The transformation of charitable activity from relief to the vital task of addressing the causes of a social and political breakdown brings us to the second major question facing charitable workers. Once it was thought that the provision of food, blankets, medicine, and shelter constituted charity. Then it became the fashion to encourage the development of local self-help initiatives. Now, in the language of international economic assistance, one speaks of "sustainable development" achieved through the creation of financially viable organizations that represent the poor of a given society. Some argue that even this is not enough. To help one community while the surrounding areas or communities are untouched is to create a Potemkin village which, upon the departure of the foreign donor, will be immediately set upon by the predatory bureaucrats, politicians, or middlemen who still control the particular environment of oppression.

There are now many who promote the idea of developing associations of empowered groups. This classic political strategy is a hallmark of the rise of not-for-profit interest groups in the United States. In many other parts of the world, it is equally a strategy worth pursuing, provided it is understood that the greater the power transferred to some group, the greater the temptation for the authorities, undoubtedly threatened, to coopt its leadership.

In this thoroughly worthy refinement of charity there arises the lingering worry that "empowerment" may actually reinforce certain forms of indigenous social stratification. At the most elementary level, the problem is apparent in a household. When a family benefits financially from some income-generating project, who benefits within the family? Many a project will extol its own benefits, citing the rise in income of a family, without tracking whether the nutritional status of the child has improved, for example, or whether the girls in the family are now going to school. In a society in which the adult male gets precedence to the best of the food on the table, followed by the male son, inequity can be easily perpetuated by the best intentioned of projects. This is the lowest common denominator that proves the fallacy of trickle-down in charity. How one guarantees equal access to charity in communities becomes a constant source of uncertainty.

The issue can be illustrated by a problem within the many programs now trying to address gender issues. Efforts are now being made to target only the central woman in a household, for example, by giving her access to cash so that she can dispose of income for the benefit of the family and thus strengthen her own position in society. Likewise, the link between poverty and the degradation of environment has spawned an entirely new category of organization whose sole purpose is to benefit those communities that care for their immediate physical environment so that the mutual benefit of increased wealth and improved environmental conditions become self-evident.

(iii) Paradoxically, these are the issues which also highlight the third issue we have to face—the question of the degree to which a donor's wishes are to influence the course of charity. The greatest amount of assistance available for charity is from governments or international organizations like the United Nations. Private organizations, will, with few exceptions, draw on these funds. When issues like women's programs, environment, or population are deemed politically attractive, the funds flow accordingly. One of the most dramatic examples of this influence is in the debate over population control, when there were massive cuts in federal funds from the United States because successive administrations were opposed to a variety of birth control programs. Today, the rage is "civil society" or "democratization" for societies which have had civility bludgeoned out of them and in which the experience of democracy, in the Western parliamentary tradition, is scant.

Proposals for funding are often developed to meet the new criteria, and are written and reviewed mainly for their relevance to the strategy of the donor institution. In preparing such proposals an organization will frequently, and unconsciously, adopt the language and philosophy of the donor institution, skewing the substance of the project in favor of the donor's wishes. Indeed, throughout the Third World today, seminars are conducted at great expense on how to write proposals, often well before those seeking funds have been given the most elementary training in management and planning. This may provide access for, and thus empower, some indigenous group. But, at the risk of being a little too cavalier with Franz Fanon, it is another way of asking the Black Face to put on the White Mask. It encourages assimilation of donor ideologies rather than the elaboration of what is in the best interest of the group it is meant to benefit.

A particularly painful debate in the world of international private philanthropy centers on the use of food aid. Huge programs of food assistance were built up during the 1950s and 1960s by private organizations thanks to the massive agricultural surpluses in the United States and, later, in Europe. The food was used not only for famines but also for addressing the crisis of structural malnourishment. By the 1970s a growing body of opinion questioned the value of these programs. It was contended that in benefiting the American farmer, they undermined the local market system, especially in societies desperately trying to establish a viable domestic agricultural market. Critics also contended that the aid programs had no discernible long-term impact in making the intended beneficiaries more independent socially or economically.

Food, however, is a very visible form of charity and in recipient societies it is an asset to those who appropriate political credit for acquiring the food. It is also a very easy way of making a charitable organization look big. Since food programs are accompanied by substantial financial support that helps to cover the administrative costs of an organization, they become attractive to those organizations that are willing to invest in the human infrastructure needed for so heavy a logistical responsibility.

Herein lies the key to understanding how a charity survives and what that does to the relationship between donor and recipient needs. Without funds to cover administrative costs, the organization cannot sustain the expertise with which to develop proposals, with which, in turn, to ask for more money.

Other agencies have forgone the opportunity to take public funds on the grounds that their mission might be compromised, especially in areas where, during the Cold War era, the U.S. government funds were clearly directed at programs that suited the political desires of Washington rather than the needs as known on the ground.

In these circumstances one limits one's financial base, developing a constituency of supporters who are educated and cultivated over time to understand and support one's mission. This is the most pristine form of charity. Such organizations inevitably are small, though highly effective. Others develop what might be regarded as an assembly line approach to charity. They identify themselves with a particular type of activity—providing emergency medicine in a disaster, sponsoring children, or creating credit schemes for impoverished women. For purposes of cost efficiency, they develop elaborately described and designed "models" which are then peddled in recipient societies where the temptation is to accept the model because there is money attached to it. Thus the cycle of model, compliant recipient and fund-raising action acquires a repetitive momentum of its own. Inevitably, such a practice generates expectations in recipient communities. There is the well-known and certainly apocryphal tale of the village chief in Africa who would give a different account of the height of his corn that year depending on what he thought the particular inquiring agency might be able to offer. This is the perverse end of charity, where the prospective recipient assumes the availability of a particular type or quantity of assistance and thus tailors the request appropriately.

Finally, there are the parachute philanthropists who live off emergencies,

flying in with plane loads of goods, many of which could normally be purchased locally, clogging up the few airstrips available, but always accompanied
by television cameras. They usually leave once the pictures have been taken. It
is exciting; it sells well among many donors. Its impact is minimal because the
supplies do not last long and the delivery of emergency assistance by air is too
expensive to sustain, even for governments. Anyway, donor governments, with
their own air forces at their disposal, are much more efficient at doing this.

Since taxpayers have already contributed by helping finance their government's contribution to the dispatch of aircraft, it would make more sense to divert charitable dollars to those programs of more lasting benefit which do not
usually attract large quantities of private contributions. The fact remains that
raising funds to provide management training for a women's group in Peru, let
us say, is much more difficult than getting gifts for a program where one can
show starvation. Famines are telegenic, management is not.

(iv) The needs or predilections of the donor also create our fourth question,
an issue that affects all organizations trying to do charity overseas, namely, the
operationally stifling and financially costly need to maintain ever higher standards of accountability. The proliferation of charitable groups has been accompanied by growing pressure from donors for greater accountability. This presents itself in various forms. The traditional one is to ask that an organization
guarantee that assistance "will get to the mouths of those who are hungry." Or
it is represented by much more stringent audit requirements. It is also represented by a growing predisposition among donors to designate their donations.
Complicating matters, more donors want to give only to those organizations
which maintain a low administrative overhead, leaving agencies trapped between the demand to reduce administrative costs and the need to live up to ever
higher standards of financial and programmatic accountability. With the explo-
sion in the number of charities, there has been a proportionate increase in publicity about excesses and abuses within charities.

Fearful of publicity over a poor project and, certainly, terrified of the appearance of ubiquitous government auditors, there is the danger that many
charitable organizations may shrink from the challenge of taking on initiatives
that are risky. Private charity has always prided itself on reaching those whom
others cannot reach, and on taking risks on behalf of the poor. Indeed, one could
argue that it is the role of an international charity to serve as a buffer and scapegoat in the struggle between the development of small indigenous initiatives—
which generally requires learning through error—and the inquisitorial donor.
At a personal level, the charitable bureaucrat will question the value of putting
his or her job on the line. Most agencies react by creating larger bureaucracies
to protect themselves, thus incurring greater costs for administration. Others
invest in very sophisticated public relations. The most dangerous consequence,
however, is that charities will shrink from the test of standing by a small or-

ganization, whose accountability is weak, but whose growth is vital to the development of pluralism and the protection of those who suffer.

(v) The tests that confront any professional in the work of charity will only grow with the years. Some of the key tensions in the conduct of charity in foreign countries have been outlined in the previous pages. But they distill themselves into the even larger moral dilemma: the triage in the selection of who is to be helped or not helped. The moral, political, and technical elements involved in the choice of a recipient of assistance occurs from the global to the local act of charity. It is, as it should be, the most contentious and personally searing aspect of the profession because the proper identification of who is most deserving of charity is the very raison d'etre of the charitable mission.

Large-scale philanthropic initiatives, whether in response to disasters and war or to address long-term poverty alleviation, depend entirely upon funding, the availability of which is dictated by current ideological or political fashion and the astonishing increase in the role of the media.

By early 1995, it was clear that, in the global triage of funding available from public sources, the poorest continent, Africa, was going to receive diminishing attention while the former Eastern Bloc was drawing away significant investment and aid funds. There is now grave concern that funds will dry up just when the momentum of civic initiative in Africa is developing and could begin to produce a degree of social stability. Many private charities that receive matching funds from public sources see their impact significantly diminished as a consequence. Conversely, charities have been forced to dilute their concentration on the poorest of nations in order to seize the opportunity of funding that is available for Eastern Europe or the former Soviet Union.

To a large extent such policies are driven by public perception. Foreign aid is deemed politically unpopular in the United States, which in relative terms gives less—under 1 percent—of its annual budget to foreign aid than many other Western nations. Yet, opinion polls taken in late 1994 and early 1995 showed that the public believed that up to 20 percent of the budget went to foreign aid. This has shaped the ambience in which politicians can speak of foreign aid being wasteful and of little use to the interests of the United States.

This perception is compounded by the belief that foreign aid has a limited impact, except in disasters where the issue is a very visible battle between life and death. Thus emergency relief programs receive more support from the public at the expense of those programs that have a long-term beneficial impact on society but which lack the visceral immediacy of a disaster. It is in this context that so many organizations are forced to succumb to vulgar televised advertising of the indignity of a starving child in which we are somehow assured by some current representative of Hollywood that this agency or that will save this child's life. Viewed from the inside of the profession—and admittedly this is a personal reflection—one does ask whether we dishonor those whom we are meant to help to preserve our own image of self-appointed and very public Samaritans. Triage creates its own unseemliness. And the justice, moreover, of preserving life supersedes the justice implicit in eradicating the cause of the threat to life.

Of greater influence, however, is the role of the media in shaping our understanding of poverty or disaster. For one year, throughout most of 1984, agencies were trying to tell the public and authorities that a catastrophe of monumental proportions was occurring in Ethiopia. The official reaction was to downplay the crisis as one exaggerated and manufactured by a thoroughly nasty government beholden to its master, the Soviet Union. Then, in one week in November of that year, a single television network devoted five minutes of each evening of its national news to the scenes in Ethiopia. Overnight a neglected disaster had become a Disaster.

A decade later, the agony of Sarajevo is so thoroughly televised that it has become an emblem of a modern form of warfare and humanitarian emergency. Money that could save entire cities in Africa has been collected for Sarajevo. Meanwhile, the city of Juba in southern Sudan—with as many inhabitants as Sarajevo—has also been besieged; malnutrition is very high, the city is bombed regularly. Relief agencies have to raise private funds to run an airlift into Juba from neighboring Kenya. Much of the city of Grozny, the capital of Chechnya in southern Russia, has been destroyed, most of its inhabitants, except the elderly, forced to flee. Frightened old women in dark, dank cellars do not make good television. The international reaction has been constrained to say the least. These are the raw human sufferings that international triage is about.

It would be wrong, nonetheless, to assume that fault lies with the donor alone, or with charities that try to weave a productive course through the shoals of public perception and the fickleness of politicians. There is a local aspect to triage. Foreign charities are not at liberty to enter another country and start operations without some degree of access granted by the authorities, who, invariably, are the cause of the crisis in the first place. Selection of who will live or die usually begins with the willingness of any local authority to admit that there is a crisis. No public official wants to admit that there is hunger in his district. It suggests that he is incompetent. From the point of view of the authorities, any public admission might create a panic and hoarding and thus aggravate the crisis. "The fear of famine creates famine," the high minister Necker warned Louis XVI. A foreign charity which may be aware of the situation can do little. For at that very early stage, to provoke an international outcry would antagonize an embarrassed government which must still be coaxed into admitting that there is a famine, or at the least a threat of one. A more subtle, but no less noxious, triage appeared recently in Russia during the refugee crisis created by the war in Chechnya. The refugees were both Chechens and Russians. The Federal Ministry responsible for refugees in the Russian Federation maintains copious lists of who is eligible from all ethnic groups; somehow most Russians appeared in the highest category of eligibility.

People call this the "politics" of foreign aid. To many of us who work "in the field," the politics are a reality that one takes for granted. The crises are caused by human political mismanagement or plain malevolence. It is the triage that becomes the constant source of tension. Just like the battlefield surgeon, one asks who has the best chance to live or die, and what resources, given the limited flow, are best applied to the preservation of which social limb. It becomes a cyclical debate over who is really poor, who is most deserving, of how one moves from treating the symptom to attacking the cause.

The five tensions I have discussed reemerge with shocking consistency, but they are never finally resolved. In each new crisis administrators and workers in charitable organizations are forced to see them from a slightly different angle. Man seems to have an infinite capacity for inventing new variations of injustice.

Bibliography

Adam, Paul. 1964. *La Vie paroissiale en France au XIVe siècle*. Histoire et sociologie de l'église, 3. Paris: Sirey.

———. 1982. *Charité et assistance en Alsace au moyen âge*. Société savante d'Alsace et des régions de l'est, Série "Grandes Publications," vol. 22. Strasbourg: Librairie Istra.

Addams, Jane. 1910. *Twenty Years at Hull-House*. New York.

Adkins, A. W. H. 1972. *Moral Values and Political Behavior in Ancient Greece*. New York: Norton.

Ambrose of Milan. 1979-. *On the Duties of the Clergy*. Trans. H. De Romestin. A Select Library of the Nicene and Post-Nicene Fathers of the Christian Church, vol. 10. Grand Rapids, MI: Eerdmans.

Andreoni, James. 1986. "Private Giving to Public Goods: The Limits to Altruism." University of Michigan Department of Economics Working Paper.

Annas, Julia. 1993. *The Morality of Happiness*. Oxford: Oxford University Press.

Aptheker, Herbert. 1964. *A Documentary History of the Negro People in the United States*. 2 vols. New York: Citadel.

Aquinas, Thomas. 1989. *Summa Theologica*. Trans. the Fathers of the English Dominican Province. 5 vols. Westminster, MD: Christian Classics.

Aristotle. 1975. *Nichomachean Ethics*. Trans. H. Rackham. Cambridge, MA: Harvard University Press.

Aristotle. 1984. *Complete Works*, ed. Jonathan Barnes. Princeton: Princeton University Press.

Armstrong, A. H., ed. 1970. *The Cambridge History of Later Greek and Early Medieval Philosophy*. Revised edition. Cambridge: Cambridge University Press.

Athanasius. 1952. *The Life of St. Anthony*. In DeFerrari, ed. (1952): 133–216.

Augustine of Hippo. 1948a. *The City of God*. Trans. Marcus Dods. In *The Basic Works of St. Augustine* (1984), ed. Whitney J. Oates. Vol. II, pp. 3–663.

———. 1948b. *On the Morals of the Catholic Church*. Trans. R. Stothert. In *The Basic Works of St. Augustine* (1984), ed. Whitney J. Oates. Vol. I, pp. 317–57.

———. 1992. *Confessions*. Trans. Henry Chadwick. Oxford: Oxford University Press.

Bahmueller, Charles F. 1981. *The National Charity Company: Jeremy Bentham's Silent Revolution*. Berkeley: University of California Press.

Bailward, W. A. 1912. "Some Recent Developments of Poor Relief." *Economic Journal* 22.

Barkley Brown, Elsa. 1988. "Womanist Consciousness: Maggie Lena Walker and the Independent Order of Saint Luke." In Malson et al., eds. (1988): 173–96.

Barry, Brian. 1989. *Theories of Justice*. Vol. 1 of *A Treatise on Social Justice*. Berkeley: University of California Press.

Battersea, Constance. 1922. *Reminiscences*. London: Macmillan.

Baynes, Norman H. 1955. *Byzantine Studies and Other Essays*. London: Athlone.

Benedict of Nursia. 1958. *The Rule of St. Benedict*. Trans. Owen Chadwick. In Chadwick (1958): 290–337.

Benton, John F., ed. 1970. *Self and Society in Medieval France: The Memoirs of Abbot Guibert of Nogent*. New York: Harper & Row.

Berry, Mary Frances, and John Blassingame. 1982. *Long Memory*. New York: Oxford Unversity Press.

Besant, Walter. 1889. *Children of Gibeon*. New York: Harper.

Beveridge, Sir William. 1928. *British Food Control*. Oxford: Oxford University Press.

Billingsley, Andrew. 1968. *Black Families in White America*. Englewood Cliffs, NJ: Prentice Hall.

Birkett, Dea. 1989. *Spinsters Abroad: Victorian Lady Explorers*. Oxford: Blackwell.

Booth, Charles. 1969. *Life and Labour of the People in London*, 1st series: *Poverty*, vol. 2 (1902–04). New York: Kelley.

Bourdieu, Pierre. 1990. *The Logic of Practice*. Trans. Richard Nice. Stanford: Stanford University Press.

Brentano, Robert. 1988. *The Two Churches: England and Italy in the Thirteenth Century*. 2nd ed. Berkeley: University of California Press.

Brown, Peter. 1967. *Augustine of Hippo*. Berkeley: University of California Press.

Buchanan, Allen. 1984. "What's So Special about Rights?" *Social Philosophy and Policy* 2, no. 1. (Autumn): 61–83.

———. 1987. "Justice and Charity." *Ethics* 97 (April): 558–75.

———. 1990. "Justice as Reciprocity versus Subject-Centered Justice." *Philosophy and Public Affairs* 19, no. 3: 227–52.

———. 1993. "The Morality of Inclusion." In Paul, Miller, and Paul, eds. (1993): 233–57.

Bulkley, M. E. 1914. *The Feeding of School Children*. London: Bell.

Bullock, Henry Allen. 1970. *A History of Negro Education in the South*. New York: Praeger.

Butler, Joseph. 1900. *Works*. 2 Vols. J. H. Bernard, ed. London: Macmillan.

Caille, Jacqueline. 1977. *Hôpitaux et charité publique à Narbonne au Moyen Age de la fin du XIe à la fin du XVe*. Toulouse: Privat.

———. 1978. "Hospices et assistance à Narbonne (XIIIe–XIVe s.)." *Assistance et charité en Languedoc au XIIIe et au début du XIVe siècles*. Cahiers de Fanjeaux, 13. Toulouse: Privat.

Calvin, Jean. 1961. *Institutes of the Christian Religion*. John T. McNeill, ed. London: S. C. M. Press.

Carson, Emmett D. 1989. "The Evolution of Black Philanthropy: Patterns of Giving and Voluntarism." In Magat, ed. (1989).

———. 1990. "Black Volunteers as Givers and Fund-raisers." Working paper prepared for the Center for the Study of Philanthropy, Conference on "Volunteers and Fund-raisers," November 14, 1990, City University of New York.

Carson, Mina. 1990. *Settlement Folk*. Chicago: University of Chicago Press.

Cassian, John. 1958. *The Conferences of Cassian*. Trans. Owen Chadwick. In Chadwick, ed. (1958): 190–289.

Chadwick, Henry. 1986. *Augustine*. Oxford: Oxford University Press.

Chadwick, Owen, ed. 1958. *Western Asceticism*. Philadelphia: Westminster.

Chase, Ellen. 1929. *Tenant Friends in Old Deptford*. London: Williams & Norgate.

Chenu, M. D. 1964. *Toward Understanding St. Thomas.* Trans. A. M. Landry & D. Hughes. Chicago: Regnery.

———. 1968. *Nature, Man, and Society in the Twelfth Century: Essays on New Theological Perspectives in the Latin West.* Trans. Jerome Taylor and Lester K. Little. Chicago: University of Chicago Press.

Chiffoleau, Jacques. 1978. "Charité et assistance en Avignon et dans le Comtat Venaissin (fin XIIIe–fin XIVe siècle)." *Assistance et charité en Languedoc au XIIIe et au début du XIVe siècles.* Cahiers de Fanjeaux, 13. Toulouse: Privat.

Chinn, Carl. 1988. *They Worked All Their Lives: Women of the Urban Poor in England, 1880–1939.* Manchester: Manchester University Press.

Chitty, Derwas J. 1966. *The Desert a City: An Introduction to the Study of Egyptian and Palestinian Monasticism under the Christian Empire.* Oxford: Blackwell.

Cicero, Marcus Tullius. 1961. *De Officiis.* Trans. Walter Miller. Loeb Classical Library. Cambridge, MA: Harvard University Press.

Cipolla, Carlo M., ed. 1972. *The Fontana Economic History of Europe: The Middle Ages.* New York: Barnes & Noble.

Cohn, Samuel. 1992. *The Cult of Remembrance and the Black Death: Six Renaissance Cities in Central Italy.* Baltimore: Johns Hopkins University Press.

Collet, E., and M. Robertson. 1896. *Family Budgets: Being the Income and Expenses of 28 British Households, 1891–1894.* London: P. S. King.

Constantelos, Demetrios J. 1991. *Byzantine Philanthropy and Social Welfare.* 2nd ed. New Rochelle, NY: Caratzas.

Coulet, Noel. 1978. "Hôpitaux et oeuvres d'assistance dans le diocèse et la ville d'Aix-en-Provence." *Assistance et charité en Languedoc au XIIIe et au début du XIVe siècles.* Cahiers de Fanjeaux, 13. Toulouse: Privat.

Courtenay, William J. 1972. "Token Coinage and the Administration of Poor Relief during the late Middle Ages." *Journal of Interdisciplinary History* III: 2 (Autumn): 275–95.

Cox, Jeffrey. 1982. *The English Churches in a Secular Society, Lambeth, 1870–1930.* New York: Oxford University Press.

Craske, May. 1908. "Girl Life in a Slum." *Economic Review* 18 (April).

Dahrendorf, Ralf. 1979. *Life Chances: Approaches to Social and Political Theory.* Chicago: University of Chicago Press.

Danielou, Jean, and Henri Marrou. 1964. *The Christian Centuries: The First Six Hundred Years.* London: Darton, Longman & Todd.

Davidoff, Leonore, and Catherine Hall. 1987. *Family Fortunes: Men and Women of the English Middle Class 1850–1870.* Chicago: University of Chicago Press.

Davis, Elizabeth Lindsay. 1933. *Lifting as They Climb.* Washington: National Association of Colored Women.

Davis, G. Scott. 1991. " 'Et Quod Vis Fac': Paul Ramsey and Augustinian Ethics." *Journal of Religious Ethics* 19, no. 2: 31–69.

———. 1992. *Warcraft and the Fragility of Virtue: An Essay in Aristotelian Ethics.* Moscow, Idaho: University of Idaho Press.

Davis, King E. 1975. *Fund Raising in the Black Community.* Metuchen, NJ: Scarecrow.

Davis, Natalie Zemon. 1968. "Poor Relief Humanism and Heresy, the Case of Lyon." *Studies in Medieval and Renaissance History,* V.

DeFerrari, Roy J., ed. 1952. *Early Christian Biographies.* Washington, DC: Fathers of the Church.

Dendy, Helen (Bosanquet). 1893. "The Industrial Residuum." *Economic Journal* 3: 612–13.

Dennett, Daniel. 1988. *The Intentional Stance*. Cambridge, MA: MIT Press.

Dewart, Janet, ed. 1990. *The State of Black America 1990*. Washington, DC: National Urban League.

Dewey, John. 1908. *Ethics*. New York: Holt.

Domat, Jean. 1828. *Oeuvres*. Vol. I. Joseph Remy, ed. Paris.

Douglas, James. 1983. *Why Charity? The Case for a Third Sector*. Sage.

Douglas, Mary. 1980. *Edward Evans-Pritchard*. New York: Viking Press.

——. 1982. *The World of Goods*. New York: Basic.

——. 1985. *Risk Acceptability According to the Social Sciences*. New York: Russell Sage Foundation.

——. 1992. "Thought Style Exemplified: The Idea of the Self." *Risk and Blame*. New York: Routledge.

——. 1993. "Emotion and Culture in Theories of Justice." *Economy and Society* 22, no. 4: 501–14.

DuBois, W. E. B. 1900. *The College Bred Negro*. Atlanta University Press Series.

——. 1970 (1899). *The Philadelphia Negro*. 3rd ed. New York: Schocken.

Duby, Georges. 1962. *Rural Economy and Country Life in the Medieval West*. Trans. Cynthia Postan. London: Edwin Arnold.

——. 1985. *William Marshal: The Flower of Chivalry*. Trans. Richard Howard. New York: Pantheon.

——, ed. 1988. *A History of Private Life, Volume II: Revelations of the Medieval World*. Trans. Arthur Goldhammer. Cambridge, MA: Harvard University Press.

Duffus, R. L. 1939. *Lillian Wald*. New York: Macmillan.

Duffy, Eamon. 1992. *The Stripping of the Altars: Traditional Religion in England, c. 1400–1580*. New York: Yale University Press.

Dunn, John. 1984. *Locke*. Oxford: Oxford University Press.

Durkheim, Emile. 1951. *Suicide*. Glencoe: Free Press.

Elliott, Sir Charles. 1909. "State Feeding of School Children in London." *The Nineteenth Century and After* 65 (May).

Epicurus. 1987. *Kuriai Doxai (Key Doctrines)*. Key Doctrine 32 and 33. In Long and Sedley (1987): 127.

F., S. S. J. 1911. "The New Pensioner in the East End." *Toynbee Record* (February).

Fleming, John V. 1977. *An Introduction to the Franciscan Literature of the Middle Ages*. Chicago: Franciscan Herald Press.

Foakes, Grace. 1972. *Between High Walls: A London Childhood*. Oxford: Pergamon.

de Fortanier, A. Ramière. 1978. "Hospitalité et charité à Fanjeaux et dans sa région: les confréries de Notre-Dame." *Assistance et charité en Languedoc au XIIIe et au début du XIVe siècles*. Cahiers de Fanjeaux, 13. Toulouse: Privat.

Fox, Robin Lane. 1986. *Pagans and Christians*. New York: Knopf.

Frank, Robert H. 1985. *Choosing the Right Pond*. New York: Oxford University Press.

——. 1988. *Passions within Reason*. New York: Norton.

Franklin, John Hope. 1991. *From Slavery to Freedom*. New York: Knopf.

Franklin, Vincent P. 1992. *Black Self-Determination*. Brooklyn: Lawrence Hill.

Free, Richard. 1907. *On the Wall: Joan and I in the East End*. London: John Lane.

Freeman, Flora Lucy. 1901. *Religious and Social Work amongst Girls*. London: Skeffington.

Freeman, Richard B. 1993. "Me Give to Charity? Well, Since You Ask." Paper delivered at the Conference on the Economics and Psychology of Happiness and Fairness, London School of Economics, November 1993.

Freud, Sigmund. 1960. *Jokes and Their Relation to the Unconscious*. Trans. James Strachey. New York: Norton.

Friedman, Milton. 1957. *A Theory of the Consumption Function*. Princeton: Princeton University Press.

Furse, Dame Katherine. 1940. *Hearts and Pomegranates: The Story of Fifty-Five Years 1875 to 1920*. London: Peter Davies.

Garrow, David J. 1987. "Philanthropy and the Civil Rights Movement." Working Papers for the Center of Philanthropy, City University of New York.

Gates, Henry Louis, ed. 1991. *Bearing Witness*. New York: Pantheon.

Gatewood, Willard B. 1993. *Aristocrats of Color*. Bloomington: Indiana University Press.

Gauthier, David. 1986. *Morals by Agreement*. Oxford: Oxford University Press.

Gauthier, R. A., and J. Y. Jolif. 1970. *Aristote: L'Éthique à Nicomaque*. 2nd ed., 4 vols. Louvain: Publications Universitaires de Louvain.

Gayles, Gloria Wade. 1993. *Pushed Back to Strength*. Boston: Beacon.

Giddings, Paula. 1984. *When and Where I Enter*. New York: Morrow.

Gilovich, Thomas. 1991. *How We Know What Isn't So*. New York: Free Press.

Gissing, George. 1976 (1884). *The Unclassed*. Brighton, Sussex: Harvester.

Glazer, Amihai, and Kai Konrad. 1992. "A Signalling Explanation for Private Charity." UC-Irvine Department of Economics Working Paper.

Gluckman, Max. 1954. "Succession and Civil War among the Bemba." *Rhodes-Livingstone Journal* 16:6: 6–25.

Godwin, William. 1971. *Political Justice*. K. Codell Carter, ed. Oxford: Oxford University Press.

Goodman, Nelson. 1978. *Ways of Worldmaking*. Indianapolis: Hackett.

Goody, J. 1966. "Circulating Succession among the Gonja." In *Succession to High Office*. Cambridge: Cambridge University Press.

Gordon, Peter. 1974. *The Victorian School Manager: A Study in the Management of Education, 1800–1902*. London: Woburn.

Gramain, Monique. 1978. "Les Institutions charitables dans les villages du Biterrois aux XIIe et XIIIe siècles." *Assistance et charité en Languedoc au XIIIe et au début du XIVe siècles*. Cahiers de Fanjeaux, 13. Toulouse: Privat.

Granovetter, Mark. 1972. "The Strength of Weak Ties." *American Journal of Sociology*.

———. 1985. "Economic Action and Social Structure: The Problem of Embeddedness." *American Journal of Sociology* 91: 481–510.

Grant, Clara. 1930. *Farthing Bundles*. London: Fern Street Settlement.

———. 193–?. *From "Me" to "We."* London: C. E. Grant.

Gregory, C. A. 1982. *Gifts and Commodities*. London: Academic.

Grotius, Hugo. 1925. *Laws of War and Peace*. Trans. Francis W. Kelsey. Oxford: Clarendon.

Haakonssen, Knut. 1985. "Hugo Grotius and the History of Political Thought." *Political Theory* 13 (May): 239–65.

Habig, Marion, ed. 1973. *St. Francis of Assisi: Writings and Early Biographies*. Chicago: Franciscan Herald Press.

Haines, Herbert. 1992. "Racial Crisis and Foundation Support of Civil Rights in the 1960's." Presented at Rockefeller Archives Center, "Philanthropy in the African-American Experience," September 24–26, 1992.

Hands, A. R. 1968. *Charities and Social Aid in Greece and Rome*. Ithaca: Cornell University Press.

Harrison, Brian. 1966. "Philanthropy and the Victorians." *Victorian Studies* 9 (June).

Heers, Jacques. 1970. *L'Occident aux XIVe et XVe siècles: Aspects économiques et sociaux.* Nouvelle Clio, 23. Paris: Presses Universitaires de France.

Hegel, G. W. F. 1942. *The Philosophy of Right.* Trans. T. M. Knox. Oxford: Clarendon.

Hildesheimer, Françoise, and Christian Gut. 1992. *L'Assistance hospitalière en France.* Paris: Publisud.

Hill, Christopher, ed. 1973 (1983). *Winstanley: "The Law of Freedom" and Other Writings.* Cambridge: Cambridge University Press.

Hill, Robert B. 1971. *The Strengths of Black Families.* New York: Emerson Hall.

Himmelfarb, Gertrude. 1991. *Poverty and Compassion: The Social Ethic of the Late Victorians.* New York: Knopf.

Hine, Lillian. 1980. "A Poplar Childhood." *East London Record* 3.

Hobbes, Thomas. 1958. *Leviathan.* Indianapolis: Bobbs-Merrill.

Hont, Istvan, and Michael Ignatieff. 1983. "Needs and Justice in 'The Wealth of Nations.'" In their *Wealth and Virtue.* Cambridge: Cambridge University Press.

Horowitz, Donald. 1985. *Ethnic Groups in Conflict.* Berkeley: University of California Press.

Horton, James O., and Lois E. Horton. 1979. *Black Bostonians.* New York: Holmes and Meier.

Hume, David. 1975. *Enquiries concerning Human Understanding and concerning the Principles of Morals.* Ed. L. A. Selby-Bigge and P. H. Nidditch. 3rd ed. Oxford: Clarendon.

———. 1983. *Treatise of Human Nature.* Ed. L. A. Selby-Bigge and Peter Nidditch. Oxford: Oxford University Press.

Hurt, J. S. 1979. *Elementary Schooling and the Working Classes 1860–1918.* London: Routledge.

Hutcheson, Francis. 1725; 4th ed., London, 1738. *An Inquiry into the Original of Our Ideas of Beauty and Virtue.*

Imbert, Jean. 1947. *Les Hôpitaux en droit canonique (du décret de Gratien à la sécularisation de l'administration de l'Hôtel-Dieu de Paris en 1505): Histoire des hôpitaux français. L'Eglise et l'état au moyen âge, VIII.* Paris: Librairie philosophique J. Vrin.

Ione, Carole. 1991. *Pride of Family: Four Generations of American Women of Color.* New York: Summit.

Irwin, Terence. 1985. *Aristotle: Nicomachean Ethics.* Translated with notes and annotated glossary. Indianapolis: Hackett.

Jephson, Arthur. 1910. *My Work in London.* London: Isaac Pitman.

Jones, Adrienne Lash. 1984. "Abolitionism and Feminism: Black Women in the Antebellum North." In Lewis, ed. (1984): 81–100.

———. 1990a. *Jane Edna Hunter: A Case Study of Black Leadership, 1905–1950.* In Darlene Clark Hine, ed., *Black Women in United States History,* vol. 12. Brooklyn: Carlson.

———. 1990b. "Struggle among the Saints: Black Women in the YWCA." Unpublished paper.

Jones, A. H. M. 1964. *The Later Roman Empire, 284–602.* Johns Hopkins Press.

Jones, Enid Huws. 1973. *Mrs. Humphrey Ward.* New York: St. Martin's.

Jones, Gareth Stedman. 1976. *Outcast London: A Study in the Relationship between Classes in Victorian Society.* Harmondsworth: Penguin.

Jordan, W. H. 1959. *Philanthropy in England, 1480–1660: A Study of the Changing Pattern of English Social Aspirations*. London: Allen and Unwin.

Julianus, Flavius Claudius. 1954. *Works*. Trans. W. C. Wright. 3 vols. Loeb Classical Library. Cambridge, MA: Harvard University Press.

Kahneman, Daniel, and A. Tversky. 1984. "Choices, Values and Frames." *American Psychologist* 39: 341–50.

Kahneman, Daniel, Jack Knetsch, and Richard Thaler. 1986. "Fairness as a Constraint on Profit Seeking: Entitlements in the Market." *American Economic Review* 76, no. 4: 728–41.

Kant, Immanuel. 1959. *Foundations of the Metaphysics of Morals*. Trans. Lewis White Beck. Indianapolis: Bobbs-Merrill Co.

———. 1965. *The Metaphysical Elements of Justice*. Trans. John Ladd. Indianapolis: Bobbs-Merrill.

———. 1974. *Gesammelte Schriften*. Berlin: de Gruyter.

———. 1991. *The Metaphysics of Morals*. Trans. Mary Gregor. Cambridge: Cambridge University Press.

Kapp, Yvonne. 1972. *Eleanor Marx*. 2 vols. London: Lawrence & Wishart.

Kenny, Anthony. 1980. *Aquinas*. New York: Hill & Wang.

Knowles, David. 1948. *The Religious Orders in England*, vol. 1. Cambridge: Cambridge University Press.

———. 1963. *The Monastic Order in England*. 2nd ed. Cambridge: Cambridge University Press.

———. 1969. *Christian Monasticism*. New York: McGraw Hill.

Knowles, David, and Dimitri Obolensky. 1969. *The Christian Centuries: The Middle Ages*. London: Darnton, Longman & Todd.

Koditschek, Theodore. 1990. *Class Formation and Urban Industrial Society: Bradford, 1750–1850*. Cambridge: Cambridge University Press.

Koven, Seth. 1992. "From Rough Lads to Hooligans: Boy Life, National Culture and Social Reform." In Andrew Parker, Mary Russo, Doris Sommer, and Patricia Yaeger, eds., *Nationalisms and Sexualities*. New York: Routledge.

———. 1994. "Henrietta Barnett: The (Auto)biography of a Late-Victorian Marriage." In Susan Petersen and Peter Mandler, eds., *After the Victorians*. New York: Routledge.

Kraut, Richard. 1989. *Aristotle on the Human Good*. Princeton: Princeton University Press.

Kretzmann, Norman, Anthony Kenny, and Jan Pinborg, eds. 1982. *The Cambridge History of Later Medieval Philosophy, from the Rediscovery of Aristotle to the Disintegration of Scholasticism 1100–1600*. Cambridge: Cambridge University Press.

Lawrence, C. H. 1989. *Medieval Monasticism: Forms of Religious Life in Western Europe in the Middle Ages*. London: Longman.

LeClercq, Dom Jean. 1961. *The Love of Learning and the Desire for God: A Study of Monastic Culture*. Trans. Catharine Misrahi. New York: Fordham University Press.

Le Grand, Léon. 1901. *Statuts d'hôtels-Dieu et de léproseries: Recueil de textes du XIIe au XIVe siècle*. Collection de textes pour servir à l'étude et à l'enseignement de l'histoire. Paris: A. Picard.

Leibniz, G. W. 1988. *Political Writings*, ed. Patrick Riley. Cambridge: Cambridge University Press.

Lerner, Gerda. 1972. *Black Women in White America*. New York: Vintage.

Lewis, Gene D., ed. 1984. *Essays on the Black Experience in Antebellum America.* Cincinnati: Friends of Harriet Beecher Stowe House and Citizens Committee on Youth.

Lincoln, C. Eric, and Lawrence H. Mamiya. 1990. *The Black Church in the African American Experience.* Durham, NC: Duke University Press.

Linklater, Andro. 1980. *An Unhusbanded Life: Charlotte Despard, Suffragette, Socialist, and Sinn Feiner.* London: Hutchinson.

Little, Lester K. 1978. *Religious Poverty and the Profit Economy in Medieval Europe.* Ithaca: Cornell University Press.

———. 1988. *Liberty, Charity, Fraternity: Lay Religious Confraternities at Bergamo in the Age of the Commune.* Bergamo: Pierluigi Lubrina Editore.

Locke, John. 1963. *Two Treatises of Government.* Peter Laslett, ed. Cambridge: Cambridge University Press.

Long, A. A., and D. N. Sedley, trans. 1987. *The Hellenistic Philosophers.* Cambridge: Cambridge University Press.

MacMullen, Ramsey. 1984. *Christianizing the Roman Empire: A.D. 100–400.* New Haven: Yale University Press.

MacPherson, C. B. 1962. *The Political Theory of Possessive Individualism.* Oxford: Clarendon.

Magat, Richard, ed. 1989. *Philanthropic Giving.* New York: Oxford University Press.

Malson, Micheline R., et al., eds. 1988. *Black Women in America.* Chicago: University of Chicago Press.

Manin, Ethel. 1930. *Confessions and Impressions.* Garden City, NY: Doubleday.

Markus, Robert A. 1988. *Saeculum: History and Society in the Theology of St. Augustine.* Rev. ed. Cambridge: Cambridge University Press.

Martène, E., and U. Durand, eds. 1717. *Thesaurus novus anecdotorum.* 5 vols. Paris.

Martin, Anna. 1911. *The Married Working Woman: A Study.* London: National Union of Women's Suffrage Societies.

Mauss, Marcel. 1990. *The Gift: The Form and Reason for Exchange in Archaic Societies.* Trans. W. D. Halls with a foreword by Mary Douglas. New York: Norton.

Mbiti, John S. 1991. *Introduction to African Religion,* 2nd ed. Garden City, NJ: Anchor.

McAdoo, Harriette Pipes. 1981. *Black Families.* Beverly Hills, CA: Sage.

McInerny, Ralph. 1982. *Ethica Thomistica: The Moral Philosophy of Thomas Aquinas.* Washington, DC: Catholic University of America.

McLeod, Hugh. 1974. *Class and Religion in the Late Victorian City.* London: Croom Helm.

McMillan, Margaret, and A. Cobden Sanderson. 1909. *London's Children: How to Feed Them and How Not to Feed Them.* London: Independent Labour Party.

Meacham, Standish. 1987. *Toynbee Hall and Social Reform.* New Haven: Yale University Press.

Messner, Johannes. 1949. *Social Ethics.* Trans. J. J. Doherty. St. Louis: Herder.

Miller, Maureen C. 1993. *The Formation of a Medieval Church: Ecclesiastical Change in Verona, 950–1150.* Ithaca: Cornell University Press.

Mjagkij, Nina. 1992. "Julius Rosenwald and African-American YMCA's." Presented at the Rockefeller Center Archives Conference, "Philanthropy in the African-American Experience." September 24–26, 1992.

Mollat, Michel. 1978. "Conclusion." *Assistance et charité en Languedoc au XIIIe et au début du XIVe siècles.* Cahiers de Fanjeaux, 13. Toulouse: Privat.

———. 1986. *The Poor in the Middle Ages: An Essay in Social History.* Trans. Arthur Goldhammer. New Haven: Yale University Press.

————, ed. 1974. *Etudes sur l'histoire de la pauvreté au moyen âge–XVIe siècle.* 2 vols. Publications de la Sorbonne, Serie "Etudes," no. 8. Paris.

Momigliano, Arnaldo, ed. 1963. *The Conflict between Paganism and Christianity in the Fourth Century.* Oxford: Oxford University Press.

Montefiore, Lt. Col. 1903. "Uses and Abuses of Medical Charities." *Charity Organisation Review,* n.s. 13 (July).

Moorman, John. 1968. *A History of the Franciscan Order from Its Origins to the Year 1517.* Oxford: Oxford University Press.

Morley, Charles. 1897. "A Little Dinner in the Borough." *Studies in Board Schools.* London: Smith, Elder.

Morris, Alton D. 1984. *The Origins of the Civil Rights Movement.* New York: Free Press.

Morris, Colin. 1989. *The Papal Monarchy: The Western Church from 1050 to 1250.* Oxford: Oxford University Press.

Morris, Robert J. 1983. "Voluntary Societies and British Urban Elites 1780–1850: An Analysis." *Historical Journal* 26:1.

————. 1990. *Class, Sect and Party: The Making of the British Middle Class 1820–1850.*

Mundy, John H. 1955. "Hospitals and Leprosaries in Twelfth and Early Thirteenth-Century Toulouse." In John H. Mundy, Richard W. Emery, and Benjamin N. Nelson, eds., *Essays in Medieval Lifeand Thought Presented in Honor of Austin Patterson Evans.* New York: Columbia University Press.

————. 1966. "Charity and Social Work in Toulouse, 1100–1250." *Traditio* 22.

Muraskin, William A. 1975. *Middle Class Blacks in a White Society: Prince Hall Freemasonry in America.* Berkeley: University of California Press.

Neverdon-Morton, Cynthia. 1989. *Afro-American Women of the South and the Advancement of the Race, 1895–1925.* Knoxville: University of Tennessee Press.

Nord, Deborah E. 1990. " 'Neither Pairs Nor Odd': Female Community in Late Nineteenth-Century London." *Signs* 15:4 (Summer): 733–54.

Nozick, Robert. 1971. *Anarchy, State, and Utopia.* New York: Basic.

Nye, Peter. 1993. "Mental Accounting and the Sunk Cost Effect: A Field Experiment." Paper presented at the annual meeting of the Association for Consumer Research, October 1993.

Owen, David. 1964. *English Philanthropy, 1660–1960.* Cambridge, MA: Harvard University Press.

Paley, William. 1785. *Principles of Moral and Political Philosophy.* London.

Paul, Ellen Frankel, Fred D. Miller, Jr., and Jeffrey Paul, eds. 1993. *Liberalism and the Economic Order.* Cambridge: Cambridge University Press.

Pember Reeves, Maud. 1979 (1913). *Round about a Pound a Week.* London: Virago.

Peterson, M. Jeanne. 1989. *Family, Love, and Work in the Lives of Victorian Gentlewomen.* Bloomington: Indiana University Press.

Plato. 1979. *Republic.* Trans. and ed. Raymond Larson. Arlington Heights, IL: AHM.

Podolny, Joel. 1993. "A Status-Based Model of Market Competition." *American Journal of Sociology* 98 (January): 829–72.

Pollard, William L. 1978. *A Study of Black Self-Help.* San Francisco: R&E Research Associates.

Price, A. R. 1893. "Meals for School Children." *Toynbee Record* (January).

Prochaska, F. K. 1980. *Women and Philanthropy in Nineteenth-Century England.* Oxford: Clarendon.

————. 1990. "Philanthropy." In *The Cambridge Social History of Britain 1750–1950.* Vol. 3. Cambridge: Cambridge University Press.

Pufendorf, Samuel. 1934. *On the Law of Nature and of Nations.* Trans. Oldfather and Oldfather. Oxford: Clarendon.

Pugh, Edwin. 1914. *The Cockney at Home.* London: Chapman & Hall.

Rachleff, Peter J. 1984. *Black Labor in the South: Richmond, Virginia, 1860–1890.* Philadelphia: Temple University Press.

Rawls, John. 1971. *A Theory of Justice.* Cambridge, MA: Harvard University Press.

Revel, Michèle. 1978. "Le Rayonnement à Rome et en Italie de l'ordre du Saint-Esprit de Montpellier." *Assistance et charité en Languedoc au XIIIe et au début du XIVe siècles.* Cahiers de Fanjeaux, 13. Toulouse: Privat.

Ricci, Giovanni. 1983. "Naissance du pauvre honteux: entre l'histoire des idées et l'histoire sociale." *Annales: Economies, Sociétés, Civilisations* 38.

Richards, Audrey. 1939. *Land Labour and Diet in Northern Rhodesia.* London: Oxford University Press.

Richter, Melvin. 1964. *The Politics of Conscience: T. H. Green and His Age.* London: Weidenfeld & Nicolson.

Ritchie, D. G. 1952. *Natural Rights.* London: G. Allen & Unwin.

Roberts, Suzanne F. 1973. "Testamentary Bequests and the Laicization of Charity in the Rouergue, 1280–1350." Paper delivered at the Midwest Medieval Conference, Milwaukee, Wisconsin, October 6, 1973.

——. 1977. "Hospitality and Charity in the Rouergue, 1100–1350." Ph.D. dissertation, Harvard University.

Rorty, Amélie, ed. 1980. *Essays on Aristotle's Ethics.* Berkeley: University of California Press.

Rorty, Richard, J. B. Schneewind, and Quentin Skinner, eds. 1984. *Philosophy in History: Essays on the Historiography of Philosophy.* Cambridge: Cambridge University Press.

Ross, Edyth L. 1978. *Black Heritage in Social Welfare, 1869–1930.* Metuchen, NJ: Scarecrow.

Ross, Ellen. 1983. "Survival Networks: Women's Neighbourhood Sharing in London before World War One." *History Workshop* 15 (Spring): 4–27.

——. 1990. "Hungry Children: Housewives and London Charity, 1870–1918." In Peter Mandler, ed., *The Uses of Charity: The Poor on Relief in the Nineteenth-Century Metropolis.* Philadelphia: University of Pennsylvania Press.

——. 1993. *Love and Toil: Motherhood in Outcast London, 1870–1918.* New York: Oxford University Press.

Rouse, Jacqueline Anne. 1989. *Lugenia Burns Hope.* Athens, GA: University of Georgia Press.

Rubin, Miri. 1987. *Charity and Community in Medieval Cambridge.* Cambridge Studies in Medieval Life and Thought, 4th series, no. 4. Cambridge: Cambridge University Press.

Ryan, Alan. 1987. "Introduction." *Mill and Bentham: Utilitarianism and Other Works.* Harmondsworth: Penguin.

——. 1995. *John Dewey and the High Tide of American Liberalism.* New York: Norton.

——, ed. 1979. *The Idea of Freedom: Essays in Honour of Isaiah Berlin.* Oxford: Oxford University Press.

Saint-Denis, Alain. 1983. *L'Hôtel-Dieu de Laon, 1150–1300: Institution hospitalière et société au XIIe et XIIIe siècles.* Nancy: Presses Universitaires de Nancy.

Samuel, Raphael. 1981. *East End Underworld: Chapters in the Life of Arthur Harding*. London: Routledge.

Sartorius, Rolf E., ed. 1983. *Paternalism*. Minneapolis: University of Minnesota Press.

Schelling, Thomas C. 1984. *Choice and Consequence*. Cambridge, MA: Harvard University Press.

Schneewind, J. B. 1987. "Pufendorf's Place in the History of Ethics." *Synthese* 72: 123–55.

———. 1990. "The Misfortunes of Virtue." *Ethics* 101:1, pp. 42–63.

Sen, A. K. 1981. *Poverty and Famines: An Essay on Entitlement and Deprivation*. Oxford: Clarendon.

Seneca, Lucius Annaeus. 1979. *De Beneficiis*. Trans. John Basore. In *Moral Essays*, vol. 3. Loeb Classical Library. Cambridge, MA: Harvard University Press.

Shaw, David Gary. 1993. *The Creation of a Community: The City of Wells in the Middle Ages*. Oxford: Clarendon.

Sherman, Nancy. 1989. *The Fabric of Character: Aristotle's Theory of Virtue*. Oxford: Oxford University Press.

Simon, Brian. 1974. *Education and the Labour Movement, 1870–1920*. London: Lawrence & Wishart.

Sinton, David H. 1990. "The Economic Status of Black Americans during the 1980's: A Decade of Limited Progress." In Dewart, ed., 1990.

Smart, J. C. C., and Bernard Williams. 1971. *Utilitarianism For and Against*. Cambridge: Cambridge University Press.

Smith, Adam. 1976. *The Theory of Moral Sentiments*. Ed. D. D. Raphael and A. L. Macfie. Oxford: Clarendon.

Société des Lettres de l'Aveyron. Archives de Sévérac, 52, no. 8 (1305).

Southern, Richard W. 1970. *Western Society and the Church in the Middle Ages*. Harmondsworth: Penguin.

Stocks, Mary. 1970. *My Commonplace Book*. London: Peter Davies.

Straw, Carole. 1988. *Gregory the Great: Perfection in Imperfection*. Berkeley: University of California Press.

Stuckey, Sterling. 1987. *Slave Culture*. New York: Oxford University Press.

Tallents, S. G. 1909. "Inquiry into the State Feeding of School Children." *Toynbee Record* (March).

Thaler, Richard H. 1980. "Toward a Positive Theory of Consumer Choice." *Journal of Economic Behavior and Organization*.

———. 1985. "Mental Accounting and Consumer Choice." *Marketing Science* 4.

Thane, Pat. 1984. "The Working Class and State 'Welfare' in Britain, 1880–1914." *Historical Journal* 27: 877–900.

Theophrastus. 1953. *Characters*. Ed. and trans. J. M. Edmonds. Loeb Classical Library. Cambridge, MA: Harvard University Press.

Thompson, J. A. F. 1965. "Piety and Charity in Late Medieval London." *Journal of Ecclesiastical History* 16.

Thorne, R. Thorne. 1888. *The Progress of Preventative Medicine in the Victorian Era*. London: Shaw.

Tierney, Brian. 1958–59. "The Decretists and the 'Deserving Poor.'" *Comparative Studies in Society and History* I.

———. 1959. *Medieval Poor Law: A Sketch of Canonical Theory and Its Application in England*. Berkeley: University of California Press.

Titmuss, Richard. 1971. *The Gift Relationship.* New York: Pantheon.

Trexler, Richard. 1973. "Charity and the Defense of Urban Elites in the Italian Communes." In Frederic Cople Jaher, ed., *The Rich, the Well-Born, and the Powerful.* Urbana: University of Illinois Press, pp. 64–109.

Tuck, Richard. 1979. *Natural Rights Theories.* Cambridge: Cambridge University Press.

Tully, James. 1980. *A Discourse on Property.* Cambridge: Cambridge University Press.

Tversky, Amos, and Daniel Kahneman. 1981. "The Framing of Decisions and the Psychology of Choice." *Science* 211: 453–58.

Veyne, Paul. 1990. *Bread and Circuses: Historical Sociology and Political Pluralism.* Trans. Brian Pearce with an Introduction by Oswyn Murray. London: Penguin.

———, ed. 1987. *A History of Private Life, Volume I: From Pagan Rome to Byzantium.* Trans. Arthur Goldhammer. Cambridge, MA: Harvard University Press.

Vicaire, Marie-Humbert. 1978. "La Place des oeuvres de miséricorde dans las pastorale en pays d'oc." *Assistance et charité en Languedoc au XIIIe et au début du XIVe siècles.* Cahiers de Fanjeaux, 13. Toulouse: Privat.

Vicinus, Martha. 1985. *Independent Women: Work and Community for Single Women 1850–1920.* Chicago: University of Chicago Press.

Vincent, Andrew, and Raymond Plant. 1984. *Philosophy, Politics, and Citizenship: The Life and Thought of the British Idealists.* Oxford: Blackwell.

Wald, Lillian D. 1933. *Windows on Henry Street.* Boston: Little, Brown.

Walzer, Michael. 1994. *Thick and Thin.* Notre Dame: University of Notre Dame Press.

Washington, Booker T. 1965. "Up from Slavery." In *Three Negro Classics.* New York: Avon.

Webb, Beatrice. 1979 (1926). *My Apprenticeship.* Cambridge: Cambridge University Press.

Webb, Sidney. 1907. *The Decline of the Birthrate.* London: Fabian Society.

Webb, Sidney, and Beatrice Webb. 1927. *English Poor Law History,* I. London.

Weisheipl, James A. 1974. *Friar Thomas D'Aquino, His Life, Thought and Works.* Garden City, NY: Doubleday.

Wetzel, James. 1992. *Augustine and the Limits of Virtue.* Cambridge: Cambridge University Press.

Wikler, Daniel I. 1983. "Paternalism and the Mildly Retarded." In Sartorius (1983): 83–94.

Wildavsky, A. 1993. "Freud on Jokes, A Postconscious Evaluation." Unpublished paper.

Williams, Bernard. 1987. *Ethics and the Limits of Philosophy.* London: Fontana.

Williams, Lillian S. 1992. "Making a Way Out of No Way." Presented at the Rockefeller Center Archives Conference, "Philanthropy in the African American Experience," September 24–26, 1992.

Contributors

Allen Buchanan is Professor of Philosophy and Grainger Professor of Business Ethics at the University of Wisconsin. He has taught at the University of Arizona and the University of Minnesota. His books include *Marx and Justice, Ethics, Efficiency and the Market, Deciding for Others: The Ethics of Surrogate Decision Making* (with Dan Brock), and *Secession: The Morality of Political Divorce*. He has written numerous articles, on Kantianism, Marxism, medical ethics, health insurance, and justice. In 1982 he was Staff Philosopher on the President's Commission on Ethical Problems in Medicine.

Scott Davis is Associate Professor in the Department of Religion at the University of Richmond and formerly in the Department of Religion at Princeton. Davis has also taught at the University of Southern California and Columbia. He wrote the section "Early Mediaeval Ethics" for the Becker and Becker *Encyclopedia of Ethics* and has published a number of essays on systematic and historical topics in religious ethics.

Mary Douglas is Avalon Foundation Professor in the Humanities Emeritus and author of *Food in the Social Order, Purity and Danger*, and *Essays in the Sociology of Perception*. Witchcraft, pollution, risk and responsibility, and the social meanings of food are among the topics which she has examined from an anthropological viewpoint.

Robert Frank is Goldwin Smith Professor of Economics, Ethics, and Public Policy at Cornell University, where he has taught since 1972 except for a two-year stint as Chief Economist for the Civil Aeronautics Board. He has written *Choosing the Right Pond: Human Behavior and the Quest for Status, Passions within Reason: The Strategic Role of the Emotions*, and *Microeconomics and Behavior*. Some of his articles offer an economist's perspective on the moral sense, honesty, and the sense of justice; others examine issues in the more abstract aspects of economic theory.

Adrienne Lash Jones is Associate Professor and Chair of the Department of Black Studies at Oberlin. She has published many studies of black women leaders, including the book *Jane Edna Hunter: A Case Study of Black Leadership, 1910–1950*. She is currently working on philanthropy among African Americans and on a history of black women in the YWCA.

Robert L. Payton is Professor of Philanthropy and former director of the Center on Philanthropy, Indiana University. He served as Ambassador to the Republic of Cameroon, was president of C. W. Post College and of Hofstra University, and president of the Exxon Education Foundation for ten years. He has written extensively on philanthropy, most recently *Philanthropy: Voluntary Action for the Public Good*.

Suzanne Roberts taught at Wooster College before becoming Bibliographer for Western European History at the Yale University Library. She has published two articles, in French, on charitable work in the Middle Ages and has also written on bibliographic problems and issues concerning book preservation.

Alex Rondos is Director of the International Orthodox Christian Charities, an international relief and development organization created by the Eastern Orthodox Churches in North America. Until 1992 he served with Catholic Relief Services, as consultant in Ethiopia, as Middle East director with responsibility for programs from Morocco to Lebanon, and on his return to the United States as Congressional Liaison and Public Affairs officer. He was assistant editor of *West Africa* magazine, and has written various newspaper articles and contributed to numerous radio and TV programs on issues of international aid.

Ellen Ross taught for several years at Connecticut College and is now Professor of Women's Studies at Ramapo College. She has done several series for educational television. Her writings include *Love and Toil: Motherhood in Outcast London 1870–98* and a number of articles on gender and history. She has also edited *Lady Explorers in "Darkest London,"* an anthology of source materials drawn from writings by social workers, district nurses, and others who knew the London poor at first hand.

Alan Ryan taught at New College, Oxford, before joining the Department of Politics at Princeton, where he teaches political philosophy. His books include *The Philosophy of John Stuart Mill, Property and Political Theory,* and *Russell: A Political Life.* He has written extensively on topics and authors in the history of liberal democratic theory. His essays often appear in such nonacademic publications as the *New York Review of Books.* Currently he is working on a study of John Dewey.

J. B. Schneewind is Professor of Philosophy at Johns Hopkins University. He previously taught at the University of Pittsburgh and at Hunter College CUNY. He works on the history of moral philosophy, his main publications being *Sidgwick's Ethics and Victorian Moral Philosophy* and an anthology of source material, *Moral Philosophy from Montaigne to Kant.* He is writing a book on the development of moral philosophy in the seventeenth and eighteenth centuries.

Index